Testing for Language Teachers

Second Edition

CAMBRIDGE LANGUAGE TEACHING LIBRARY

A series covering central issues in language teaching and learning, by authors who have expert knowledge in their field.

Testing for Language Teachers

Second Edition

Arthur Hughes

CAMBRIDGE
UNIVERSITY PRESS

PUBLISHED BY THE PRESS SYNDICATE OF THE UNIVERSITY OF CAMBRIDGE
The Pitt Building, Trumpington Street, Cambridge, United Kingdom

CAMBRIDGE UNIVERSITY PRESS
The Edinburgh Building, Cambridge CB2 2RU, UK
40 West 20th Street, New York, NY10011–4211, USA
477 Williamstown Road, Port Melbourne, VIC 3207, Australia
Ruiz de Alarcón 13, 28014 Madrid, Spain
Dock House, The Waterfront, Cape Town 8001, South Africa

http://www.cambridge.org

First published 1989
Second edition 2003

Printed in the United Kingdom at the University Press, Cambridge

Typeface Sabon 10.5/12. *System* QuarkXPress® [OD&I]

A catalogue record for this book is available from the British Library

ISBN 0 521 823250 hardback
ISBN 0 521 484952 paperback

For Vicky, Meg and Jake

Contents

Contents

Acknowledgements

The publishers and I are grateful to the authors, publishers and others who have given permission for the use of copyright material identified in the text. It has not been possible to identify, or trace, sources of all the materials used and in such cases the publishers would welcome information from copyright owners.

American Council on the Teaching of Foreign Languages Inc. for extracts from ACTFL Proficiency Guidelines; ARELS Examination Trust for extracts from examinations; A. Hughes for extracts from the New Bogazici University Language Proficiency Test (1984); Cambridge University Press for M. Swan and C. Walter: Cambridge English Course 3, p.16 (1988); Filmscan Lingual House for M. Garman and A. Hughes for English Cloze Exercises Chapter 4 (1983); The Foreign Service Institute for the Testing Kit pp. 35–8 (1979), Harper & Row; *The Independent* for N. Timmins: 'Passive smoking comes under fire', 14 March 1987; Language Learning, and J. W. Oller Jr and C. A. Conrad for the extract from 'The cloze technique and ESL proficiency'; Macmillan London Ltd for Colin Dexter: The Secret of Annexe 3 (1986); *The ©Guardian* for S. Limb: 'One-sided headache', 9 October 1983; The Royal Society of Arts Examinations Board/ University of Cambridge Local Examinations Syndicate (UCLES) for extracts from the examination in The Communicative Use of English as a Foreign Language; UCLES for the extract from Testpack 1 paper 3; UCLES for extracts from the Oxford Examination in English as a Foreign Language, CCSE, FCE, and Young learners ARELS handbooks and papers, Interagency Language Roundtable Speaking Levels. Oxford University Press for extract from *Speaking* by Martin Bygate © Oxford University Press 1987; TOEFL© materials are reprinted by permission of Educational Testing Service, the copyright owner. However, the test questions and any other testing information are provided in their entirety by Cambridge University Press. No endorsement of this publication by Educational

Acknowledgements

Testing Service should be inferred; *Cloze test* by Christine Klein-Braley and Ulrich Raatz 1984, used by permission of Grotjahn and Raatz; Kartlegging av Kommunikativ Kompetanse i Engelsk (Testing of Communicative Ability in English), reproduced by permission of Angela Hasselgren; *International English 4th Edition 2002* by Trudgill and Hannah i NEAB/AQA examination questions are reproduced by permission of the Assessment and Qualifications Alliance.

Preface

The objective of this book is to help language teachers write better tests. It takes the view that test construction is essentially a matter of problem solving, with every teaching situation setting a different testing problem. In order to arrive at the best solution for any particular problem – the most appropriate test or testing system – it is not enough to have at one's disposal a collection of test techniques from which to choose. It is also necessary to understand the principles of testing and how they can be applied in practice.

It is relatively straightforward to introduce and explain the desirable qualities of tests: validity, reliability, practicality, and beneficial backwash; this last referring to the favourable effects testing can have on teaching and learning. It is much less easy to give realistic advice on how to achieve them in teacher-made tests. One is tempted either to ignore the issue or to present as a model the not always appropriate methods of large-scale testing organisations. In resisting this temptation, I have made recommendations that I hope teachers will find practical but which I have also tried to justify in terms of language testing theory.

Exemplification throughout the book is from the testing of English as a foreign language. This reflects both my own experience in language testing and the fact that English will be the one language known by all readers. I trust that it will not prove too difficult for teachers of other languages to find or construct parallel examples of their own.

Because the objective and general approach of the book remain those of the first edition, much of the text remains. However, I have made changes throughout. These include the inclusion of greater detail in the writing of specifications and the provision of outlines of training programmes for interviewers and raters. In response to the now widespread availability of powerful and relatively inexpensive computers, as well as ready access to the Internet, I have made extensive reference to resources on the Internet and have written a completely new chapter on the statistical treatment of test data, using an inexpensive program which is available to readers via the book's own website www.cambridge.org/elt/tflt.

Links to all of the websites mentioned in the book can be found there. The increasing tendency throughout the world for language learning (and testing) to begin at primary school has led me to include a chapter on the testing of young learners. While one might have reservations about such testing (as opposed to other forms of assessment), since testing does take place, it seemed better to offer advice in the area rather than simply ignore the issue.

Perhaps the most striking development in language testing since the publication of the first edition has been the great increase in the number of published articles and books. Many – perhaps most – of the articles have been of a theoretical or technical nature, not directly relevant to the concerns of language teachers. Even where their relevance is clear, in order to keep the text accessible to newcomers to the field, I have usually restricted references to them to the Further reading sections. These sections are intended to act as a guide for those readers who wish to go more deeply into the issues raised in the book, and also to provide an outline of the state of language testing today. They also contain recommendations of a number of recent books which, in an accessible fashion, treat areas of language testing (such as the testing of a particular skill) in greater depth than is possible in the present volume.

I must acknowledge the contributions of others: MA and research students at Reading University, too numerous to mention by name, who have taught me much, usually by asking questions that I found difficult to answer; my friends and colleagues, Paul Fletcher, Michael Garman, Don Porter, Tony Woods, who all read parts of the manuscript of the first edition and made many helpful suggestions; Angela Hasselgren who shared thoughts on the testing of young learners and provided me with copies of the materials used in the Norwegian EVA project; my friends Cyril Weir and Russanne Hozayin, with whom I've collaborated on testing projects in recent years; and finally my wife, who drew the cartoon series on page 209, and whose patience during the writing of this second edition was almost endless.

1 Teaching and testing

Many language teachers harbour a deep mistrust of tests and of testers. The starting point for this book is the admission that this mistrust is frequently well-founded. It cannot be denied that a great deal of language testing is of very poor quality. Too often language tests have a harmful effect on teaching and learning, and fail to measure accurately whatever it is they are intended to measure.

Backwash

The effect of testing on teaching and learning is known as *backwash*, and can be harmful or beneficial. If a test is regarded as important, if the stakes are high, preparation for it can come to dominate all teaching and learning activities. And if the test content and testing techniques are at variance with the objectives of the course, there is likely to be harmful backwash. An instance of this would be where students are following an English course that is meant to train them in the language skills (including writing) necessary for university study in an English-speaking country, but where the language test that they have to take in order to be admitted to a university does not test those skills directly. If the skill of writing, for example, is tested only by multiple choice items, then there is great pressure to practise such items rather than practise the skill of writing itself. This is clearly undesirable.

We have just looked at a case of harmful backwash. However, backwash can be positively beneficial. I was once involved in the development of an English language test for an English medium university in a non-English-speaking country. The test was to be administered at the end of an intensive year of English study there and would be used to determine which students would be allowed to go on to their undergraduate courses (taught in English) and which would have to leave the university. A test was devised which was based directly on an analysis of the English language needs of first year undergraduate students, and which included tasks as similar as possible to those which they would have to perform as undergraduates (reading textbook materials, taking notes during lectures, and so on).

The introduction of this test, in place of one which had been entirely multiple choice, had an immediate effect on teaching: the syllabus was redesigned, new books were chosen, classes were conducted differently. The result of these changes was that by the end of their year's training, in circumstances made particularly difficult by greatly increased numbers and limited resources, the students reached a much higher standard in English than had ever been achieved in the university's history. This was a case of beneficial backwash.

Davies (1968:5) once wrote that 'the good test is an obedient servant since it follows and apes the teaching'. I find it difficult to agree, and perhaps today Davies would as well. The proper relationship between teaching and testing is surely that of partnership. It is true that there may be occasions when the teaching programme is potentially good and appropriate but the testing is not; we are then likely to suffer from harmful backwash. This would seem to be the situation that led Davies in 1968 to confine testing to the role of servant to the teaching. But equally there may be occasions when teaching is poor or inappropriate and when testing is able to exert a beneficial influence. We cannot expect testing only to follow teaching. Rather, we should demand of it that it is supportive of good teaching and, where necessary, exerts a corrective influence on bad teaching. If testing always had a beneficial backwash on teaching, it would have a much better reputation among teachers. Chapter 6 of this book is devoted to a discussion of how beneficial backwash can be achieved.

One last thing to be said about backwash in the present chapter is that it can be viewed as part of something more general – the *impact* of assessment. The term 'impact', as it is used in educational measurement, is not limited to the effects of assessment on learning and teaching but extends to the way in which assessment affects society as a whole, and has been discussed in the context of the ethics of language testing (see Further Reading).

Inaccurate tests

The second reason for mistrusting tests is that very often they fail to measure accurately whatever it is that they are intended to measure. Teachers know this. Students' true abilities are not always reflected in the test scores that they obtain. To a certain extent this is inevitable. Language abilities are not easy to measure; we cannot expect a level of accuracy comparable to those of measurements in the physical sciences. But we can expect greater accuracy than is frequently achieved.

Why are tests inaccurate? The causes of inaccuracy (and ways of minimising their effects) are identified and discussed in subsequent chapters, but a short answer is possible here. There are two main sources of inaccuracy. The first of these concerns test content and test techniques. To return to an earlier example, if we want to know how well someone can write, there is absolutely no way we can get a really accurate measure of their ability by means of a multiple choice test. Professional testers have expended great effort, and not a little money, in attempts to do it, but they have always failed. We may be able to get an approximate measure, but that is all. When testing is carried out on a very large scale, when the scoring of tens of thousands of compositions might not seem to be a practical proposition, it is understandable that potentially greater accuracy is sacrificed for reasons of economy and convenience. But this does not give testing a good name! And it does set a bad example.

While few teachers would wish to follow that particular example in order to test writing ability, the overwhelming practice in large-scale testing of using multiple choice items does lead to imitation in circumstances where such items are not at all appropriate. What is more, the imitation tends to be of a very poor standard. Good multiple choice items are notoriously difficult to write. A great deal of time and effort has to go into their construction. Too many multiple choice tests are written where the necessary care and attention are not given. The result is a set of poor items that cannot possibly provide accurate measurements. One of the principal aims of this book is to discourage the use of inappropriate techniques and to show that teacher-made tests can be superior in certain respects to their professional counterparts.

The second source of inaccuracy is lack of *reliability*. This is a technical term that is explained in Chapter 5. For the moment it is enough to say that a test is reliable if it measures consistently. On a reliable test you can be confident that someone will get more or less the same score, whether they happen to take it on one particular day or on the next; whereas on an unreliable test the score is quite likely to be considerably different, depending on the day on which it is taken. Unreliability has two origins. The first is the interaction between the person taking the test and features of the test itself. Human beings are not machines and we therefore cannot expect them to perform in exactly the same way on two different occasions, whatever test they take. As a result, we expect some variation in the scores a person gets on a test, depending on when they happen to take it, what mood they are in, how much sleep they had the night before. However, what we can do is ensure that the tests themselves don't increase this variation by having unclear instructions, ambiguous questions, or items that result in guessing on the part of the test takers. Unless we minimise these features, we cannot have confidence in the scores that people obtain on a test.

The second origin of unreliability is to be found in the scoring of a test. Scoring can be unreliable in that equivalent test performances are accorded significantly different scores. For example, the same composition may be given very different scores by different markers (or even by the same marker on different occasions). Fortunately, there are ways of minimising such differences in scoring. Most (but not all) large testing organisations, to their credit, take every precaution to make their tests, and the scoring of them, as reliable as possible, and are generally highly successful in this respect. Small-scale testing, on the other hand, tends to be less reliable than it should be. Another aim of this book, then, is to show how to achieve greater reliability in testing. Advice on this is to be found in Chapter 5.

The need for tests

So far this chapter has been concerned with understanding why tests are so mistrusted by many language teachers, and how this mistrust is often justified. One conclusion drawn from this might be that we would be better off without language tests. Teaching is, after all, the primary activity; if testing comes in conflict with it, then it is testing that should go, especially when it has been admitted that so much testing provides inaccurate information. However, information about people's language ability is often very useful and sometimes necessary. It is difficult to imagine, for example, British and American universities accepting students from overseas without some knowledge of their proficiency in English. The same is true for organisations hiring interpreters or translators. They certainly need dependable measures of language ability. Within teaching systems, too, so long as it is thought appropriate for individuals to be given a statement of what they have achieved in a second or foreign language, tests of some kind or another will be needed. They will also be needed in order to provide information about the achievement of groups of learners, without which it is difficult to see how rational educational decisions can be made. While for some purposes teachers' informal assessments of their own students are both appropriate and sufficient, this is not true for the cases just mentioned. Even without considering the possibility of bias, we have to recognise the need for a common yardstick, which tests provide, in order to make meaningful comparisons.

Testing and assessment

The focus of this book is on more or less formal testing. But testing is not, of course, the only way in which information about people's language ability can be gathered. It is just one form of assessment, and other methods will often be more appropriate. It is helpful here to make clear the difference between *formative* and *summative* assessment. Assessment is formative when teachers use it to check on the progress of their students, to see how far they have mastered what they should have learned, and then use this information to modify their future teaching plans. Such assessment can also be the basis for feedback to the students. Informal tests or quizzes may have a part to play in formative assessment but so will simple observation (of performance on learning tasks, for example) and the study of portfolios that students have made of their work. Students themselves may be encouraged to carry out *self-assessment* in order to monitor their progress, and then modify their own learning objectives.

Summative assessment is used at, say, the end of the term, semester, or year in order to measure what has been achieved both by groups and by individuals. Here, for the reasons given in the previous section, formal tests are usually called for. However, the results of such tests should not be looked at in isolation. A complete view of what has been achieved should include information from as many sources as possible. In an ideal world, the different pieces of information from all sources, including formal tests, should be consistent with each other. If they are not, the possible sources of these discrepancies need to be investigated.

What is to be done?

I believe that the teaching profession can make three contributions to the improvement of testing: they can write better tests themselves; they can enlighten other people who are involved in testing processes; and they can put pressure on professional testers and examining boards, to improve *their* tests. This book aims to help them do all three. The first aim is easily understood. One would be surprised if a book with this title did not attempt to help teachers write better tests. The second aim is perhaps less obvious. It is based on the belief that the better all of the stakeholders in a test or testing system understand testing, the better the testing will be and, where relevant, the better it will be integrated with teaching. The stakeholders I have in mind include test takers, teachers, test writers, school or college administrators, education authorities, examining bodies and testing institutions. The more they interact and cooperate on the basis of shared knowledge and understanding, the better and more appropriate should be the testing in which they all have a stake. Teachers are probably in the best position to understand the issues, and then to share their knowledge with others.

For the reader who doubts the relevance of the third aim, let this chapter end with a further reference to the testing of writing through multiple choice items. This was the practice followed by those responsible for TOEFL (Test of English as a Foreign Language) – the test taken by most non-native speakers of English applying to North American universities. Over a period of many years they maintained that it was simply not possible to test the writing ability of hundreds of thousands of candidates by means of a composition: it was impracticable and the results, anyhow, would be unreliable. Yet in 1986 a writing test (Test of Written English), in which candidates actually have to write for thirty minutes, was introduced as a supplement to TOEFL. The principal reason given for this change was pressure from English language teachers who had finally convinced those responsible for the TOEFL of the overriding need for a writing task that would provide beneficial backwash.

Reader activities

1. Think of tests with which you are familiar (the tests may be international or local, written by professionals or by teachers). What do you think the backwash effect of each of them is? Harmful or beneficial? What are your reasons for coming to these conclusions?
2. Consider these tests again. Do you think that they give accurate or inaccurate information? What are your reasons for coming to these conclusions?

Further reading

Rea-Dickens (1997) considers the relationship between stakeholders in language testing and Hamp-Lyons (1997a) raises ethical concerns relating to backwash, impact and validity. These two papers form part of a special issue of *Language Testing* (Volume 14, Number 3) devoted to ethics in language testing. For an early discussion of the ethics of language testing, see Spolsky (1981). The International Language Testing Association has developed a code of ethics (adopted in 2000) which can be downloaded from the Internet (see the book's website). Kunnan (2000) is concerned with fairness and validation in language testing. Rea-Dickens and Gardner (2000) examine the concept and practice of formative assessment. Alderson and Clapham (1995) make recommendations for classroom assessment. Brown and Hudson (1998) present teachers with alternative ways of assessing language. Nitko (1989) offers advice on the designing of tests which are integrated with instruction. Ross (1998) reviews research into self assessment. DeVicenzi (1995) gives advice to teachers on how to learn from standardised tests. Gipps (1990) and Raven (1991) draw attention to the possible dangers of inappropriate assessment. For an account of how the introduction of a new test can have a striking beneficial effect on teaching and learning, see Hughes (1988a).

2 Testing as problem solving: an overview of the book

Language testers are sometimes asked to say what is 'the best test' or 'the best testing technique'. Such questions reveal a misunderstanding of what is involved in the practice of language testing. A test that proves ideal for one purpose may be quite useless for another; a technique that may work very well in one situation can be entirely inappropriate in another. As we saw in the previous chapter, what suits large testing corporations may be quite out of place in the tests of teaching institutions. Equally, two teaching institutions may require very different tests, depending on the objectives of their courses, the purpose of the tests, and the resources available. Each testing situation is unique and sets a particular testing problem. And so the first step must be to state this testing problem as clearly as possible. Whatever test or testing system we then create should be one that:

- consistently provides accurate measures of precisely the abilities[1] in which we are interested;
- has a beneficial effect on teaching (in those cases where the test is likely to influence teaching);
- is economical in terms of time and money.

The first thing that testers have to be clear about is the purpose of testing in any particular situation. Different purposes will usually require different kinds of tests. This may seem obvious but it is something that is not always recognised. The purposes of testing discussed in this book are:

- To measure language proficiency.
- To discover how successful students have been in achieving the objectives of a course of study.
- To diagnose students' strengths and weaknesses, to identify what they know and what they don't know.
- To assist placement of students by identifying the stage or part of a teaching programme most appropriate to their ability.

All of these purposes are discussed in the next chapter. That chapter also introduces different kinds of testing and test techniques: direct as opposed to indirect testing; discrete-point versus integrative testing; criterion-referenced testing as against norm-referenced testing; objective and subjective testing. In stating the testing problem in general terms above, we spoke of providing consistent measures of precisely the abilities we are interested in. A test that does this is said to be *valid*. Chapter 4 addresses itself to various kinds of validity. It provides advice on the achievement of validity in test construction and shows how validity is measured.

The word 'consistently' was used in the statement of the testing problem. The consistency with which accurate measurements are made is in fact an essential ingredient of validity. If a test measures consistently (if, for example a person's score on the test is likely to be very similar regardless of whether they happen to take it on, say, Monday morning rather than on Tuesday afternoon, assuming that there has been no significant change in their ability) it is said to be reliable. Reliability, already referred to in the previous chapter, is an absolutely essential quality of tests – what use is a test if it will give widely differing estimates of an individual's (unchanged) ability? – yet it is something which is distinctly lacking in very many teacher-made tests. Chapter 5 gives advice on how to achieve reliability and explains how it can be measured.

The concept of backwash effect was introduced in the previous chapter. Chapter 6 identifies a number of conditions for tests to meet in order to achieve beneficial backwash.

All tests cost time and money – to prepare, administer, score and interpret. As both are in limited supply, there is often likely to be a conflict between what appears to be a perfect testing solution in a particular situation and considerations of practicality. This issue is also discussed in Chapter 6.

The second half of the book is devoted to more detailed advice on the construction and use of tests – the putting into practice of the principles outlined in earlier chapters. Chapter 7 outlines and exemplifies the various stages of test development. Chapter 8 discusses a number of common testing techniques. Chapters 9–13 show how a variety of language abilities can best be tested, particularly within teaching institutions. Chapter 14 discusses 'overall ability' and how it may be measured. Chapter 15 considers the particular problems that have to be faced when young learners are tested. Chapter 16 gives straightforward advice on the administration of tests.

We have to say something about statistics. Some understanding of statistics is useful, indeed necessary, for a proper appreciation of testing matters and for successful problem solving. In the chapters on validity and reliability, simple statistical notions are presented in terms that it is hoped everyone should be able to grasp. Appendix 1 deals in some detail with the statistical analysis of test results. Even here, however, the emphasis is on interpretation rather than on calculation. In fact, given the computing power and statistics software that is readily available these days, there is no real need for any calculation on the part of language testers. They simply need to understand the output of the computer programs which they (or others) use. Appendix 1 attempts to develop this understanding and, just as important, show how valuable statistical information can be in developing better tests.

Further reading

The collection of critical reviews of nearly 50 English language tests (mostly British and American), edited by Alderson, Krahnke and Stansfield (1987), reveals how well professional test writers are thought to have solved their problems. A full understanding of the reviews will depend to some degree on an assimilation of the content of Chapters 3, 4, and 5 of this book. Alderson and Buck (1993) and Alderson et al (1995) investigate the test development procedures of certain British testing institutions.

1. 'Abilities' is not being used here in any technical sense. It refers simply to what people can do in, or with, a language. It could, for example, include the ability to converse fluently in a language, as well as the ability to recite grammatical rules (if that is something which we are interested in measuring!). It does not, however, refer to language aptitude, the talent which people have, in differing degrees, for learning languages. The measurement of this talent in order to predict how well or how quickly individuals will learn a foreign language, is beyond the scope of this book. The interested reader is referred to Pimsleur (1968), Carroll (1981), and Skehan (1986), Sternberg (1995), MacWhinney (1995), Spolsky (1995), Mislevy (1995), McLaughlin (1995).

3 Kinds of tests and testing

This chapter begins by considering the purposes for which language testing is carried out. It goes on to make a number of distinctions: between direct and indirect testing, between discrete point and integrative testing, between norm-referenced and criterion-referenced testing, and between objective and subjective testing. Finally there are notes on computer adaptive testing and communicative language testing.

Tests can be categorised according to the types of information they provide. This categorisation will prove useful both in deciding whether an existing test is suitable for a particular purpose and in writing appropriate new tests where these are necessary. The four types of test which we will discuss in the following sections are: proficiency tests, achievement tests, diagnostic tests, and placement tests.

Proficiency tests

Proficiency tests are designed to measure people's ability in a language, regardless of any training they may have had in that language. The content of a proficiency test, therefore, is not based on the content or objectives of language courses that people taking the test may have followed. Rather, it is based on a specification of what candidates have to be able to do in the language in order to be considered proficient. This raises the question of what we mean by the word 'proficient'.

In the case of some proficiency tests, 'proficient' means having sufficient command of the language for a particular purpose. An example of this would be a test designed to discover whether someone can function successfully as a United Nations translator. Another example would be a test used to determine whether a student's English is good enough to follow a course of study at a British university. Such a test may even attempt to take into account the level and kind of English needed to follow courses in particular subject areas. It might, for example, have one form of the test for arts subjects, another for sciences, and so on.

Whatever the particular purpose to which the language is to be put, this will be reflected in the specification of test content at an early stage of a test's development.

There are other proficiency tests which, by contrast, do not have any occupation or course of study in mind. For them the concept of proficiency is more general. British examples of these would be the Cambridge First Certificate in English examination (FCE) and the Cambridge Certificate of Proficiency in English examination (CPE). The function of such tests is to show whether candidates have reached a certain standard with respect to a set of specified abilities. The examining bodies responsible for such tests are independent of teaching institutions and so can be relied on by potential employers, etc. to make fair comparisons between candidates from different institutions and different countries. Though there is no particular purpose in mind for the language, these general proficiency tests should have detailed specifications saying just what it is that successful candidates have demonstrated that they can do. Each test should be seen to be based directly on these specifications. All users of a test (teachers, students, employers, etc.) can then judge whether the test is suitable for them, and can interpret test results. It is not enough to have some vague notion of proficiency, however prestigious the testing body concerned. The Cambridge examinations referred to above are linked to levels in the ALTE (Association of Language Testers in Europe) framework, which draws heavily on the work of the Council of Europe (see Further Reading).

Despite differences between them of content and level of difficulty, all proficiency tests have in common the fact that they are not based on courses that candidates may have previously taken. On the other hand, as we saw in Chapter 1, such tests may themselves exercise considerable influence over the method and content of language courses. Their back-wash effect – for this is what it is – may be beneficial or harmful. In my view, the effect of some widely used proficiency tests is more harmful than beneficial. However, the teachers of students who take such tests, and whose work suffers from a harmful backwash effect, may be able to exercise more influence over the testing organisations concerned than they realise. The supplementing of TOEFL with a writing test, referred to in Chapter 1, is a case in point.

Achievement tests

Most teachers are unlikely to be responsible for proficiency tests. It is much more probable that they will be involved in the preparation and use of achievement tests. In contrast to proficiency tests, achievement tests are directly related to language courses, their purpose being to establish how successful individual students, groups of students, or the courses themselves have been in achieving objectives. They are of two kinds: final achievement tests and progress achievement tests.

Final achievement tests are those administered at the end of a course of study. They may be written and administered by ministries of education, official examining boards, or by members of teaching institutions. Clearly the content of these tests must be related to the courses with which they are concerned, but the nature of this relationship is a matter of disagreement amongst language testers.

In the view of some testers, the content of a final achievement test should be based directly on a detailed course syllabus or on the books and other materials used. This has been referred to as the *syllabus-content approach*. It has an obvious appeal, since the test only contains what it is thought that the students have actually encountered, and thus can be considered, in this respect at least, a fair test. The disadvantage is that if the syllabus is badly designed, or the books and other materials are badly chosen, the results of a test can be very misleading. Successful performance on the test may not truly indicate successful achievement of course objectives. For example, a course may have as an objective the development of conversational ability, but the course itself and the test may require students only to utter carefully prepared statements about their home town, the weather, or whatever. Another course may aim to develop a reading ability in German, but the test may limit itself to the vocabulary the students are known to have met. Yet another course is intended to prepare students for university study in English, but the syllabus (and so the course and the test) may not include listening (with note taking) to English delivered in lecture style on topics of the kind that the students will have to deal with at university. In each of these examples – all of them based on actual cases – test results will fail to show what students have achieved in terms of course objectives.

The alternative approach is to base the test content directly on the objectives of the course. This has a number of advantages. First, it compels course designers to be explicit about objectives. Secondly, it makes it possible for performance on the test to show just how far students have achieved those objectives. This in turn puts pressure on those responsible for the syllabus and for the selection of books and materials to ensure that these are consistent with the course objectives. Tests based on objectives work against the perpetuation of poor teaching practice, something which course-content-based tests, almost as if part of a conspiracy, fail to do. It is my belief that to base test content on course objectives is much to be preferred; it will provide more accurate information about individual and group achievement, and it is likely to promote a more beneficial backwash effect on teaching[1].

Now it might be argued that to base test content on objectives rather than on course content is unfair to students. If the course content does not fit well with objectives, they will be expected to do things for which they have not been prepared. In a sense this is true. But in another sense it is not. If a test is based on the content of a poor or inappropriate course, the students taking it will be misled as to the extent of their achievement and the quality of the course. Whereas if the test is based on objectives, not only will the information it gives be more useful, but there is less chance of the course surviving in its present unsatisfactory form. Initially some students may suffer, but future students will benefit from the pressure for change. The long-term interests of students are best served by final achievement tests whose content is based on course objectives.

The reader may wonder at this stage whether there is any real difference between final achievement tests and proficiency tests. If a test is based on the objectives of a course, and these are equivalent to the language needs on which a proficiency test is based, there is no reason to expect a difference between the form and content of the two tests. Two things have to be remembered, however. First, objectives and needs will not typically coincide in this way. Secondly, many achievement tests are not in fact based on course objectives. These facts have implications both for the users of test results and for test writers. Test users have to know on what basis an achievement test has been constructed, and be aware of the possibly limited validity and applicability of test scores. Test writers, on the other hand, must create achievement tests that reflect the objectives of a particular course, and not expect a general proficiency test (or some imitation of it) to provide a satisfactory alternative.

Progress achievement tests, as their name suggests, are intended to measure the progress that students are making. They contribute to formative assessment (referred to in Chapter 1). Since 'progress' is towards the achievement of course objectives, these tests, too, should relate to objectives. But how? One way of measuring progress would be repeatedly to administer final achievement tests, the (hopefully) increasing scores indicating the progress made. This is not really feasible, particularly in the early stages of a course. The low scores obtained would be discouraging to students and quite possibly to their teachers. The alternative is to establish a series of well-defined short-term objectives. These should make a clear progression towards the final achievement test based on course objectives. Then if the syllabus and teaching are appropriate to these objectives, progress tests based on short-term objectives will fit well with what has been taught. If not, there will be pressure to create a better fit. If it is the syllabus that is at fault, it is the tester's responsibility to make clear that it is there that change is needed, not in the tests.

In addition to more formal achievement tests that require careful preparation, teachers should feel free to set their own 'pop quizzes'. These serve both to make a rough check on students' progress and to keep students on their toes. Since such tests will not form part of formal assessment procedures, their construction and scoring need not be too rigorous. Nevertheless, they should be seen as measuring progress towards the intermediate objectives on which the more formal progress achievement tests are based. They can, however, reflect the particular 'route' that an individual teacher is taking towards the achievement of objectives.

It has been argued in this section that it is better to base the content of achievement tests on course objectives rather than on the detailed content of a course. However, it may not be at all easy to convince colleagues of this, especially if the latter approach is already being followed. Not only is there likely to be natural resistance to change, but such a change may represent a threat to many people. A great deal of skill, tact and, possibly, political manoeuvring may be called for – topics on which this book cannot pretend to give advice.

Diagnostic tests

Diagnostic tests are used to identify learners' strengths and weaknesses. They are intended primarily to ascertain what learning still needs to take place. At the level of broad language skills this is reasonably straightforward. We can be fairly confident of our ability to create tests that will tell us that someone is particularly weak in, say, speaking as opposed to reading in a language. Indeed existing proficiency tests may often prove adequate for this purpose.

We may be able to go further, and analyse samples of a person's performance in writing or speaking in order to create profiles of the student's ability with respect to such categories as 'grammatical accuracy' or 'linguistic appropriacy'. Indeed Chapters 9 and 10 suggest that raters of writing and oral test performance should provide feedback to the test takers as a matter of course.

But it is not so easy to obtain a detailed analysis of a student's command of grammatical structures – something that would tell us, for example, whether she or he had mastered the present perfect/past tense distinction in English. In order to be sure of this, we would need a number of examples of the choice the student made between the two structures in every different context that we thought was significantly different and important enough to warrant obtaining information on. A single example of each would not be enough, since a student might give the correct response by chance. Similarly, if one wanted to test control of the English article system, one would need several items for each of the twenty or so uses of the articles (including the 'zero' article') listed in Collins Cobuild English Usage (1992). Thus, a comprehensive diagnostic test of English grammar would be vast (think of what would be involved in testing the modal verbs, for instance). The size of such a test would make it impractical to administer in a routine fashion. For this reason, very few tests are constructed for purely diagnostic purposes, and those that there are tend not to provide very detailed or reliable information.

The lack of good diagnostic tests is unfortunate. They could be extremely useful for individualised instruction or self-instruction. Learners would be shown where gaps exist in their command of the language, and could be directed to sources of information, exemplification and practice. Happily, the ready availability of relatively inexpensive computers with very large memories should change the situation. Well-written computer programs will ensure that the learner spends no more time than is absolutely necessary to obtain the desired information, and without the need for a test administrator. Tests of this kind will still need a tremendous amount of work to produce. Whether or not they become generally available will depend on the willingness of individuals to write them and of publishers to distribute them. In the meantime, there is at least one very interesting web-based development, DIALANG. Still at the trialling stage as I write this, this project is planned to offer diagnostic tests in fourteen European languages, each having five modules: reading, writing, listening, grammatical structures, and vocabulary.

Placement tests

Placement tests, as their name suggests, are intended to provide information that will help to place students at the stage (or in the part) of the teaching programme most appropriate to their abilities. Typically they are used to assign students to classes at different levels. Placement tests can be bought, but this is to be recommended only when the institution concerned is sure that the test being considered suits its particular teaching programme. No one placement test will work for every institution, and the initial assumption about any test that is commercially available must be that it will not work well. One possible exception is placement tests designed for use by language schools, where the similarity of popular text books used in them means that the schools' teaching programmes also tend to resemble each other.

The placement tests that are most successful are those constructed for particular situations. They depend on the identification of the key features at different levels of teaching in the institution. They are tailor-made rather than bought off the peg. This usually means that they have been produced 'in house'. The work that goes into their construction is rewarded by the saving in time and effort through accurate placement. An example of how a placement test might be developed is given in Chapter 7; the validation of placement tests is referred to in Chapter 4.

Direct versus indirect testing

So far in this chapter we have considered a number of uses to which test results are put. We now distinguish between two approaches to test construction.

Testing is said to be *direct* when it requires the candidate to perform precisely the skill that we wish to measure. If we want to know how well candidates can write compositions, we get them to write compositions. If we want to know how well they pronounce a language, we get them to speak. The tasks, and the texts that are used, should be as authentic as possible. The fact that candidates are aware that they are in a test situation means that the tasks cannot be really authentic. Nevertheless every effort is made to make them as realistic as possible.

Direct testing is easier to carry out when it is intended to measure the productive skills of speaking and writing. The very acts of speaking and writing provide us with information about the candidate's ability. With listening and reading, however, it is necessary to get candidates not only to listen or read but also to demonstrate that they have done this successfully. Testers have to devise methods of eliciting such evidence accurately and without the method interfering with the performance of the skills in which they are interested. Appropriate methods for achieving this are discussed in Chapters 11 and 12. Interestingly enough, in many texts on language testing it is the testing of productive skills that is presented as being most problematic, for reasons usually connected with reliability. In fact these reliability problems are by no means insurmountable, as we shall see in Chapters 9 and 10.

Direct testing has a number of attractions. First, provided that we are clear about just what abilities we want to assess, it is relatively straightforward to create the conditions which will elicit the behaviour on which to base our judgements. Secondly, at least in the case of the productive skills, the assessment and interpretation of students' performance is also quite straightforward. Thirdly, since practice for the test involves practice of the skills that we wish to foster, there is likely to be a helpful backwash effect.

Indirect testing attempts to measure the abilities that underlie the skills in which we are interested. One section of the TOEFL, for example, was developed as an indirect measure of writing ability. It contains items of the following kind where the candidate has to identify which of the underlined elements is erroneous or inappropriate in formal standard English:

> <u>At first</u> the old woman seemed unwilling <u>to accept</u> anything <u>that</u> was offered her by my friend and <u>I</u>.

While the ability to respond to such items has been shown to be related statistically to the ability to write compositions (although the strength of the relationship was not particularly great), the two abilities are far from being identical. Another example of indirect testing is Lado's (1961) proposed method of testing pronunciation ability by a paper and pencil test in which the candidate has to identify pairs of words which rhyme with each other.

Perhaps the main appeal of indirect testing is that it seems to offer the possibility of testing a representative sample of a finite number of abilities which underlie a potentially indefinite large number of manifestations of them. If, for example, we take a representative sample of grammatical structures, then, it may be argued, we have taken a sample which is relevant for all the situations in which control of grammar is necessary. By contrast, direct testing is inevitably limited to a rather small sample of tasks, which may call on a restricted and possibly unrepresentative range of grammatical structures. On this argument, indirect testing is superior to direct testing in that its results are more generalisable.

The main problem with indirect tests is that the relationship between performance on them and performance of the skills in which we are usually more interested tends to be rather weak in strength and uncertain in nature. We do not yet know enough about the component parts of, say, composition writing to predict accurately composition writing ability from scores on tests that measure the abilities that we believe underlie it. We may construct tests of grammar, vocabulary, discourse markers, handwriting, punctuation, and what we will. But we will still not be able to predict accurately scores on compositions (even if we make sure of the validity of the composition scores by having people write many compositions and by scoring these in a valid and highly reliable way).

It seems to me that in our present state of knowledge, at least as far as proficiency and final achievement tests are concerned, it is preferable to rely principally on direct testing. Provided that we sample reasonably widely (for example require at least two compositions, each calling for a different kind of writing and on a different topic), we can expect more accurate estimates of the abilities that really concern us than would be obtained through indirect testing. The fact that direct tests are generally easier to construct simply reinforces this view with respect to institutional tests, as does their greater potential for beneficial backwash. It is only fair to say, however, that many testers are reluctant to commit themselves entirely to direct testing and will always include an indirect element in their tests. Of course, to obtain diagnostic information on underlying abilities, such as control of particular grammatical structures, indirect testing may be perfectly appropriate.

Before ending this section, it should be mentioned that some tests are referred to as *semi-direct*. The most obvious examples of these are speaking tests where candidates respond to tape-recorded stimuli, with their own responses being recorded and later scored. These tests are semi-direct in the sense that, although not direct, they simulate direct testing.

Discrete point versus integrative testing

Discrete point testing refers to the testing of one element at a time, item by item. This might, for example, take the form of a series of items, each testing a particular grammatical structure. *Integrative testing*, by contrast, requires the candidate to combine many language elements in the completion of a task. This might involve writing a composition, making notes while listening to a lecture, taking a dictation, or completing a cloze passage. Clearly this distinction is not unrelated to that between indirect and direct testing. Discrete point tests will almost always be indirect, while integrative tests will tend to be direct. However, some integrative testing methods, such as the cloze procedure, are indirect. Diagnostic tests of grammar of the kind referred to in an earlier section of this chapter will tend to be discrete point.

Norm-referenced versus criterion-referenced testing

Imagine that a reading test is administered to an individual student. When we ask how the student performed on the test, we may be given two kinds of answer. An answer of the first kind would be that the student obtained a score that placed her or him in the top 10 per cent of candidates who have taken that test, or in the bottom 5 per cent; or that she or he did better than 60 per cent of those who took it. A test which is designed to give this kind of information is said to be *norm-referenced*. It relates one candidate's performance to that of other candidates. We are not told directly what the student is capable of doing in the language.

The other kind of answer we might be given is exemplified by the following, taken from the Interagency Language Roundtable (ILR) language skill level descriptions for reading:

> Sufficient comprehension to read simple, authentic written materials in a form equivalent to usual printing or typescript on subjects within a familiar context. Able to read with some misunderstandings straightforward, familiar, factual material, but in general insufficiently experienced with the language to draw inferences directly from the linguistic aspects of the text. Can locate and understand the main ideas and details in materials written for the general reader . . . The individual can read uncomplicated but authentic prose on familiar subjects that are normally presented in a predictable sequence which aids the reader in understanding. Texts may include descriptions and narrations in contexts such as news items describing frequently occurring events, simple biographical information, social notices, formulaic business letters, and simple technical information written for the general reader. Generally the prose that can be read by the individual is predominantly in straightforward/high-frequency sentence patterns. The individual does not have a broad active vocabulary . . . but is able to use contextual and real-world clues to understand the text.

Similarly, a candidate who is awarded the Berkshire Certificate of Proficiency in German Level 1 can 'speak and react to others using simple language in the following contexts':

- to greet, interact with and take leave of others; – to exchange information on personal background, home, school life and interests;
- to discuss and make choices, decisions and plans; – to express opinions, make requests and suggestions; – to ask for information and understand instructions.

In these two cases we learn nothing about how the individual's performance compares with that of other candidates. Rather we learn something about what he or she can actually do in the language. Tests that are designed to provide this kind of information directly are said to be *criterion-referenced*[2].

The purpose of criterion-referenced tests is to classify people according to whether or not they are able to perform some task or set of tasks satisfactorily. The tasks are set, and the performances are evaluated. It does not matter in principle whether all the candidates are successful, or none of the candidates is successful. The tasks are set, and those who perform them satisfactorily 'pass'; those who don't, 'fail'. This means that students are encouraged to measure their progress in relation to meaningful criteria, without feeling that, because they are less able than most of their fellows, they are destined to fail. In the case of the Berkshire German Certificate, for example, it is hoped that all students who are entered for it will be successful. Criterion-referenced tests therefore have two positive virtues: they set meaningful standards in terms of what people can do, which do not change with different groups of candidates, and they motivate students to attain those standards.

The need for direct interpretation of performance means that the construction of a criterion-referenced test may be quite different from that of a norm-referenced test designed to serve the same purpose. Let us imagine that the purpose is to assess the English language ability of students in relation to the demands made by English medium universities. The criterion-referenced test would almost certainly have to be based on an analysis of what students had to be able to do with or through English at university. Tasks would then be set similar to those to be met at university. If this were not done, direct interpretation of performance would be impossible. The norm-referenced test, on the other hand, while its content might be based on a similar analysis, is not so restricted. The Michigan Test of English Language Proficiency, for instance, has multiple choice grammar, vocabulary, and reading comprehension components. A candidate's score on the test does not tell us directly what his or her English ability is in relation to the demands that would be made on it at an English medium university. To know this, we must consult a table which makes recommendations as to the academic load that a student with that score should be allowed to carry, this being based on experience over the years of students with similar scores, not on any meaning in the score itself. In the same way, university administrators have learned from experience how to interpret TOEFL scores and to set minimum scores for their own institutions. The fact that these minimum scores can be thought of as criterial for entry does not, however, make the TOEFL criterion-referenced.

Books on language testing have tended to give advice which is more appropriate to norm-referenced testing than to criterion-referenced testing. One reason for this may be that procedures for use with norm-referenced tests (particularly with respect to such matters as the analysis of items and the estimation of reliability) are well established, while those for criterion-referenced tests are not. The view taken in this book, and argued for in Chapter 6, is that criterion-referenced tests are often to be preferred, not least for the beneficial backwash effect they are likely to have. The lack of agreed procedures for such tests is not sufficient reason for them to be excluded from consideration. Chapter 5 presents one method of estimating the consistency (more or less equivalent to 'reliability') of criterion-referenced tests.

The Council of Europe publications referred to in Further reading are a valuable resource for those wishing to write specifications for criterion-referenced tests. The highly detailed learning objectives specified in those publications, expressed in terms of notions and functions, lend themselves readily to the writing of 'can do' statements, which can be included in test specifications.

Objective testing versus subjective testing

The distinction here is between methods of scoring, and nothing else. If no judgement is required on the part of the scorer, then the scoring is *objective*. A multiple choice test, with the correct responses unambiguously identified, would be a case in point. If judgement is called for, the scoring is said to be *subjective*. There are different degrees of subjectivity in testing. The impressionistic scoring of a composition may be considered more subjective than the scoring of short answers in response to questions on a reading passage.

Objectivity in scoring is sought after by many testers, not for itself, but for the greater reliability it brings. In general, the less subjective the scoring, the greater agreement there will be between two different scorers (and between the scores of one person scoring the same test paper on different occasions). However, there are ways of obtaining reliable subjective scoring, even of compositions. These are discussed first in Chapter 5.

Computer adaptive testing

In most paper and pencil tests, the candidate is presented with all the items, usually in ascending order of difficulty, and is required to respond to as many of them as possible. This is not the most economical way of collecting information on someone's ability. People of high ability (in relation to the test as a whole) will spend time responding to items that are very easy for them – all, or nearly all, of which they will get correct. We would have been able to predict their performance on these items from their correct response to more difficult items. Similarly, we could predict the performance of people of low ability on difficult items, simply by seeing their consistently incorrect response to easy items. There is no real need for strong candidates to attempt easy items, and no need for weak candidates to attempt difficult items.

Computer adaptive testing offers a potentially more efficient way of collecting information on people's ability. All candidates are presented initially with an item of average difficulty. Those who respond correctly are presented with a more difficult item; those who respond incorrectly are presented with an easier item. The computer goes on in this way to present individual candidates with items that are appropriate for their apparent level of ability (as estimated by their performance on previous items), raising or lowering the level of difficulty until a dependable estimate of their ability is achieved. This dependable estimate, which will normally be arrived at after collecting responses to a relatively small number of items, is based on statistical analysis (item response theory) which most language teachers may find daunting but which is presented briefly in Appendix 1. Before leaving this topic, it is perhaps worth noting that oral interviews are typically a form of adaptive testing, with the interviewer's prompts and language being adapted to the apparent level of the candidate.

Communicative language testing

Much has been written about 'communicative language testing'. Discussions have centred on the desirability of measuring the ability to take part in acts of communication (including reading and listening) and on the best way to do this. It is assumed in this book that it is usually communicative ability that we want to test. As a result, what I believe to be the most significant points made in discussions of communicative testing are to be found throughout. A recapitulation under a separate heading would therefore be redundant.

Reader activities

Consider a number of language tests with which you are familiar. For each of them, answer the following questions:
1. What is the purpose of the test?
2. Does it represent direct or indirect testing (or a mixture of both)?
3. Are the items discrete point or integrative (or a mixture of both)?

4. Which items are objective, and which are subjective? Can you order the subjective items according to degree of subjectivity?
5. Is the test norm-referenced or criterion-referenced?
6. Does the test measure communicative abilities? Would you describe it as a communicative test? Justify your answers.
7. What relationship is there between the answers to question 6 and the answers to the other questions?

Further reading

Handbooks for the various Cambridge proficiency tests can be obtained from UCLES, Syndicate Buildings, 1 Hills Road, Cambridge, CB1 2EU (information is also on their website www.cambridge-efl.org). For a discussion of the two approaches towards achievement test content specification, see Pilliner (1968). Nitko (2001) includes a chapter on diagnostic assessment. DIALANG can be found at www.dialang.org. Council of Europe (2001) provides details of the feedback given by DIALANG. Fulcher (2000) discusses the role of computers in language testing. Wall et al (1994) and Fulcher (1997) discuss issues in placement test development. Direct testing calls for texts and tasks to be as authentic as possible: Vol. 2, No. 1 (1985) of the journal *Language Testing* is devoted to articles on authenticity in language testing. Lewkowicz (2000) discusses authenticity in language testing. An account of the development of an indirect test of writing is given in Godshalk et al. (1966). Hudson and Lynch (1984) was an early discussion of criterion-referenced language testing; Brown and Hudson's (2002) book is the first full length treatment of the subject. Classic short papers on criterion-referencing and norm-referencing (not restricted to language testing) are by Popham (1978), favouring criterion-referenced testing, and Ebel (1978), arguing for the superiority of norm-referenced testing. Doubts about the applicability of criterion-referencing to language testing are expressed by Skehan (1984); for a different view, see Hughes (1986). Examples of criterion-referenced tests are: The ACTFL Oral Proficiency Interview (http://www.actfl.org); the FBI Listening summary translation exam (Scott et al, 1996); the Canadian Academic English Language (CAEL) Assessment (Jennings et al, 1999). The description of reading ability given in this chapter comes from the Interagency Language Roundtable Language Skill Level Descriptions. Comparable descriptions at a number of levels for the four skills, intended for assessing students in academic contexts, have been devised by the American Council for the teaching of Foreign Languages (ACTFL). The ILR and ACTFL scales are to be found on the Internet. The ALTE levels, which are used by 18 testing institutions in Europe, representing 15 languages, are also to be found on the Internet. Carroll (1961) made the distinction between discrete point and integrative language testing. Oller (1979) discusses integrative testing techniques. Chalhoub-Deville and Deville (1999) looks at computer adaptive language testing. Chalhoub-Deville (1999) is a collection of papers discussing issues in computer adaptive testing of reading proficiency. Morrow (1979) is a seminal paper on communicative language testing. Further discussion of the topic is to be found in Canale and Swain (1980), Alderson and Hughes (1981, Part 1), Hughes and Porter (1983), and Davies (1988). Weir's (1990) book has as its title *Communicative Language Testing*.

1. Of course, if objectives are unrealistic, then tests will also reveal a failure to achieve them. This, too, can only be regarded as salutary. There may be disagreement as to why there has been a failure to achieve the objectives, but at least this provides a starting point for necessary discussion which otherwise might never have taken place.
2. People differ somewhat in their use of the term 'criterion-referenced'. This is unimportant provided that the sense intended is made clear. The sense in which it is used here is the one which I feel will be most useful to the reader in analysing testing problems.

4 Validity

We already know from Chapter 2 that a test is said to be valid if it measures accurately what it is intended to measure. We create language tests in order to measure such essentially theoretical constructs as 'reading ability', 'fluency in speaking', 'control of grammar', and so on. For this reason, in recent years the term *construct validity*[1] has been increasingly used to refer to the general, overarching notion of validity.

It is not enough to assert that a test has construct validity; empirical evidence is needed. Such evidence may take several forms, including the subordinate forms of validity, *content validity* and *criterion-related validity*. We shall begin by looking at these two forms of evidence in turn, and attempt to show their relevance for the solution of language testing problems. We shall then turn to other forms of evidence.

Content validity

The first form of evidence relates to the content of the test. A test is said to have content validity if its content constitutes a representative sample of the language skills, structures, etc. with which it is meant to be concerned. It is obvious that a grammar test, for instance, must be made up of items relating to the knowledge or control of grammar. But this in itself does not ensure content validity. The test would have content validity only if it included a proper sample of the relevant structures. Just what are the relevant structures will depend, of course, upon the purpose of the test. We would not expect an achievement test for intermediate learners to contain just the same set of structures as one for advanced learners. In order to judge whether or not a test has content validity, we need a specification of the skills or structures, etc. that it is meant to cover. Such a specification should be made at a very early stage in test construction. It isn't to be expected that everything in the specification will always appear in the test; there may simply be too many things for all of them to appear in a single test. But it will provide the test constructor with the basis for making a principled selection of elements for inclusion in the test. A comparison of test specification and test content is the basis for judgements as to content validity. Ideally these judgements should be made by people who are familiar with language teaching and testing but who are not directly concerned with the production of the test in question.

What is the importance of content validity? First, the greater a test's content validity, the more likely it is to be an accurate measure of what it is supposed to measure, i.e. to have construct validity. A test in which major areas identified in the specification are under-represented – or not represented at all – is unlikely to be accurate. Secondly, such a test is likely to have a harmful backwash effect. Areas that are not tested are likely to become areas ignored in teaching and learning. Too often the content of tests is determined by what is easy to test rather than what is important to test. The best safeguard against this is to write full test specifications and to ensure that the test content is a fair reflection of these. For this reason, content validation should be carried out while a test is being developed; it should not wait until the test is already being used. Advice on the writing of specifications is to be found in Chapter 7.

Criterion-related validity

The second form of evidence of a test's construct validity relates to the degree to which results on the test agree with those provided by some independent and highly dependable assessment of the candidate's ability. This independent assessment is thus the criterion measure against which the test is validated.

There are essentially two kinds of criterion-related validity: *concurrent validity* and *predictive validity*. Concurrent validity is established when the test and the criterion are administered at about the same time. To exemplify this kind of validation in achievement testing, let us consider a situation where course objectives call for an oral component as part of the final achievement test. The objectives may list a large number of 'functions' which students are expected to perform orally, to test all of which might take 45 minutes for each student. This could well be impractical. Perhaps it is felt that only ten minutes can be devoted to each student for the oral component. The question then arises: can such a ten-minute session give a sufficiently accurate estimate of the student's ability with respect to the functions specified in the course objectives? Is it, in other words, a valid measure?

From the point of view of content validity, this will depend on how many of the functions are tested in the component, and how representative they are of the complete set of functions included in the objectives. Every effort should be made when designing the oral component to give it content validity. Once this has been done, however, we can go further. We can attempt to establish the concurrent validity of the component.

To do this, we should choose at random a sample of all the students taking the test. These students would then be subjected to the full 45 minute oral component necessary for coverage of all the functions, using perhaps four scorers to ensure reliable scoring (see next chapter). This would be the criterion test against which the shorter test would be judged. The students' scores on the full test would be compared with the ones they obtained on the ten-minute session, which would have been conducted and scored in the usual way, without knowledge of their performance on the longer version. If the comparison between the two sets of scores reveals a high level of agreement, then the shorter version of the oral component may be considered valid, inasmuch as it gives results similar to those obtained with the longer version. If, on the other hand, the two sets of scores show little agreement, the shorter version cannot be considered valid; it cannot be used as a dependable measure of achievement with respect to the functions specified in the objectives. Of course, if ten minutes really is all that can be spared for each student, then the oral component may be included for the contribution that it makes to the assessment of students' overall achievement and for its backwash effect. But it cannot be regarded as an accurate measure in itself.

References to 'a high level of agreement' and 'little agreement' raise the question of how the level of agreement is measured. There are, in fact, standard procedures for comparing sets of scores in this way, which generate what is called a 'correlation coefficient' (or, when we are considering validity, a 'validity coefficient') – a mathematical measure of similarity. Perfect agreement between two sets of scores will result in a coefficient of 1. Total lack of agreement will give a coefficient of zero. To get a feel for the meaning of a coefficient between these two extremes, read the contents of the box on page 29.

Whether or not a particular level of agreement is regarded as satisfactory will depend upon the purpose of the test and the importance of the decisions that are made on the basis of it. If, for example, a test of oral ability was to be used as part of the selection procedure for a high level diplomatic post, then a coefficient of 0.7 might well be regarded as too low for a shorter test to be substituted for a full and thorough test of oral ability. The saving in time would not be worth the risk of appointing someone with insufficient ability in the relevant foreign language. On the other hand, a coefficient of the same size might be

To get a feel for what a coefficient means in terms of the level of agreement between two sets of scores, it is best to square that coefficient. Let us imagine that a coefficient of 0.7 is calculated between the two oral tests referred to in the main text. Squared, this becomes 0.49. If this is regarded as a proportion of one, and converted to a percentage, we get 49 per cent. On the basis of this, we can say that the scores on the short test predict 49 per cent of the variation in scores on the longer test. In broad terms, there is almost 50 per cent agreement between one set of scores and the other. A coefficient of 0.5 would signify 25 per cent agreement; a coefficient of 0.8 would indicate 64 per cent agreement. It is important to note that a 'level of agreement' of, say, 50 per cent does not mean that 50 per cent of the students would each have equivalent scores on the two versions. We are dealing with an overall measure of agreement that does not refer to the individual scores of students. This explanation of how to interpret validity coefficients is very brief and necessarily rather crude. For a better understanding, the reader is referred to the Further reading section at the end of the chapter.

perfectly acceptable for a brief interview forming part of a placement test[2].

It should be said that the criterion for concurrent validation is not necessarily a proven, longer test. A test may be validated against, for example, teachers' assessments of their students, provided that the assessments themselves can be relied on. This would be appropriate where a test was developed that claimed to be measuring something different from all existing tests.

The second kind of criterion-related validity is predictive validity. This concerns the degree to which a test can predict candidates' future performance. An example would be how well a proficiency test could predict a student's ability to cope with a graduate course at a British university. The criterion measure here might be an assessment of the student's English as perceived by his or her supervisor at the university, or it could be the outcome of the course (pass/fail etc.). The choice of criterion measure raises interesting issues. Should we rely on the subjective and untrained judgements of supervisors? How helpful is it to use final outcome as the criterion measure when so many factors other than ability in English (such as subject knowledge, intelligence, motivation, health and happiness) will have contributed to every outcome? Where outcome is used as the criterion measure, a validity coefficient of around 0.4 (only 20 per cent agreement) is about as high as one can expect. This is partly because of the other factors, and partly because those students whose English the test predicted would be inadequate are not normally permitted to take the course, and so the test's (possible) accuracy in predicting problems for those students goes unrecognised[3].

As a result, a validity coefficient of this order is generally regarded as satisfactory. The Further reading section at the end of the chapter gives references to the reports on the validation of the British Council's ELTS test (the predecessor of IELTS), in which these issues are discussed at length.

Another example of predictive validity would be where an attempt was made to validate a placement test. Placement tests attempt to predict the most appropriate class for any particular student. Validation would involve an enquiry, once courses were under way, into the proportion of students who were thought to be misplaced. It would then be a matter of comparing the number of misplacements (and their effect on teaching and learning) with the cost of developing and administering a test that would place students more accurately.

Content validity, concurrent validity and predictive validity all have a part to play in the development of a test. For instance, in developing an English placement test for language schools, Hughes et al (1996) validated test content against the content of three popular course books used by language schools in Britain, compared students' performance on the test with their performance on the existing placement tests of a number of language schools, and then examined the success of the test in placing students in classes. Only when this process was complete (and minor changes made on the basis of the results obtained) was the test published.

Other forms of evidence for construct validity

Investigations of a test's content validity and criterion-related validity provide evidence for its overall, or construct validity. However, they are not the only source of evidence. One could imagine a test that was meant to measure reading ability, the specifications for which included reference to a variety of reading sub-skills, including, for example, the ability to guess the meaning of unknown words from the context in which they are met. Content validation of the test might confirm that these sub-skills were well represented in the test. Concurrent validation might reveal a strong relationship between students' performance on the test and their supervisors' assessment of their reading ability. But one would still not be sure that the items in the test were 'really' measuring the sub-skills listed in the specifications.

The word 'construct' refers to any underlying ability (or trait) that is hypothesised in a theory of language ability. The ability to guess the meaning of unknown words from context, referred to above, would be an example. It is a matter of empirical research to establish whether or not such a distinct ability exists, can be measured, and is indeed measured in that test. Without confirming evidence from such research, it would not be possible to say that the part of a test that attempted to measure that ability has construct validity. If all of the items in a test were meant to measure specified abilities, then, without evidence that they were actually measuring those abilities, the construct validity of the whole test would be in question.

The reader may ask at this point whether such a demanding require-ment for validity is appropriate for practical testing situations. It is easy to see the relevance of content validity in developing a test. And if a test has criterion related validity, whether concurrent or predictive, surely it is doing its job well. But does it matter if we can't demonstrate that parts of the test are measuring exactly what we say they are measuring?

I have some sympathy for this view. What is more, I believe that gross, commonsense constructs like 'reading ability' and 'writing ability' are unproblematic. Similarly, the direct measurement of writing ability, for instance, should not cause us too much concern: even without research we can be fairly confident that we are measuring a distinct and mean-ingful ability (albeit a quite general and not closely defined ability)[4]. Once we try to measure such an ability indirectly, however, we can no longer take for granted what we are doing. We need to look to a theory of writing ability for guidance as to the form an indirect test should take, its content and techniques.

Let us imagine that we are indeed planning to construct an indirect test of writing ability that must for reasons of practicality be multiple choice. Our theory of writing tells us that underlying writing ability are a number of sub-abilities, such as control of punctuation, sensitivity to demands on style, and so on. We construct items that are meant to measure these sub-abilities and administer them as a pilot test. How do we know that this test really is measuring writing ability? One step we would almost certainly take is to obtain extensive samples of the writing ability of the group to whom the test is first administered, and have these reliably scored. We would then compare scores on the pilot test with the scores given for the samples of writing. If there is a high level of agreement (and a coefficient of the kind described in the previous section can be calculated), then we have evidence that we are measuring writing ability with the test.

So far, however, although we may have developed a satisfactory indirect test of writing, we have not demonstrated the reality of the underlying constructs (control of punctuation, etc.). To do this we might administer a series of specially constructed tests, measuring each of the constructs by a number of different methods. In addition, compositions written by the people who took the tests could be scored separately for performance in relation to the hypothesised constructs (control of punctuation, for example). In this way, for each person, we would obtain a set of scores for each of the constructs. Coefficients could then be calculated between the various measures. If the coefficients between scores on the same construct are consistently higher than those between scores on different constructs, then we have evidence that we are indeed measuring separate and identifiable constructs. This knowledge would be particularly valuable if we wanted to use the test for diagnostic purposes.

Another way of obtaining evidence about the construct validity of a test is to investigate what test takers actually *do* when they respond to an item. Two principal methods are used to gather such information: *think aloud* and *retrospection*. In the think aloud method, test takers voice their thoughts as they respond to the item. In retrospection, they try to recollect what their thinking was as they responded. In both cases their thoughts are usually tape-recorded, although a questionnaire may be used for the latter. The problem with the think aloud method is that the very voicing of thoughts may interfere with what would be the natural response to the item. The drawback to retrospection is that thoughts may be misremembered or forgotten. Despite these weaknesses, such research can give valuable insights into how items work (which may be quite different from what the test developer intended).

All test validation is to some degree a research activity. When it goes beyond content and criterion related validation, theories are put to the test and are confirmed, modified, or abandoned. It is in this way that language testing can be put on a sounder, more scientific footing. But it will not all happen overnight; there is a long way to go. In the meantime, the practical language tester should try to keep abreast of what is known. When in doubt, where it is possible, direct testing of abilities is recommended.

Validity in scoring

It is worth pointing out that if a test is to have validity, not only the items but also the way in which the responses are scored must be valid. It is no use having excellent items if they are scored invalidly. A reading test may call for short written responses. If the scoring of these responses takes into account spelling and grammar, then it is not valid (assuming the reading test is meant to measure reading ability!). By measuring more than one ability, it makes the measurement of the one ability in question less accurate. There may be occasions when, because of misspelling or faulty grammar, it is not clear what the test taker intended. In this case, the problem is with the item, not with the scoring. Similarly, if we are interested in measuring speaking or writing ability, it is not enough to elicit speech or writing in a valid fashion. The rating of that speech or writing has to be valid too. For instance, overemphasis on such mechanical features as spelling and punctuation can invalidate the scoring of written work (and so the test of writing).

Face validity

A test is said to have face validity if it looks as if it measures what it is supposed to measure. For example, a test that pretended to measure pronunciation ability but which did not require the test taker to speak (and there have been some) might be thought to lack face validity. This would be true even if the test's construct and criterion-related validity could be demonstrated. Face validity is not a scientific notion and is not seen as providing evidence for construct validity, yet it can be very important. A test which does not have face validity may not be accepted by candidates, teachers, education authorities or employers. It may simply not be used; and if it is used, the candidates' reaction to it may mean that they do not perform on it in a way that truly reflects their ability. Novel techniques, particularly those which provide indirect measures, have to be introduced slowly, with care, and with convincing explanations.

How to make tests more valid

In the development of a high stakes test, which may significantly affect the lives of those who take it, there is an obligation to carry out a full validation exercise before the test becomes operational.

In the case of teacher-made tests, full validation is unlikely to be possible. In these circumstances, I would recommend the following:

First, write explicit specifications for the test (see Chapter 7) which take account of all that is known about the constructs that are to be measured. Make sure that you include a representative sample of the content of these in the test.

Second, whenever feasible, use direct testing. If for some reason it is decided that indirect testing is necessary, reference should be made to the research literature to confirm that measurement of the relevant underlying constructs has been demonstrated using the testing techniques that are to be employed (this may often result in disappointment, another reason for favouring direct testing!).

Third, make sure that the scoring of responses relates directly to what is being tested.

Finally, do everything possible to make the test reliable. If a test is not reliable, it cannot be valid. Reliability is dealt with in the next chapter.

Last word

Test developers must make every effort to make their tests as valid as possible.

Any published test should supply details of its validation, without which its validity (and suitability) can hardly be judged by a potential purchaser. Tests for which validity information is not available should be treated with caution.

Reader activities

Consider any tests with which you are familiar. Assess each of them in terms of the various kinds of validity that have been presented in this chapter. What empirical evidence is there that the test is valid? If evidence is lacking, how would you set about gathering it?

Further reading

At first sight, validity seems a quite straightforward concept. On closer examination, however, it can seem impossibly complex, with some writers even finding it difficult to separate it from the notion of reliability in some circumstances. In the present chapter, I have tried to present validity in a form which can be grasped by newcomers to the field and which will prove useful in thinking about and developing tests. For those who would like to explore the concept in greater depth, I would recommend: Anastasi and Urbina (1997) for a general discussion of test validity and ways of measuring it; Nitko (2001) for validity in the context of educational measurement; and Messick (1989) for a long, wide ranging and detailed chapter on validity which is much cited in language testing literature. His 1996 paper discusses the relationship between validity and backwash.

Bachman and Palmer (1981) was a notable early attempt to introduce construct validation to language testing. A still interesting example of test validation (of the British Council ELTS test) in which a number of important issues are raised, is described and evaluated in Criper and Davies (1988) and Hughes, Porter and Weir (1988). More recent accounts of validation can be found in Wall et al (1994) and Fulcher (1997). Cohen (1984) describes early use of 'think-aloud' and retrospection. Buck (1991) and Wu (1998) provide more recent examples of the use of introspection. Storey (1997) uses 'think-aloud'. Bradshaw (1990) investigates the face validity of a placement test. Weir et al. (1993) and Weir and Porter (1995) disagree with Alderson (1990a, 1990b) about the evidence for certain reading comprehension skills. Cumming and Berwick (1996) is a collection of papers on validation in language testing. Bachman and Cohen (1998) is a collection of papers concerned with the relationship between second language acquisition and language testing research. For the argument (with which I do not agree) that there is no criterion against which 'communicative' language tests can be validated (in the sense of criterion-related validity), see Morrow (1986). Bachman's (1990) book – much referred to and influential in the field of language testing – discusses validity and other theoretical issues in depth.

1. When the term 'construct validity' was first used, it was in the context of psychological tests, particularly of personality tests. There was real concern at that time at the number of such tests which purported to measure psychological constructs, without offering evidence that these constructs existed in a measurable form. The demand was therefore that such evidence of these constructs be provided as part of demonstrating a test's validity.

2. Sometimes the size of a correlation coefficient can be misleading, an accident of the particular sample of people taking the test(s). If, for example, there are 'extreme' scores from outstandingly good or outstandingly poor takers of the test(s), the coefficient may be higher than the performance of the group as a whole warrants. See Nitko (2001) for details.

3. Because the full range of ability is not included, the validity coefficient is an underestimate (see previous footnote).

4. However, one may question the validity of the scales used to assess performance in, say, writing. How far do they reflect the development or acquisition of the skills they refer to? This may not be important in proficiency testing, where the scales may be based on levels of skill needed for a particular purpose (a job, for example). In achievement testing, scales that are not consistent with patterns of development may lack validity.

5 Reliability

Imagine that a hundred students take a 100-item test at three o'clock one Thursday afternoon. The test is not impossibly difficult or ridiculously easy for these students, so they do not all get zero or a perfect score of 100. Now what if, in fact, they had not taken the test on the Thursday but had taken it at three o'clock the previous afternoon? Would we expect each student to have got exactly the same score on the Wednesday as they actually did on the Thursday? The answer to this question must be no. Even if we assume that the test is excellent, that the conditions of administration are almost identical, that the scoring calls for no judgement on the part of the scorers and is carried out with perfect care, and that no learning or forgetting has taken place during the one-day interval, nevertheless we would not expect every individual to get precisely the same score on the Wednesday as they got on the Thursday. Human beings are not like that; they simply do not behave in exactly the same way on every occasion, even when the circumstances seem identical.

But if this is the case, it implies that we can never have complete trust in any set of test scores. We know that the scores would have been different if the test had been administered on the previous or the following day. This is inevitable, and we must accept it. What we have to do is construct, administer and score tests in such a way that the scores actually obtained on a test on a particular occasion are likely to be very similar to those which would have been obtained if it had been administered to the same students with the same ability, but at a different time. The more similar the scores would have been, the more reliable the test is said to be.

Look at the hypothetical data in Table 1(a). They represent the scores obtained by ten students who took a 100-item test (A) on a particular occasion, and those that they would have obtained if they had taken it a day later. Compare the two sets of scores. (Do not worry for the moment about the fact that we would never be able to obtain this information. Ways of estimating what scores people would have got on

36

another occasion are discussed later. The most obvious of these is simply to have people take the same test twice.) Note the size of the difference between the two scores for each student.

Table 1(a): *Scores on test A (Invented data)*

Student	Score obtained	Score which would have been obtained on the following day
Bill	68	82
Mary	46	28
Ann	19	34
Harry	89	67
Cyril	43	63
Pauline	56	59
Don	43	35
Colin	27	23
Irene	76	62
Sue	62	49

Now look at Table 1(b), which displays the same kind of information for a second 100-item test (B). Again note the difference in scores for each student.

Table 1(b): *Scores on test B (Invented data)*

Student	Score obtained	Score which would have been obtained on the following day
Bill	65	69
Mary	48	52
Ann	23	21
Harry	85	90
Cyril	44	39
Pauline	56	59
Don	38	35
Colin	19	16
Irene	67	62
Sue	52	57

Which test seems the more reliable? The differences between the two sets of scores are much smaller for Test B than for Test A. On the evidence that we have here (and in practice we would not wish to make claims about reliability on the basis of such a small number of individuals), Test B appears to be more reliable than Test A.

Look now at Table 1(c), which represents scores of the same students on an interview using a five-point scale.

Table 1(c): *Scores on interview (Invented data)*

Student	Score obtained	Score which would have been obtained on the following day
Bill	5	3
Mary	4	5
Ann	2	4
Harry	5	2
Cyril	2	4
Pauline	3	5
Don	3	1
Colin	1	2
Irene	4	5
Sue	3	1

In one sense the two sets of interview scores are very similar. The largest difference between a student's actual score and the one which would have been obtained on the following day is 3. But the largest possible difference is only 4! Really the two sets of scores are very different. This becomes apparent once we compare the size of the differences between students with the size of differences between scores for individual students. They are of about the same order of magnitude. The result of this can be seen if we place the students in order according to their interview score, the highest first. The order based on their actual scores is markedly different from the one based on the scores they would have obtained if they had had the interview on the following day. This interview turns out in fact not to be very reliable at all.

The reliability coefficient

It is possible to quantify the reliability of a test in the form of a *reliability coefficient*. Reliability coefficients are like validity coefficients

(Chapter 4). They allow us to compare the reliability of different tests. The ideal reliability coefficient is 1. A test with a reliability coefficient of 1 is one which would give precisely the same results for a particular set of candidates regardless of when it happened to be administered. A test which had a reliability coefficient of zero (and let us hope that no such test exists!) would give sets of results quite unconnected with each other, in the sense that the score that someone actually got on a Wednesday would be no help at all in attempting to predict the score he or she would get if they took the test the day after. It is between the two extremes of 1 and zero that genuine test reliability coefficients are to be found.

Certain authors have suggested how high a reliability coefficient we should expect for different types of language tests. Lado (1961), for example, says that good vocabulary, structure and reading tests are usually in the .90 to .99 range, while auditory comprehension tests are more often in the .80 to .89 range. Oral production tests may be in the .70 to .79 range. He adds that a reliability coefficient of .85 might be considered high for an oral production test but low for a reading test. These suggestions reflect what Lado sees as the difficulty in achieving reliability in the testing of the different abilities. In fact the reliability coefficient that is to be sought will depend also on other considerations, most particularly the importance of the decisions that are to be taken on the basis of the test. The more important the decisions, the greater reliability we must demand: if we are to refuse someone the opportunity to study overseas because of their score on a language test, then we have to be pretty sure that their score would not have been much different if they had taken the test a day or two earlier or later. The next section will explain how the reliability coefficient can be used to arrive at another figure (the standard error of measurement) to estimate likely differences of this kind. Before this is done, however, something has to be said about the way in which reliability coefficients are arrived at.

The first requirement is to have two sets of scores for comparison. The most obvious way of obtaining these is to get a group of subjects to take the same test twice. This is known as the *test-retest method*. The drawbacks are not difficult to see. If the second administration of the test is too soon after the first, then subjects are likely to recall items and their responses to them, making the same responses more likely and the reliability spuriously high. If there is too long a gap between administrations, then learning (or forgetting!) will have taken place, and the coefficient will be lower than it should be. However long the gap, the subjects are unlikely to be very motivated to take the same test twice, and this too is likely to have a depressing effect on the coefficient. These effects are reduced somewhat by the use of two different forms of the same test (the *alternate forms method*). However, alternate forms are often simply not available.

It turns out, surprisingly, that the most common methods of obtaining the necessary two sets of scores involve only one administration of one test. Such methods provide us with a *coefficient of internal consistency*. The most basic of these is the *split half method*. In this the subjects take the test in the usual way, but each subject is given two scores. One score is for one half of the test, the second score is for the other half. The two sets of scores are then used to obtain the reliability coefficient as if the whole test had been taken twice. In order for this method to work, it is necessary for the test to be split into two halves which are really equivalent, through the careful matching of items (in fact where items in the test have been ordered in terms of difficulty, a split into odd-numbered items and even-numbered items may be adequate). It can be seen that this method is rather like the alternate forms method, except that the two 'forms' are only half the length[1].

It has been demonstrated empirically that this altogether more economical method will indeed give good estimates of alternate forms coefficients, provided that the alternate forms are closely equivalent to each other[2].

The standard error of measurement and the true score

While the reliability coefficient allows us to compare the reliability of tests, it does not tell us directly how close an individual's actual score is to what he or she might have scored on another occasion. With a little further calculation, however, it is possible to estimate how close a person's actual score is to what is called their 'true score'. Imagine that it were possible for someone to take the same language test over and over again, an indefinitely large number of times, without their performance being affected by having already taken the test, and without their ability in the language changing. Unless the test is perfectly reliable, and provided that it is not so easy or difficult that the student always gets full marks or zero, we would expect their scores on the various administrations to vary. If we had all of these scores we would be able to calculate their average score, and it would seem not unreasonable to think of this average as the one that best represents the student's ability with respect to this particular test. It is this score, which for obvious reasons we can never know for certain, which is referred to as the candidate's *true score*.

We are able to make statements about the probability that a candidate's true score (the one which best represents their ability on the test) is within a certain number of points of the score they actually obtained on the test. In order to do this, we must first know the *standard error of measurement* of the particular test. The calculation of the standard error of measurement is based on the reliability coefficient and a measure of the spread of all the scores on the test (for a given spread of scores, the greater the reliability coefficient, the smaller will be the standard error of measurement). How such statements can be made using the standard error of measurement of the test is best illustrated by an example.

Suppose that a test has a standard error of measurement of 5. An individual scores 56 on that test. We are then in a position to make the following statements[3]:

We can be about 68 per cent certain that the person's true score lies in the range of 51–61 (i.e. within one standard error of measurement of the score actually obtained on this occasion).

We can be about 95 per cent certain that their true score is in the range 46–66 (i.e. within two standard errors of measurement of the score actually obtained).

We can be 99.7 per cent certain that their true score is in the range 41–71 (i.e. within three standard errors of measurement of the score actually obtained).

These statements are based on what is known about the pattern of scores that would occur if it were in fact possible for someone to take the test repeatedly in the way described above. About 68 per cent of their scores would be within one standard error of measurement, and so on. If in fact they only take the test once, we cannot be sure how their score on that occasion relates to their true score, but we are still able to make probabilistic statements as above[4].

In the end, the statistical rationale is not important. What is important is to recognise how we can use the standard error of measurement to inform decisions that we take on the basis of test scores. We should, for example, be very wary of taking important negative decisions about people's future if the standard error of measurement indicates that their true score is quite likely to be equal to or above the score that would lead to a positive decision, even though their actual score is below it. For this reason, all published tests should provide users with not only the reliability coefficient but also the standard error of measurement.

A relatively new approach to the statistical analysis of test data, known as *Item Response Theory (IRT)* allows an even better estimate of how far an individual test taker's actual score is likely to diverge from their true score. While classical analysis gives us a single estimate for all test takers, IRT gives an estimate for each individual, basing this estimate on that individual's performance on each of the items on the test. Examples of this estimate, usually referred to as the 'standard error' of the individual's score, can be found in Appendix 1.

What has been said so far in this chapter has been concerned with the consistency of *scores* that candidates obtain on a test. In criterion-referenced testing, we are often less interested in scores than in whether a candidate has reached the criterion which has been set. In this case, the consistency which we are looking for is referred to as 'decision consistency' (rather than 'reliability')[5].

We want to know whether a test is consistent in deciding whether or not the candidates have or have not reached the criterion. Imagine a case where 50 candidates take a test (perhaps two alternate forms of it) twice. Those who reach a criterion may be called 'masters' (in the sense of having mastered the skills, or whatever, that are being tested) and those who do not reach it may be called 'non-masters'. Of the 50 candidates:

18 are masters on both occasions

15 are non-masters on both occasions

9 are masters on the first occasion but non-masters on the second

8 are non-masters on the first occasion but masters on the second

So, out of 50 candidates, 33 are assigned to the same category (master or non-master on both occasions. Thirty-three out of 50 can be expressed as a percentage (66%) or as a proportion (0.66). This last value, 0.66, is known as the 'per cent agreement' and is an accepted estimate of decision consistency. For other methods for estimating decision consistency (and they are not limited to just two groups, masters and non-masters), see the Further reading section.

We have seen the importance of reliability. If a test is not reliable then we know that the actual scores of many individuals are likely to be quite different from their true scores. This means that we can place little reliance on those scores. Even where reliability is quite high, the standard error of measurement (or the standard errors obtained through IRT) serves to remind us that in the case of some individuals there is quite possibly a large discrepancy between actual score and true score. This should make us very cautious about making important decisions on the basis of the test scores of candidates whose actual scores place them close to the cut-off point (the point that divides 'passes' from 'fails'). We should at least consider the possibility of gathering further relevant information on the language ability of such candidates.

Having seen the importance of reliability, we shall consider, later in the chapter, how to make our tests more reliable. Before that, however, we shall look at another aspect of reliability.

Scorer reliability

In the first example given in this chapter we spoke about scores on a multiple choice test. It was most unlikely, we thought, that every candidate would get precisely the same score on both of two possible administrations of the test. We assumed, however, that scoring of the test would be 'perfect'. That is, if a particular candidate did perform in exactly the same way on the two occasions, they would be given the same score on both occasions. That is, any one scorer would give the same score on the two occasions, and this would be the same score as would be given by any other scorer on either occasion[6].

It is possible to quantify the level of agreement given by the same or different scorers on different occasions by means of a scorer reliability coefficient which can be interpreted in a similar way as the test reliability coefficient. In the case of the multiple choice test just described, the scorer reliability coefficient would be 1. As we noted in Chapter 3, when scoring requires no judgement, and could in principle or in practice be carried out by a computer, the test is said to be objective. Only carelessness should cause the scorer reliability coefficients of objective tests to fall below 1.

However, we did not make the assumption of perfectly consistent scoring in the case of the interview scores discussed earlier in the chapter. It would probably have seemed to the reader an unreasonable assumption. We can accept that scorers should be able to be consistent when there is only one easily recognised correct response. But when a degree of judgement is called for on the part of the scorer, as in the scoring of performance in an interview, perfect consistency is not to be expected. Such subjective tests will not have scorer reliability coefficients of 1! Indeed there was a time when many people thought that scorer reliability coefficients (and also the reliability of the test) would always be too low to justify the use of subjective measures of language ability in serious language testing. This view is less widely held today. While the perfect reliability of objective tests is not obtainable in subjective tests, there are ways of making it sufficiently high for test results to be valuable. It is possible, for instance, to obtain scorer reliability coefficients of over 0.9 for the scoring of compositions.

It is perhaps worth making explicit something about the relationship between scorer reliability and test reliability. If the scoring of a test is not reliable, then the test results cannot be reliable either. Indeed the test reliability coefficient will almost certainly be lower than scorer reliability, since other sources of unreliability will be additional to what enters through imperfect scoring. In a case I know of, the scorer reliability coefficient on a composition writing test was .92, while the reliability coefficient for the test was .84. Variability in the performance of individual candidates accounted for the difference between the two coefficients.

How to make tests more reliable

As we have seen, there are two components of test reliability: the performance of candidates from occasion to occasion, and the reliability of the scoring. We will begin by suggesting ways of achieving consistent performances from candidates and then turn our attention to scorer reliability.

Take enough samples of behaviour

Other things being equal, the more items that you have on a test, the more reliable that test will be. This seems intuitively right. If we wanted to know how good an archer someone was, we wouldn't rely on the evidence of a single shot at the target. That one shot could be quite unrepresentative of their ability. To be satisfied that we had a really reliable measure of the ability we would want to see a large number of shots at the target.

The same is true for language testing. It has been demonstrated empirically that the addition of further items will make a test more reliable. There is even a formula (the Spearman-Brown formula, see Appendix 1) that allows one to estimate how many extra items similar to the ones already in the test will be needed to increase the reliability coefficient to a required level. One thing to bear in mind, however, is that the additional items should be independent of each other and of existing items. Imagine a reading test that asks the question: 'Where did the thief hide the jewels?' If an additional item following that took the form, 'What was unusual about the hiding place?', it would not make a full contribution to an increase in the reliability of the test. Why not? Because it is hardly possible for someone who got the original question wrong to get the supplementary question right. Such candidates are effectively prevented from answering the additional question; for them, in reality, there is no additional question. We do not get an additional sample of their behaviour, so the reliability of our estimate of their ability is not increased.

Each additional item should as far as possible represent a fresh start for the candidate. By doing this we are able to gain additional information on all of the candidates – information that will make test results more reliable. The use of the word 'item' should not be taken to mean only brief questions and answers. In a test of writing, for example, where candidates have to produce a number of passages, each of those passages is to be regarded as an item. The more independent passages there are, the more reliable will be the test. In the same way, in an interview used to test oral ability, the candidate should be given as many 'fresh starts' as possible. More detailed implications of the need to obtain sufficiently large samples of behaviour will be outlined later in the book, in chapters devoted to the testing of particular abilities.

While it is important to make a test long enough to achieve satisfactory reliability, it should not be made so long that the candidates become so bored or tired that the behaviour they exhibit becomes unrepresentative of their ability. At the same time, it may often be necessary to resist pressure to make a test shorter than is appropriate. The usual argument for shortening a test is that it is not practical for it to be longer. The answer to this is that accurate information does not come cheaply: if such information is needed, then the price has to be paid. In general, the more important the decisions based on a test, the longer the test should be. Jephthah used the pronunciation of the word 'shibboleth' as a test to distinguish his own men from Ephraimites, who could not pronounce *sh*. Those who failed the test were executed. Any of Jephthah's own men killed in error might have wished for a longer, more reliable test.

Exclude items which do not discriminate well between weaker and stronger students.

Items on which strong students and weak students perform with similar degrees of success contribute little to the reliability of a test. Statistical analysis of items (Appendix 1) will reveal which items do not discriminate well. These are likely to include items which are too easy or too difficult for the candidates, but not only such items. A small number of easy, non-discriminating items may be kept at the beginning of a test to give candidates confidence and reduce the stress they feel.

Do not allow candidates too much freedom

In some kinds of language test there is a tendency to offer candidates a choice of questions and then to allow them a great deal of freedom in the way that they answer the ones that they have chosen. An example would be a test of writing where the candidates are simply given a selection of titles from which to choose. Such a procedure is likely to have a depressing effect on the reliability of the test. The more freedom that is given, the greater is likely to be the difference between the performance actually elicited and the performance that would have been elicited had the test been taken, say, a day later. In general, therefore, candidates should not be given a choice, and the range over which possible answers might vary should be restricted. Compare the following writing tasks:

1. Write a composition on tourism.
2. Write a composition on tourism in this country.
3. Write a composition on how we might develop the tourist industry in this country.
4. Discuss the following measures intended to increase the number of foreign tourists coming to this country:
    i) More/better advertising and/or information (Where? What form should it take?).
    ii) Improve facilities (hotels, transportation, communication, etc.).
    iii) Training of personnel (guides, hotel managers, etc.).

The successive tasks impose more and more control over what is written. The fourth task is likely to be a much more reliable indicator of writing ability than the first. The general principle of restricting the freedom of candidates will be taken up again in chapters relating to particular skills. It should perhaps be said here, however, that in restricting the students we must be careful not to distort too much the task that we really want to see them perform. The potential tension between reliability and validity is addressed at the end of the chapter.

Write unambiguous items

It is essential that candidates should not be presented with items whose meaning is not clear or to which there is an acceptable answer which the test writer has not anticipated. In a reading test I once set the following open-ended question, based on a lengthy reading passage about English accents and dialects: Where does the author direct the reader who is interested in non-standard dialects of English? The expected answer was the Further reading section of the book. A number of candidates answered 'page 3', which was the place in the text where the author actually said that the interested reader should look in the Further reading section. Only the alertness of those scoring the test revealed that there was a completely unanticipated correct answer to the question. If that had not happened, a correct answer would have been scored as incorrect. The fact that an individual candidate might interpret the question in different ways on different occasions means that the item is not contributing fully to the reliability of the test.

The best way to arrive at unambiguous items is, having drafted them, to subject them to the critical scrutiny of colleagues, who should try as hard as they can to find alternative interpretations to the ones intended. If this task is entered into in the right spirit – one of good-natured perversity – most of the problems can be identified before the test is administered. Pre-testing of the items on a group of people comparable to those for whom the test is intended (see Chapter 7) should reveal the remainder. Where pre-testing is not practicable, scorers must be on the lookout for patterns of response that indicate that there are problem items.

Provide clear and explicit instructions

This applies both to written and oral instructions. If it is possible for candidates to misinterpret what they are asked to do, then on some occasions some of them certainly will. It is by no means always the weakest candidates who are misled by ambiguous instructions; indeed it is often the better candidate who is able to provide the alternative interpretation. A common fault of tests written for the students of a particular teaching institution is the supposition that the students all know what is intended by carelessly worded instructions. The frequency of the complaint that students are unintelligent, have been stupid, have wilfully misunderstood what they were asked to do, reveals that the supposition is often unwarranted. Test writers should not rely on the students' powers of telepathy to elicit the desired behaviour. Again, the use of colleagues to criticise drafts of instructions (including those which will be spoken) is the best means of avoiding problems. Spoken instructions should always be read from a prepared text in order to avoid introducing confusion.

Ensure that tests are well laid out and perfectly legible

Too often, institutional tests are badly typed (or handwritten), have too much text in too small a space, and are poorly reproduced. As a result, students are faced with additional tasks which are not ones meant to measure their language ability. Their variable performance on the unwanted tasks will lower the reliability of a test.

Make candidates familiar with format and testing techniques

If any aspect of a test is unfamiliar to candidates, they are likely to perform less well than they would do otherwise (on subsequently taking a parallel version, for example). For this reason, every effort must be made to ensure that all candidates have the opportunity to learn just what will be required of them. This may mean the distribution of sample tests (or of past test papers), or at least the provision of practice materials in the case of tests set within teaching institutions.

Provide uniform and non-distracting conditions of administration

The greater the differences between one administration of a test and another, the greater the differences one can expect between a candidate's performance on the two occasions. Great care should be taken to ensure uniformity. For example, timing should be specified and strictly adhered to; the acoustic conditions should be similar for all administrations of a listening test. Every precaution should be taken to maintain a quiet setting with no distracting sounds or movements.

We turn now to ways of obtaining scorer reliability, which, as we saw above, is essential to test reliability.

Use items that permit scoring which is as objective as possible

This may appear to be a recommendation to use multiple choice items, which permit completely objective scoring. This is not intended. While it would be a mistake to say that multiple choice items are never appropriate, it is certainly true that there are many circumstances in which they are quite inappropriate. What is more, good multiple choice items are notoriously difficult to write and always require extensive pre-testing. A substantial part of Chapter 8 is given over to the shortcomings of the multiple choice technique.

An alternative to multiple choice is the open-ended item which has a unique, possibly one-word, correct response which the candidates produce themselves. This too should ensure objective scoring, but in fact problems with such matters as spelling which makes a candidate's meaning unclear (say, in a listening test) often make demands on the scorer's judgement. The longer the required response, the greater the difficulties of this kind. One way of dealing with this is to structure the candidate's response by providing part of it. For example, the open-ended question, *What was different about the results?* may be designed to elicit the response, *Success was closely associated with high motivation.* This is likely to cause problems for scoring. Greater scorer reliability will probably be achieved if the question is followed by:

       .... was more closely associated with ....

Items of this kind are discussed in later chapters.

Make comparisons between candidates as direct as possible

This reinforces the suggestion already made that candidates should not be given a choice of items and that they should be limited in the way that they are allowed to respond. Scoring the compositions all on one topic will be more reliable than if the candidates are allowed to choose from six topics, as has been the case in some well-known tests. The scoring should be all the more reliable if the compositions are guided as in the example above, in the section, 'Do not allow candidates too much freedom'.

Provide a detailed scoring key

This should specify acceptable answers and assign points for acceptable partially correct responses. For high scorer reliability the key should be as detailed as possible in its assignment of points. It should be the outcome of efforts to anticipate all possible responses and have been subjected to group criticism. (This advice applies only where responses can be classed as partially or totally 'correct', not in the case of compositions, for instance.)

Train scorers

This is especially important where scoring is most subjective. The scoring of compositions, for example, should not be assigned to anyone who has not learned to score accurately compositions from past administrations. After each administration, patterns of scoring should be analysed. Individuals whose scoring deviates markedly and inconsistently from the norm should not be used again.

Agree acceptable responses and appropriate scores
at outset of scoring

A sample of scripts should be taken immediately after the administration of the test. Where there are compositions, archetypical representatives of different levels of ability should be selected. Only when all scorers are agreed on the scores to be given to these should real scoring begin. More will be said in Chapter 9 about the scoring of compositions.

For short answer questions, the scorers should note any difficulties they have in assigning points (the key is unlikely to have anticipated every relevant response), and bring these to the attention of whoever is supervising that part of the scoring. Once a decision has been taken as

49

to the points to be assigned, the supervisor should convey it to all the scorers concerned.

Identify candidates by number, not name

Scorers inevitably have expectations of candidates that they know. Except in purely objective testing, this will affect the way that they score. Studies have shown that even where the candidates are unknown to the scorers, the name on a script (or a photograph) will make a significant difference to the scores given. For example, a scorer may be influenced by the gender or nationality of a name into making predictions which can affect the score given. The identification of candidates only by number will reduce such effects.

Employ multiple, independent scoring

As a general rule, and certainly where testing is subjective, all scripts should be scored by at least two independent scorers. Neither scorer should know how the other has scored a test paper. Scores should be recorded on separate score sheets and passed to a third, senior, colleague, who compares the two sets of scores and investigates discrepancies.

Reliability and validity

To be valid a test must provide consistently accurate measurements. It must therefore be reliable. A reliable test, however, may not be valid at all. For example, as a writing test we could require candidates to write down the translation equivalents of 500 words in their own language. This might well be a reliable test; but it is unlikely to be a valid test of writing.

In our efforts to make tests reliable, we must be wary of reducing their validity. Earlier in this chapter it was admitted that restricting the scope of what candidates are permitted to write in a composition might diminish the validity of the task. This depends in part on what exactly we are trying to measure by setting the task. If we are interested in candidates' ability to structure a composition, then it would be hard to justify providing them with a structure in order to increase reliability. At the same time we would still try to restrict candidates in ways which would not render their performance on the task invalid.

There will always be some tension between reliability and validity. The tester has to balance gains in one against losses in the other.

Reader activities

1. What published tests are you familiar with? Try to find out their reliability coefficients. What method was used to arrive at these? What are the standard errors of measurement?
2. The TOEFL test has a standard error of measurement of 15. A particular American college states that it requires a score of 600 on the test for entry. What would you think of students applying to that college and making scores of 605, 600, 595, 590, 575?
3. Look at your own institutional tests. Using the list of points in the chapter, say in what ways you could improve their reliability.
4. What examples can you think of where there would be a tension between reliability and validity? In cases that you know, do you think the right balance has been struck?

Further reading

For more on reliability in general and the relationship between different estimates of reliability and the different factors that account for it, see Anastasi and Urbina (1997). For reliability in educational measurement see Nitko (2001) and Feldt and Brennan (1989) – the latter being highly technical.

For four 'relatively easy to calculate' estimates of decision consistency see Brown (1990). For further discussion of consistency in criterion-referenced testing, see Brown and Hudson (2002). Nitko (2001) also deals with decision consistency.

For what I think is an exaggerated view of the difficulty of achieving high reliability in more communicative tasks, see Lado (1961). This may have been written forty years ago, but the same beliefs are still expressed today in certain quarters.

1. Because of the reduced length, which will cause the coefficient to be less than it would be for the whole test, a statistical adjustment has to be made, using the Spearman-Brown formula (see Appendix 1).
2. Note that a reliability coefficient can be misleading if there are even just a couple of candidates that score much higher (and/or much lower) than the others. The presence of such scores will cause the reliability coefficient to be misleadingly high. This is because the statistical methods used to estimate reliability compare the size of differences between candidates with the size of differences 'within' candidates (i.e. between candidates'

two scores). The greater the relative difference between candidates, the greater will be the reliability coefficient. The difference between candidates will be exaggerated by the inclusion in the study of untypical candidates of the kind identified above. It is this which leads to an inappropriate estimate of reliability. See Nitko (2002) for details.

3. These statistical statements are based on what is known about the way a person's scores would tend to be distributed if they took the same test an indefinitely large number of times (without the experience of any test-taking occasion affecting performance on any other occasion). The scores would follow what is called a normal distribution (see Woods, Fletcher, and Hughes, 1986, for discussion beyond the scope of the present book). It is the known structure of the normal distribution which allows us to say what percentage of scores will fall within a certain range (for example about 68 per cent of scores will fall within one standard error of measurement of the true score). Since about 68 per cent of actual scores will be within one standard error of measurement of the true score, we can be about 68 per cent certain that any particular actual score will be within one standard error of measurement of the true score.

4. It should be clear that there is no such thing as a 'good' or a 'bad' standard error of measurement. It is the particular use made of particular scores in relation to a particular standard error of measurement which may be considered acceptable or unacceptable.

5. A criterion-referenced test may be very consistent yet yield a low reliability coefficient. This is because candidates' scores, although they classify the candidates consistently, may be very limited in range (see footnote 2). For this reason, it is recommended that one should use methods specifically designed for criterion-referenced tests.

6. The reliability of one person scoring the same test responses on different occasions is called 'intra-scorer reliability'; the reliability of different people scoring the same test responses is called 'inter-scorer reliability'.

6 Achieving beneficial backwash

Backwash is the effect that tests have on learning and teaching. Since the first edition of this book, there has been evidence of a much greater interest in backwash[1] than was previously the case, and its importance in language testing is generally accepted. There has been research, there have been calls for an explicit model of backwash which can be tested empirically, and an entire issue of *Language Testing* has been devoted to the topic. Backwash is now seen as a part of the impact a test may have on learners and teachers, on educational systems in general, and on society at large.

I have no doubt that over the next few years further research into backwash will result in a better understanding of the processes involved and how different variables contribute to its effect in different situations. Nevertheless, I believe that the basic practical advice which I gave in the first edition of this book for promoting beneficial backwash continues to be appropriate and, for that reason, I repeat it below. It is for readers to decide how the suggestions I make can be implemented in their own situation.

Test the abilities whose development you want to encourage

For example, if you want to encourage oral ability, then test oral ability[2]. This is very obvious, yet it is surprising how often it is not done. There is a tendency to test what is easiest to test rather than what is most important to test. Reasons advanced for not testing particular abilities may take many forms. It is often said, for instance, that sufficiently high reliability cannot be obtained when a form of testing (such as an oral interview) requires subjective scoring. This is simply not the case, and in addition to the advice already given in the previous chapter, more detailed suggestions for achieving satisfactory reliability of subjective tests are to be found in Chapters 9 and 10. The other most frequent reason given for not testing is the expense involved in terms of time and money. This is discussed later in the chapter.

It is important not only that certain abilities should be tested, but also that they should be given sufficient weight in relation to other abilities. I well remember my French master telling the class that, since the oral component of the General Certificate of Education examination in French (which we were to take later in the year) carried so few marks, we should not waste our time preparing for it. The examining board concerned was hardly encouraging beneficial backwash.

Sample widely and unpredictably

Normally a test can measure only a sample of everything included in the specifications. It is important that the sample taken should represent as far as possible the full scope of what is specified. If not, if the sample is taken from a restricted area of the specifications, then the backwash effect will tend to be felt only in that area. If, for example, a writing test were repeatedly, over the years, to include only two kinds of task: compare/contrast; describe/interpret a chart or graph, the likely outcome is that much preparation for the test will be limited to those two types of task. The backwash effect may not be as beneficial as it might have been had a wider range of tasks been used.

Whenever the content of a test becomes highly predictable, teaching and learning are likely to concentrate on what can be predicted. An effort should therefore be made to test across the full range of the specifications (in the case of achievement tests, this should be equivalent to a fully elaborated set of objectives), even where this involves elements that lend themselves less readily to testing.

Use direct testing

As we saw in Chapter 3, direct testing implies the testing of performance skills, with texts and tasks as authentic as possible. If we test directly the skills that we are interested in fostering, then practice for the test represents practice in those skills. If we want people to learn to write compositions, we should get them to write compositions in the test. If a course objective is that students should be able to read scientific articles, then we should get them to do that in the test. Immediately we begin to test indirectly, we are removing an incentive for students to practise in the way that we want them to.

Make testing criterion-referenced

If test specifications make clear just what candidates have to be able to do, and with what degree of success, then students will have a clear picture of what they have to achieve. What is more, they know that if they do perform the tasks at the criterial level, then they will be successful on the test, regardless of how other students perform. Both these things will help to motivate students. Where testing is not criterion-referenced, it becomes easy for teachers and students to assume that a certain (perhaps very high) percentage of candidates will pass, almost regardless of the absolute standard that they reach.

The possibility exists of having a series of criterion-referenced tests, each representing a different level of achievement or proficiency. The tests are constructed such that a 'pass' is obtained only by completing the great majority of the test tasks successfully. Students take only the test (or tests) on which they are expected to be successful. As a result, they are spared the dispiriting, demotivating experience of taking a test on which they can, for example, respond correctly to fewer than half of the items (and yet be given a pass). This type of testing, I believe, should encourage positive attitudes to language learning. It has been the basis of some GCSE (General Certificate of Secondary Education) examinations in Britain.

Base achievement tests on objectives

If achievement tests are based on objectives, rather than on detailed teaching and textbook content, they will provide a truer picture of what has actually been achieved. Teaching and learning will tend to be evaluated against those objectives. As a result, there will be constant pressure to achieve them. This was argued more fully in Chapter 3.

Ensure the test is known and understood by students and teachers

However good the potential backwash effect of a test may be, the effect will not be fully realised if students and those responsible for teaching do not know and understand what the test demands of them. The rationale for the test, its specifications, and sample items should be made available to everyone concerned with preparation for the test. This is particularly important when a new test is being introduced, especially if it incorporates novel testing methods. Another, equally important, reason for supplying information of this kind is to increase test reliability, as was noted in the previous chapter.

Where necessary, provide assistance to teachers

The introduction of a new test may make demands on teachers to which they are not equal. If, for example, a longstanding national test of grammatical structure and vocabulary is to be replaced by a direct test of a much more communicative nature, it is possible that many teachers will feel that they do not know how to teach communicative skills. One important reason for introducing the new test may have been to encourage communicative language teaching, but if the teachers need guidance and possibly training, and these are not given, the test will not achieve its intended effect. It may simply cause chaos and disaffection. Where new tests are meant to help change teaching, support has to be given to help effect the change.

Counting the cost

One of the desirable qualities of tests which trips quite readily off the tongue of many testers, after validity and reliability, is that of practicality. Other things being equal, it is good that a test should be easy and cheap to construct, administer, score and interpret. We should not forget that testing costs time and money that could be put to alternative uses.

It is unlikely to have escaped the reader's notice that at least some of the recommendations listed above for creating beneficial backwash involve more than minimal expense. The individual direct testing of some abilities will take a great deal of time, as will the reliable scoring of performance on any subjective test. The production and distribution of sample tests and the training of teachers will also be costly. It might be argued, therefore, that such procedures are impractical. In my opinion, this would reveal an incomplete understanding of what is involved. Before we decide that we cannot afford to test in a way that will promote beneficial backwash, we have to ask ourselves a question: What will be the cost of *not* achieving beneficial backwash? When we compare the cost of the test with the waste of effort and time on the part of teachers and students in activities quite inappropriate to their true learning goals (and in some circumstances, with the potential loss to the national economy of not having more people competent in foreign languages), we are likely to decide that we cannot afford not to introduce a test with a powerful beneficial backwash effect.

Reader activities

1. How would you improve the backwash effect of tests that you know? Be as specific as possible. (This is a follow-up to Activity 1 at the end of Chapter 1.)
2. Rehearse the arguments you would use to convince a sceptic that it would be worthwhile making the changes that you recommend.

Further reading

Alderson and Wall (1993) question the existence of backwash. Wall and Alderson (1993) investigate backwash in a project in Sri Lanka with which they were concerned, argue that that the processes involved in backwash are not straightforward, and call for a model of backwash and for further research.

Language Testing 13, 3 (1996) is a special issue devoted to backwash. In it Messick discusses backwash in relation to validity. Bailey (1996) reviews the concept of backwash in language testing, including Hughes's (1993) proposed model and Alderson and Wall's (1993) fifteen hypotheses about backwash. Shohamy et al (1996) report that two different tests have different patterns of backwash. Wall (1996) looks to developments in general education and to innovation theory for insights into backwash. Watanabe (1996) investigates the possible effect of university entrance examinations in Japan on classroom methodology. Alderson and Hamp-Lyons (1996) report on a study into TOEFL preparation courses and backwash.

Hamp-Lyons's (1997a) article raises ethical concerns in relation to backwash, impact and validity. Her 1997b article discusses ethical issues in test preparation practice for TOEFL, to which Wadden and Hilke (1999) take exception. Hamp-Lyons (1999) responds to their criticisms.

Brown and Hudson (1998) lay out the assessment possibilities for language teachers and argue that one of the criteria for choice of assessment method is potential backwash effect.

---

1. In much of this work the word 'washback', rather than 'backwash' has been used. Where 'washback' came from I do not know. What I do know is that I can find 'backwash' in dictionaries, but not 'washback'.
2. Bearing in mind what was said in Chapter 4, it is important that the scoring or rating of test performance (as well as the means of elicitation) should be valid.

7 Stages of test development

This chapter begins by briefly laying down a set of general procedures for test construction. These are then illustrated by two examples: an achievement test and a placement test.

In brief, the procedures I recommend are these:

1. Make a full and clear statement of the testing 'problem'.
2. Write complete specifications for the test.
3. Write and moderate items.
4. Trial the items informally on native speakers and reject or modify problematic ones as necessary.
5. Trial the test on a group of non-native speakers similar to those for whom the test is intended.
6. Analyse the results of the trial and make any necessary changes.
7. Calibrate scales.
8. Validate.
9. Write handbooks for test takers, test users and staff.
10. Train any necessary staff (interviewers, raters, etc.).

Before looking more closely at this set of procedures, it is worth saying that test development is best thought of as a task to be carried out by a team. It is very difficult for an individual to develop a test, if only because of the need to look objectively at what is being proposed at each stage of development. This difficulty can be seen most clearly at the stage of item writing, when faults in an item which are obvious to others are often invisible to the person who wrote the item. Writing items is a creative process, and we tend to think of our items as minor works of art or even, it sometimes seems, our babies. We do not find it easy to admit that our baby is not as beautiful as we had thought. One of the qualities to be looked for in item writers, therefore, is a willingness to accept justified criticism of the items they have written. Other desirable qualities – not only for item writers but for test developers in general – are: native or near-native command of the language, intelligence, and imagination (to create contexts in items and to foresee possible misinterpretations).

1. Stating the problem

It cannot be said too many times that the essential first step in testing is to make oneself perfectly clear about what it is one wants to know and for what purpose. The following questions, the significance of which should be clear from previous chapters, have to be answered:

   (i) What kind of test is it to be? Achievement (final or progress), proficiency, diagnostic, or placement?
  (ii) What is its precise purpose?
 (iii) What abilities are to be tested?
  (iv) How detailed must the results be?
   (v) How accurate must the results be?
  (vi) How important is backwash?
 (vii) What constraints are set by unavailability of expertise, facilities, time (for construction, administration and scoring)?

Once the problem is clear, steps can be taken to solve it. It is to be hoped that a handbook of the present kind will take readers a long way towards appropriate solutions. In addition, however, efforts should be made to gather information on tests that have been designed for similar situations. If possible, samples of such tests should be obtained. There is nothing dishonourable in doing this; it is what professional testing bodies do when they are planning a test of a kind for which they do not already have first-hand experience. Nor does it contradict the claim made earlier that each testing situation is unique. It is not intended that other tests should simply be copied; rather that their development can serve to suggest possibilities and to help avoid the need to 'reinvent the wheel'.

2. Writing specifications for the test

A set of specifications for the test must be written at the outset[1].

This will include information on: content, test structure, timing, medium/channel, techniques to be used, criterial levels of performance, and scoring procedures.

(i) Content

This refers not to the content of a single, particular version of a test, but to the entire potential content of any number of versions. Samples of this content will appear in individual versions of the test.

The fuller the information on content, the less arbitrary should be the subsequent decisions as to what to include in the writing of any version of the test. There is a danger, however, that in the desire to be highly specific, we may go beyond our current understanding of what the components of language ability are and what their relationship is to each other. For instance, while we may believe that many sub-skills contribute to the ability to read lengthy prose passages with full understanding, it seems hardly possible in our present state of knowledge to name them all or to assess their individual contributions to the more general ability. We cannot be sure that the sum of the parts that we test will amount to the whole in which we are generally most directly interested. At the same time, however, teaching practice often assumes some such knowledge, with one subskill being taught at a time. It seems to me that the safest procedure is to include in the content specifications only those elements whose contribution is fairly well established.

The way in which content is described will vary with its nature. The content of a grammar test, for example, may simply list all the relevant structures. The content of a test of a language skill, on the other hand, may be specified along a number of dimensions. The following provides a possible framework for doing this. It is not meant to be prescriptive; readers may wish to describe test content differently. The important thing is that content should be as fully specified as possible.

Operations (the tasks that candidates have to be able to carry out). For a reading test these might include, for example: scan text to locate specific information; guess meaning of unknown words from context.

Types of text For a writing test these might include: letters, forms, academic essays up to three pages in length.

Addressees of texts This refers to the kinds of people that the candidate is expected to be able to write or speak to (for example, native speakers of the same age and status); or the people for whom reading and listening materials are primarily intended (for example, native speaker university students).

Length of text(s) For a reading test, this would be the length of the passages on which items are set. For a listening test it could be the length of the spoken texts. For a writing test, the length of the pieces to be written.

Topics Topics may be specified quite loosely and selected according to suitability for the candidate and the type of test.

Readability Reading passages may be specified as being within a certain range of readability[2].

Structural range
Either: (a) a list of structures which may occur in texts
or (b) a list of structures which should be excluded
or (c) a general indication of range of structures (e.g. in terms of frequency of occurrence in the language)

Vocabulary range This may be loosely or closely specified. An example of the latter is to be found in the handbook of the Cambridge Young Learners tests, where words are listed.

Dialect, accent, style This may refer to the dialects and accents that test takers are meant to understand or those in which they are expected to write or speak. Style may be formal, informal, conversational, etc.

Speed of processing For reading this may be expressed in the number of words to be read per minute (and will vary according to type of reading to be done). For speaking it will be rate of speech, also expressed in words per minute. For listening it will be the speed at which texts are spoken.

(ii) Structure, timing, medium/channel and techniques

The following should be specified:

Test structure What sections will the test have and what will be tested in each? (for example: 3 sections – grammar, careful reading, expeditious reading)

Number of items (in total and in the various sections)

Number of passages (and number of items associated with each)

Medium/channel (paper and pencil, tape, computer, face-to-face, telephone, etc.)

Timing (for each section and for entire test)

Techniques What techniques will be used to measure what skills or subskills?

(iii) Criterial levels of performance

The required level(s) of performance for (different levels of) success should be specified. This may involve a simple statement to the effect that, to demonstrate 'mastery', 80 per cent of the items must be responded to correctly.

For speaking or writing, however, one can expect a description of the criterial level to be much more complex. For example, the handbook of the Cambridge Certificates in Communicative Skills in English (CCSE)[3] specifies the following degree of skill for the award of the Certificate in Oral Interaction at level 2:

> **Accuracy** Pronunciation must be clearly intelligible even if still obviously influenced by L1. Grammatical/lexical accuracy is generally high although some errors that do not destroy communication are acceptable.

> **Appropriacy** The use of language must be generally appropriate to function. The overall intention of the speaker must be generally clear.

> **Range** A fair range of language must be available to the candidate. Only in complex utterances is there a need to search for words.

> **Flexibility** There must be some evidence of the ability to initiate and concede a conversation and to adapt to new topics or changes of direction.

> **Size** Must be capable of responding with more than short-form answers where appropriate. Should be able to expand simple utterances with occasional prompting from the Interlocutor.

(iv) Scoring procedures

These are always important, but particularly so where scoring will be subjective. The test developers should be clear as to how they will achieve high reliability and validity in scoring. What rating scale will be used? How many people will rate each piece of work? What happens if two or more raters disagree about a piece of work?

3. Writing and moderating items

Once specifications are in place, the writing of items can begin.

(i) Sampling

It is most unlikely that everything found under the heading of 'Content' in the specifications can be covered by the items in any one version of the test. Choices have to be made. For content validity and for beneficial backwash, the important thing is to choose widely from the whole area of content. One should not concentrate on those elements known to be easy to test. Succeeding versions of the test should also sample widely and unpredictably, although one will always wish to include elements that are particularly important.

(ii) Writing items

Items should always be written with the specifications in mind. It is no use writing 'good' items if they are not consistent with the specifications. As one writes an item, it is essential to try to look at it through the eyes of test takers and imagine how they might misinterpret the item (in which case it will need to be rewritten). Even if there is no possibility of misinterpretation, test takers (especially intelligent ones) may find responses that are different from, but equally valid as, the one intended. Mention of the intended response is a reminder that the key to an item (i.e. a statement of the correct response or responses) is an integral part of the item. An item without a key is incomplete.

The writing of successful items (in the broadest sense, including, for example, the setting of writing tasks) is extremely difficult. No one can expect to be able consistently to produce perfect items. Some items will have to be rejected, others reworked. The best way to identify items that have to be improved or abandoned is through the process of moderation.

(iii) Moderating items

Moderation is the scrutiny of proposed items by (ideally) at least two colleagues, neither of whom is the author of the items being examined. Their task is to try to find weaknesses in the items and, where possible, remedy them. Where successful modification is not possible, they must reject the item. It is to be hoped, of course, that they will not find fault with most of the items that they moderate and that they can therefore accept them. A checklist of the kind in Table 1 (designed for moderating grammar items) is useful to moderators.

4. Informal trialling of items on native speakers

Items which have been through the process of moderation should be presented in the form of a test (or tests) to a number of native speakers – twenty or more, if possible. There is no need to do this formally; the 'test' can be taken in the participants' own time. The native speakers

63

Table 1 *Moderation of grammar items*

	YES	NO
1. Is the English grammatically correct?		
2. Is the English natural and acceptable?		
3. Is the English in accordance with the specifications?		
4. Does the item test what it is supposed to test, as specified?		
5. The correct response cannot be obtained without the appropriate knowledge of grammar (other than by random guessing)		
6. Is the item economical?		
7. (a) Multiple choice – is there just one correct response? (b) Gap filling – are there just one or two correct responses?		
8. Multiple choice: Are all the distractors likely to distract?		
9. Is the key complete and correct?		

should be similar to the people for whom the test is being developed, in terms of age, education, and general background. There is no need for them to be specialists in language or testing. Indeed, it is preferable that they should not be, since 'experts' are unlikely to behave in the way of naïve test takers that is being looked for.

Items that prove difficult for the native speakers almost certainly need revision or replacement. So do items where unexpected or inappropriate responses are provided. Of course, people taking a test on their own language will have lapses of attention. Where these can be recognised, the responses should not count against the item.

5. Trialling of the test on a group of non-native speakers similar to those for whom the test is intended

Those items that have survived moderation and informal trialling on native speakers should be put together into a test, which is then administered under test conditions to a group similar to that for which the test is intended[4]. Problems in administration and scoring are noted.

It has to be accepted that, for a number of reasons, trialling of this kind is often not feasible. In some situations a group for trialling may simply not be available. In other situations, although a suitable group exists, it may be thought that the security of the test might be put at risk. It is often the case, therefore, that faults in a test are discovered only after it has been administered to the target group. Unless it is intended that no part of the test should be used again, it is worthwhile noting problems that become apparent during administration and scoring, and afterwards carrying out statistical analysis of the kind referred to below and treated more fully in Appendix 1.

6. Analysis of results of the trial; making of any necessary changes

There are two kinds of analysis that should be carried out. The first – statistical – is described in Appendix 1. This will reveal qualities (such as reliability) of the test as a whole and of individual items (for example, how difficult they are, how well they discriminate between stronger and weaker candidates).

The second kind of analysis is qualitative. Responses should be examined in order to discover misinterpretations, unanticipated but possibly correct responses, and any other indicators of faulty items. Items that analysis shows to be faulty should be modified or dropped from the test. Assuming that more items have been trialled than are needed for the final test, a final selection can be made, basing decisions on the results of the analyses.

7. Calibration of scales

Where rating scales are going to be used for oral testing or the testing of writing, these should be calibrated. Essentially, this means collecting samples of performance (for example, pieces of writing) which cover the full range of the scales. A team of 'experts' then looks at these samples and assigns each of them to a point on the relevant scale. The assigned samples provide reference points for all future uses of the scale, as well as being necessary training materials.

8. Validation

The final version of the test can be validated. For a high stakes, or published test, this should be regarded as essential. For relatively low stakes tests that are to be used within an institution, this may not be thought necessary, although where the test is likely to be used many times over a period of time, informal, small-scale validation is still desirable.

9. Writing handbooks for test takers, test users and staff

Handbooks (each with rather different content, depending on audience) may be expected to contain the following:

- the rationale for the test;
- an account of how the test was developed and validated;
- a description of the test (which may include a version of the specifications);
- sample items (or a complete sample test);
- advice on preparing for taking the test;
- an explanation of how test scores are to be interpreted;
- training materials (for interviewers, raters, etc.);
- details of test administration.

10. Training staff

Using the handbook and other materials, all staff who will be involved in the test process should be trained. This may include interviewers, raters, scorers, computer operators, and invigilators (proctors).

Example of test development 1: An Achievement Test

Statement of the problem

There is a need for an achievement test to be administered at the end of a pre-sessional course of training in the reading of academic texts in the social sciences and business studies (the students are graduates who are about to follow postgraduate courses in English-medium universities). The teaching institution concerned (as well as the sponsors of the students) wants to know just what progress is

---

being made during the three-month course. The test must therefore be sufficiently sensitive to measure gain over that relatively short period. While there is no call for diagnostic information on individuals, it would be useful to know, for groups, where the greatest difficulties remain at the end of the course, so that future courses may give more attention to these areas. Backwash is considered important; the test should encourage the practice of the reading skills that the students will need in their university studies. This is, in fact, intended to be only one of a battery of tests, and a maximum of two hours can be allowed for it. It will not be possible at the outset to write separate tests for different subject areas.

Specifications

Content

Operations These are based on the stated objectives of the course, and include expeditious and slower, careful reading.

> *Expeditious reading:* Skim for main ideas; search read for information; scan to find specific items in lists, indexes, etc.

> *Slower, careful reading:* Construe the meaning of complex, closely argued passages.

> Underlying skills that are given particular attention in the course:
> - Guessing the meaning of unfamiliar words from context;
> - Identifying referents of pronouns etc., often some distance removed in the text.

Types of text The texts should be authentic, academic (taken from textbooks and journal articles).

Addressees Academics at postgraduate level and beyond.

Lengths of texts Expeditious: c. 3000 words Careful: c. 800 words.

Topics The subject areas will have to be as 'neutral' as possible, since the students are from a variety of social science and business disciplines (economics, sociology, management etc.).

Readability Not specified.

Structural range Unlimited.

Vocabulary range General academic, not specialist technical.

Dialect and style Standard American or British English dialect. Formal, academic style.

Speed of processing Expeditious: 300 words per minute (not reading all words).
Careful: 100 words per minute.

Structure, timing, medium and techniques

Test structure Two sections: expeditious reading; careful reading.

Number of items 30 expeditious; 20 careful. Total: 50 items.

Number of passages 3 expeditious; 2 careful.

Timing Expeditious: 15 minutes per passage (each passage collected after 15 minutes).
Careful: 30 minutes (passage only handed out after 45 minutes, when expeditious reading has been completed).
TOTAL: 75 minutes.

Medium Paper and pencil. Each passage in a separate booklet.

Techniques Short answer and gap filling for both sections.

Examples:

For inferring meaning from context:
For each of the following, find a single word in the text with an equivalent meaning. Note: the word in the text may have an ending such as -ing, -s, etc.
highest point (lines 20–35)

For identifying referents:
What does each of the following refer to in the text? Be very precise.
the former (line 43)

Criterial levels of performance

Satisfactory performance is represented by 80 per cent accuracy in each of the two sections.

The number of students reaching this level will be the number who have succeeded in terms of the course's objectives.

Scoring procedures

There will be independent double scoring. Scorers will be trained to ignore irrelevant (for example grammatical) inaccuracy in responses.

Sampling

Texts will be chosen from as wide a range of topics and types of writing as is compatible with the specifications. Draft items will only be written after the suitability of the texts has been agreed.

Item writing and moderation

Items will be based on a consideration of what a competent non-specialist reader should be able to obtain from the texts. Considerable time will be set aside for moderation and rewriting of items.

Informal trialling

This will be carried out on 20 native speaking postgraduate students in the university.

Trialling and analysis

Trialling of texts and items sufficient for at least two versions will be carried out with students currently taking the course, with full qualitative and statistical analysis. An overall reliability coefficient of 0.90 and a per cent agreement (see Chapter 5) of 0.85 are required.

Validation

There will be immediate content validation.

Concurrent validation will be against tutors' ratings of the students.

Predictive validation will be against subject supervisors' ratings one month after the students begin their postgraduate studies.

Handbooks

One handbook will be written for the students, their sponsors, and their future supervisors.

Another handbook will be written for internal use.

Example of test development 2: A Placement Test

Statement of the problem

A commercial English language teaching organisation (which has a number of schools) needs a placement test. Its purpose will be to assign new students to classes at five levels: false beginners; lower intermediate; middle intermediate; upper intermediate; advanced. Course objectives at all levels are expressed in rather general 'communicative' terms, with no one skill being given greater attention than any other. As well as information on overall ability in the language, some indication of oral ability would be useful. Sufficient accuracy is required for there to be little need for changes of class once teaching is under way. Backwash is not a serious consideration. More than two thousand new students enrol within a matter of days. The test must be brief (not more than 45 minutes in length), quick and easy to administer, score and interpret. Scoring by clerical staff should be possible. The organisation has previously conducted interviews but the number of students now entering the school is making this impossible.

Specifications

Content

Operations Ability to predict missing words (based on the notion of 'reduced redundancy'[5]).

Types of text Constructed 'spoken' exchanges involving two people. It is hoped that the spoken nature of the texts will, however indirectly, draw on students' oral abilities.

Length of text One turn (of a maximum of about 20 words) per person.

Topics 'Everyday'. Those found in the text books used by the organisation.

Structural range All those found in the text books (listed in the specifications but omitted here to save space).

Vocabulary range As found in the text books, plus any other common lexis.

Dialect and style Standard English English. Mostly informal style, some formal.

Structure, timing, medium and techniques

Test structure No separate sections.

Number of items 100 (though this will be decreased if the test does its job well with fewer items).

Timing 30 minutes (Note: this seems very little time, but the more advanced students will find the early passages extremely easy, and will take very little time. It does not matter whether lower level students reach the later passages.)

Medium Pencil-and-paper.

Technique All items will be gap filling. One word per gap. Contractions count as one word. Gaps will relate to vocabulary as well as structure (not always possible to distinguish what is being tested).

> Examples: A: Whose book _____ that?
> B: It's mine.
>
> A: How did you learn French?
> B: I just picked it _____ as I went along.

Criterial levels of performance

These will only be decided when comparison is made between performance on the test and (a) the current assignment of students by the interview and (b) the teachers' view of each student's suitability to the class they have been assigned to by the interview.

Scoring procedures

Responses will be on a separate response sheet. A template with a key will be constructed so that scoring can be done rapidly by clerical staff.

Informal trialling

This will be carried out on 20 first year native speaker undergraduate students.

71

Trialling and analysis

Many more items will be constructed than will finally be used. All of them (in as many as three different test forms, with linking anchor items) will be trialled on current students at all levels in the organisation. Problems in administration and scoring will be noted.

After statistical and qualitative analysis, one test form made up of the 'best' items will be constructed and trialled on a different set of current students. The total score for each of the students will then be compared with his or her level in the institution, and decisions as to criterial levels of performance made.

Validation

The final version of the test will be checked against the list of structures in the specifications. If one is honest, however, one must say that at this stage content validity will be only a matter of academic interest. What will matter is whether the test does the job it is intended for. Thus the most important form of validation will be criterion-related, the criterion being placement of students in appropriate classes, as judged by their teachers (and possibly by the students themselves). The smaller the proportion of misplacements, the more valid the test.

Handbook

A handbook will be written for distribution by the organisation to its various schools.

Reader activities

On the basis of experience or intuition, try to write a specification for a test designed to measure the level of language proficiency of students applying to study an academic subject in the medium of a foreign language at an overseas university. Compare your specification with those of tests that have actually been constructed for that purpose.

Further reading

It is useful to study existing specifications. Specifications for UCLES for many tests can be obtained from UCLES, 1 Hills Road, Cambridge, CB1 2EU and on their website. Specifications for a test designed to assess the level of English of students wishing to study at tertiary level in the UK, the Test of English for Educational Purposes (TEEP), are to be found in Weir (1988, 1990). The ALTE (Association of Language Testers in Europe) website gives details of tests in a variety of European languages. Council of Europe (2001) and van Ek and Trim (2001a, 2001b, 2001c) are excellent sources for the content section of specifications. For those writing English language tests, the British National Corpus and the COBUILD corpus (information on both to be found on the Internet) between them provide millions of utterances that can be used as a basis for items.

For other models of test development see Alderson et al (1995) and Bachman and Palmer (1996). The model used by Bachman and Palmer is highly detailed and complex but their book gives information on ten test development projects.

Alderson and Buck (1993) report on the test development procedures of certain British testing bodies.

For advice on what to include in handbooks, see AERA (1999), which is reviewed by Davidson (2000).

1. This does not mean that the specifications should never be modified. Trialling may reveal, for example, that there are too many items to be responded to in the time assigned to them. The circumstances in which the test is to be administered may change. It is also true at the time of writing specifications certain details may be unknowable. For example, we may not know how many items will be needed in a test in order to make it reliable and valid for its purpose.
2. The Flesch Reading Ease Score and the Flesch-Kincaid Grade Level Score are readily available for any passage in Microsoft Word. These measures are based on average sentence length and the average number of syllables per word. While they may not be wholly valid measures, they are at least objective.
3. In 1999 UCLES decided to merge the CCSE and Oxford EFL examinations. The Certificates in English Language Skills (CELS) have now replaced these.
4. If there are too many items for one group to take in a single sitting, more than one form of the test can be constructed, with each form containing a

subset of items common to both (known as anchor items). Using performance on the common anchor items as a basis for comparison, it is possible to put the other items on the same difficulty scale. If this is not done, differences in ability between the groups will mean that the difficulty levels of items taken by one group will not be directly comparable with the difficulty levels of items taken by another group. See Appendix 1 for statistical treatment of results when anchor items are used.

5. See Chapter 14 for a discussion of reduced redundancy.

8 Common test techniques

What are test techniques?[1]

Quite simply test techniques are means of eliciting behaviour from candidates that will tell us about their language abilities. What we need are techniques that:

- will elicit behaviour which is a reliable and valid indicator of the ability in which we are interested;
- will elicit behaviour which can be reliably scored;
- are as economical of time and effort as possible;
- will have a beneficial backwash effect, where this is relevant.

From Chapter 9 to Chapter 13, techniques are discussed in relation to particular abilities. Techniques that may be thought to test 'overall ability' are treated in Chapter 14. The present chapter introduces common techniques that can be used to test a variety of abilities, including reading, listening, grammar and vocabulary. This is to avoid having to introduce them repeatedly in the chapters in which they appear later. We begin with an examination of the multiple choice technique and then go on to look at techniques that require the test taker to construct a response (rather than just select one from a number provided by the test maker).

Multiple choice items

Multiple choice items take many forms, but their basic structure is as follows.
There is a *stem*:

Enid has been here _____ half an hour.

and a number of *options* – one of which is correct, the others being *distractors*:

A. during   B. for   C. while   D. since

It is the candidate's task to identify the correct or most appropriate option (in this case B). Perhaps the most obvious advantage of multiple choice, referred to earlier in the book, is that scoring can be perfectly reliable. Scoring should also be rapid and economical. A further considerable advantage is that, since in order to respond the candidate has only to make a mark on the paper, it is possible to include more items than would otherwise be possible in a given period of time. As we know from Chapter 5, this is likely to make for greater test reliability. Finally, it allows the testing of receptive skills without requiring the test taker to produce written or spoken language.

The advantages of the multiple choice technique were so highly regarded at one time that it almost seemed that it was the only way to test. While many laymen have always been sceptical of what could be achieved through multiple choice testing, it is only fairly recently that the technique's limitations have been more generally recognised by professional testers. The difficulties with multiple choice are as follows.

The technique tests only recognition knowledge

If there is a lack of fit between at least some candidates' productive and receptive skills, then performance on a multiple choice test may give a quite inaccurate picture of those candidates' ability. A multiple choice grammar test score, for example, may be a poor indicator of someone's ability to use grammatical structures. The person who can identify the correct response in the item above may not be able to produce the correct form when speaking or writing. This is in part a question of construct validity; whether or not grammatical knowledge of the kind that can be demonstrated in a multiple choice test underlies the productive use of grammar. Even if it does, there is still a gap to be bridged between knowledge and use; if use is what we are interested in, that gap will mean that test scores are at best giving incomplete information.

Guessing may have a considerable but unknowable effect on test scores

The chance of guessing the correct answer in a three-option multiple choice item is one in three, or roughly thirty-three per cent. On average we would expect someone to score 33 on a 100-item test purely by guesswork. We would expect some people to score fewer than that by guessing, others to score more. The trouble is that we can never know what part of any particular individual's score has come about through guessing. Attempts are sometimes made to estimate the contribution of guessing by assuming that all incorrect responses are the result of guessing, and by further assuming that the individual has had average luck in guessing. Scores are then reduced by the number of points the individual is estimated to have obtained by guessing. However, neither assumption is necessarily correct, and we cannot know that the revised score is the same as (or very close to) the one an individual would have obtained without guessing. While other testing methods may also involve guessing, we would normally expect the effect to be much less, since candidates will usually not have a restricted number of responses presented to them (with the information that one of them is correct).

If multiple choice is to be used, every effort should be made to have at least four options (in order to reduce the effect of guessing). It is important that all of the distractors should be chosen by a significant number of test takers who do not have the knowledge or ability being tested. If there are four options but only a very small proportion of candidates choose one of the distractors, the item is effectively only a three-option item.

The technique severely restricts what can be tested

The basic problem here is that multiple choice items require distractors, and distractors are not always available. In a grammar test, it may not be possible to find three or four plausible alternatives to the correct structure. The result is often that the command of what may be an important structure is simply not tested. An example would be the distinction in English between the past tense and the present perfect. For learners at a certain level of ability, in a given linguistic context, there are no other alternatives that are likely to distract. The argument that this must be a difficulty for any item that attempts to test for this distinction is difficult to sustain, since other items that do not overtly present a choice may elicit the candidate's usual behaviour, without the candidate resorting to guessing.

It is very difficult to write successful items

A further problem with multiple choice is that, even where items are possible, good ones are extremely difficult to write. Professional test writers reckon to have to write many more multiple choice items than they actually need for a test, and it is only after trialling and statistical analysis of performance on the items that they can recognise the ones that are usable. It is my experience that multiple choice tests that are produced for use within institutions are often shot through with faults. Common amongst these are: more than one correct answer; no correct answer; there are clues in the options as to which is correct (for example the correct option may be different in length to the others); ineffective distractors. The amount of work and expertise needed to prepare good multiple choice tests is so great that, even if one ignored other problems associated with the technique, one would not wish to recommend it for regular achievement testing (where the same test is not used repeatedly) within institutions. Savings in time for administration and scoring will be outweighed by the time spent on successful test preparation. It is true that the development and use of item banks, from which a selection can be made for particular versions of a test, makes the effort more worthwhile, but great demands are still made on time and expertise.

Backwash may be harmful

It should hardly be necessary to point out that where a test that is important to students is multiple choice in nature, there is a danger that practice for the test will have a harmful effect on learning and teaching. Practice at multiple choice items (especially when – as can happen – as much attention is paid to improving one's educated guessing as to the content of the items) will not usually be the best way for students to improve their command of a language.

Cheating may be facilitated

The fact that the responses on a multiple choice test (a, b, c, d) are so simple makes them easy to communicate to other candidates non-verbally. Some defence against this is to have at least two versions of the test, the only difference between them being the order in which the options are presented.

All in all, the multiple choice technique is best suited to relatively infrequent testing of large numbers of candidates. This is not to say that there should be no multiple choice items in tests produced regularly within institutions. In setting a reading comprehension test, for example, there may be certain tasks that lend themselves very readily to the multiple choice format, with obvious distractors presenting themselves in the text. There are real-life tasks (say, a shop assistant identifying which one of four dresses a customer is describing) which are essentially multiple choice. The simulation in a test of such a situation would seem to be perfectly appropriate. What the reader is being urged to avoid is the excessive, indiscriminate, and potentially harmful use of the technique. In later chapters, advice is given on writing multiple choice items.

YES/NO and TRUE/FALSE items

Items in which the test taker has merely to choose between YES and NO, or between TRUE and FALSE, are effectively multiple choice items with only two options. The obvious weakness of such items is that the test taker has a 50% chance of choosing the correct response by chance alone. In my view, there is no place for items of this kind in a formal test, although they may well have a use in assessment where the accuracy of the results is not critical. True/False items are sometimes modified by requiring test takers to give a reason for their choice. However, this extra requirement is problematic, first because it is adding what is a potentially difficult writing task when writing is not meant to be tested (validity problem), and secondly because the responses are often difficult to score (reliability and validity problem).

Short-answer items

Items in which the test taker has to provide a short answer are common, particularly in listening and reading tests.
Examples:

> (i) What does *it* in the last sentence refer to?

> (ii) How old was Hannibal when he started eating human beings?

> (iii) Why did Hannibal enjoy eating brain so much?

Advantages over multiple choice are that:

- guessing will (or should) contribute less to test scores;
- the technique is not restricted by the need for distractors (though there have to be potential alternative responses);
- cheating is likely to be more difficult;
- though great care must still be taken, items should be easier to write.

Disadvantages are:

- responses may take longer and so reduce the possible number of items;
- the test taker has to produce language in order to respond;
- scoring may be invalid or unreliable, if judgement is required;
- scoring may take longer.

The first two of these disadvantages may not be significant if the required response is really short (and at least the test takers do not have to ponder four options, three of which have been designed to distract them). The next two can be overcome by making the required response unique (i.e. there is only one possible answer) and to be found in the text (or to require very simple language). Looking at the examples above, without needing to see the text, we can see that the correct response to Item (i) should be unique and found in the text. The same could be true of Item (ii). Item (iii), however, may cause problems (which can be solved by using gap filling, below).

I believe that short-answer questions have a role to play in serious language testing. Only when testing has to be carried out on a very large scale would I think of dismissing short answer questions as a possible technique because of the time taken to score. With the increased use of computers in testing (in TOEFL, for example), where written responses can be scored reliably and quickly, there is no reason for short answer items not to have a place in the very largest testing programmes.

Gap filling items

Items in which test takers have to fill a gap with a word are also common. Examples:

> Hannibal particularly liked to eat brains because of their _____ and their _____ .

From this example, assuming that missing words (let us say they are *texture* and *colour*) can be found in the text, it can be seen that the problem of the third short answer item has been overcome. Gap filling items for reading or listening work best if the missing words are to be found in the text or are straightforward, high frequency words which should not present spelling problems.

Gap filling items can also work well in tests of grammar and vocabulary. Examples:

> He asked me for money, _____ though he knows I earn a lot less than him.

> Our son just failed another exam. He really needs to pull his _____ up.

But it does not work well where the grammatical element to be tested is discontinuous, and so needs more than one gap. An example would be where one wants to see if the test taker can provide the past continuous appropriately. None of the following is satisfactory:

> (i) While they _____ watching television, there was a sudden bang outside.

(ii) While they were _____ television, there was a sudden bang outside.

(iii) While they _____ _____ television, there was a sudden bang outside.

In the first two cases, alternative structures which the test taker might have naturally used (such as the simple past) are excluded. The same is true in the third case too, unless the test taker inserted an adverb and wrote, for example, *quietly watched*, which is an unlikely response. In all three cases, there is too strong a clue as to the structure which is needed.

Gap filling does not always work well for grammar or vocabulary items where minor or subtle differences of meaning are concerned, as the following items demonstrate.

(i) A: What will he do?

B: I think he _____ resign.

A variety of modal verbs (*will, may, might, could,* etc.) can fill the gap satisfactorily.
Providing context can help:

(ii) A: I wonder who that is.

B: It _____ be the doctor.

This item has the same problem as the previous one. But adding:

A: How can you be so certain?

means that the gap must be filled with a modal expressing certainty (*must*). But even with the added context, *will* may be another possibility.

When the gap filling technique is used, it is essential that test takers are told very clearly and firmly that only one word can be put in each gap. They should also be told whether contractions (I'm, isn't, it's, etc.) count as one word. (In my experience, counting contractions as one word is advisable, as it allows greater flexibility in item construction.)

Gap filling is a valuable technique. It has the advantages of the short answer technique, but the greater control it exercises over the test takers means that it does not call for significant productive skills. There is no reason why the scoring of gap filling should not be highly reliable, provided that it is carried out with a carefully constructed key on which the scorers can rely completely (and not have to use their individual judgement).

This chapter has only provided an introduction to certain common testing techniques. The techniques are treated in greater detail in later chapters, along with others that are relevant to the testing of particular abilities.

Reader activities

1. Examine each of the following three items. If an item is problematic, what is the problem? Can you remove the problem without changing the technique?

   (i) When she asked for an extension, they agreed _____ let her have another month to finish the report.

         a. at   b. to   c. over   d. of

   Key: b

   (ii) A: Why are you doing the work yourself?

       B: When I asked Bill, he said he _____ do it.

   Key: couldn't

   (iii) A: It's too easy for young people to make money these days.

       B: I _____ agree more.

   Key: couldn't

2. Re-write each of the above items using another technique. What do you learn from doing this?
3. Look at ten items in any test to which you have access. If any of them are problematic, can you improve them using the same technique as in the original item? See how many of the ten items can be satisfactorily re-written using a different technique.

Further reading

Heaton (1975) discusses various types of item and gives many examples for analysis by the reader.

1. Testing techniques are frequently referred to as 'formats'. I prefer the word 'technique', leaving the word 'format' for more general aspects of test structure, such as the interview.

9 Testing writing

We will make the assumption in this chapter that the best way to test people's writing ability is to get them to write[1]. This is not an unreasonable assumption. Even professional testing institutions are unable to construct indirect tests that measure writing ability accurately (see Further reading; Godshalk et al.). And if, in fact, satisfactory accuracy were a real possibility, considerations of backwash and ease of construction would still argue for the direct testing of writing within teaching institutions.

Given the decision to test writing ability directly, we are in a position to state the testing problem, in a general form, for writing. This has three parts:

1. We have to set writing tasks that are properly representative of the population of tasks that we should expect the students to be able to perform.
2. The tasks should elicit valid samples of writing (i.e. which truly represent the students' ability).
3. It is essential that the samples of writing can and will be scored validly and reliably.

We shall deal with each of these in turn, offering advice and examples.

Representative tasks

(i) Specify all possible content

In order to judge whether the tasks we set are representative of the tasks that we expect students to be able to perform, we have to be clear at the outset just what these tasks are that they should be able to perform. These should be identified in the test specifications. The following elements in the framework for the specification of content presented in Chapter 7 are relevant here: operations, types of text, addressees, length of texts, topics, dialect and style.

Let us look at the handbook of the Cambridge Certificates in Communicative Skills in English (CCSE). The description of the Certificate in Writing (Level 1) may not include the complete set of specifications for that test but it shows what specifications for a writing test may look like.

Operations[2]

Expressing	thanks, requirements, opinions, comment, attitude, confirmation, apology, want/need, information, complaints, reasons, justifications
Directing	ordering, instructing, persuading, advising, warning
Describing	actions, events, objects, people, processes
Eliciting	information, directions, service, clarification, help, permission
Narration	sequence of events
Reporting	description, comment, decisions

Types of text

Form, letter (personal, business), message, fax, note, notice, postcard, recipe, report, set of instructions.

Addressees of texts

Unspecified, although 'the target audience for each piece of writing is made clear to the candidate'.

Topics

Unspecified, although on some sets of papers all the tasks will be connected with a common theme.

Dialect and **length of texts** are also unspecified.

It is probably fair to say that the CCSE Certificate in Writing specifications (as they appear in the Handbook) account for a significant proportion of the writing tasks that students in general language courses that have communicative aims are expected to be able to perform. They ought, therefore, to be useful to readers of this book who are responsible for testing writing on such courses. Under each heading, institutional testers can identify the elements that apply to their own situation. There will be some points where perhaps more detail is called for; others where additional elements are needed. There is certainly no reason to feel limited to this particular framework or its content, but all in all these specifications should provide a good starting point for many testing purposes. For the same reason, further examples of specifications are given in the following chapters.

A second example, this time much more restricted, concerns the writing component of a test of English for academic purposes with which I was associated. The purpose of the test was to discover whether a student's written English was adequate for study through the medium of English at a particular overseas university. An analysis of needs had revealed that the most important uses of written English were for the purpose of taking notes in lectures and the writing of examination answers up to two paragraphs in length. The first of these tasks was integrated into the listening component of the test. This left the examination answers. An analysis of examination questions in the university revealed that students were required to describe, explain, compare and contrast, and argue for and against a position. Because in that university the first year undergraduate course is very general (all students study arts, science and social science subjects), almost all reasonably academic topics were appropriate. The addressees were university lecturers – both native speakers and non-native speakers of English. Using the suggested framework, we can describe the relevant tasks quite succinctly:

Operations
Describe, explain, compare and contrast, argue for and against a position.

Types of text
Examination answers up to two paragraphs in length.

Addressees of texts
Native speaker and non-native speaker university lecturers.

Topics
Any capable of academic treatment. Not specialist. Relevant to the test takers.

Dialect and Style
Any standard variety of English (e.g. American, British) or a mixture of these.

Formal style.

Length of texts
About 1 page.

(ii) Include a representative sample of the specified content

From the standpoint of content validity, the ideal test would be one which required candidates to perform all the relevant potential writing tasks. The total score obtained on that test (the sum of the scores on each of the different tasks) would be our best estimate of a candidate's ability. If it were ever possible to do this, we would not expect all of a candidate's scores to be equal, even if they were perfectly scored on the same scale. People will simply be better at some tasks than others. So, if we aren't able to include every task (and of course this is normally the case) and happen to choose just the task or tasks that a candidate is particularly good (or bad) at, then the outcome is likely to be very different. This is why we try to select a representative set of tasks. And the more tasks (within reason) that we set, the more representative of a candidate's ability (the more valid) will be the totality of the samples (of the candidate's ability) we obtain. It is also to be remembered that if a test includes a wide ranging and representative sample of specifications, the test is more likely to have a beneficial backwash effect.

Let us look at the sample below, which the CCSE examiners chose for one of their tests – the Level 1 version for May/June 2000.

This Test of Writing is about working in a Summer Camp for Children in America. Look carefully at the information on this page. Then turn to the next page.

TASK 1

You saw the advertisement for Helpers. You write a letter to American Summer Camps at the address in the advertisement.

> In your letter:
> - find out about
>   - the start and finish dates
>   - the hours of work
>   - the type of accommodation
> - ask for an application form.
>
> Write your LETTER on the next page.

TASK 2

American Summer Camps for Children sent you an application form.
Fill in the APPLICATION FORM below

AMERICAN SUMMER CAMPS FOR CHILDREN

SECTION A: Please use CAPITALS for this section.

FAMILY NAME: (Mr/Mrs/Ms)_____

FIRST NAME(S): _____

AGE: _____ DATE OF BIRTH: _____

NATIONALITY: _____

SECTION B

TICK (✓) the age group of children you would most like to work with.
(NB: Choose only ONE group)

9–10 ☐   11–13 ☐   14–16 ☐

Why did you choose this particular age group?

_____

_____

SECTION C

In about 30 words, say why you think you would be especially good at organising games and activities for children.

_____

_____

_____

Signature: _____ Date:_____

TASK 3

You are now working in the American Summer Camps for Children in Florida. You write a postcard to an English-speaking friend.

> On your postcard tell your friend:
> - where you are
> - why you are there
> - two things you like about the Summer Camp.
>
> Write your POSTCARD here.

TASK 4

You have arranged to go out tonight with Gerry and Carrie, two other Helpers at the Summer Camp in Florida. You have to change your plans suddenly, and cannot meet them. You leave them a note.

> In your note:
> - apologise and explain why you cannot meet them
> - suggest a different day to go out.
>
> Write your NOTE here.

From this it is clear that the examiners have made a serious attempt to create a representative sample of tasks (the reader might wish to check off the elements in the specification that are represented in the test). What also becomes clear is that with so many *potential* tasks and with relatively few items, the test's content validity is inevitably brought into question. Really good coverage of the range of potential tasks is not possible in a single version of the test. This is a problem to which there is no easy answer. Only research will tell us whether candidates' performance on one small set of selected tasks will result in scores very similar to those that their performance on another small, non-overlapping set would have been awarded.

In the case of the English medium university, it is not nearly as difficult to select representative writing tasks. Content validity is less of a problem than with the much wider-ranging CCSE test. Since it is only under the heading of 'operations' that there is any significant variability, a test that required the student to write four answers could cover the whole range of tasks, assuming that differences of topic really did not matter. In fact, the writing component of each version of the test contained two writing tasks, and so fifty per cent of all tasks were to be found in each version of the test. Topics were chosen with which it was expected all students would be familiar, and information or arguments were provided (see example, page 93).

Of course, the desirability of wide sampling has to be balanced against practicality; otherwise we would always try to include all (or at least a large proportion) of the potential tasks. It must be remembered, however, that if we need to know something accurate and meaningful about a person's writing ability, we have to be prepared to pay for that information. What we decide to do will depend in large part on how accurate the information has to be. This in turn depends on how high the stakes are. If the test is used simply to place students in classes from which they can easily be moved to another more appropriate one, accuracy is not so important; we may be satisfied with a single sample of writing. But if the result is going to be very important to candidates – if it could, for example, determine whether they are allowed to study overseas – then certainly more than one sample is necessary if serious injustices are not to be perpetrated.

Elicit a valid sample of writing ability

Set as many separate tasks as is feasible

This requirement is closely related to the need to include a representative sample of the specified content. As we saw in Chapter 5, people's performance even on the same task is unlikely to be perfectly consistent. Therefore we have to offer candidates as many 'fresh starts' as possible, and each task can represent a fresh start. By doing this, we will achieve greater reliability and so greater validity. Again, there has to be a balance between what is desirable and what is practical.

Test only writing ability, and nothing else

This advice assumes that we do not want to test anything other than the ability to write. In language testing we are not normally interested in knowing whether students are creative, imaginative, or even intelligent, have wide general knowledge, or have good reasons for the opinions they happen to hold. Therefore, for the sake of validity, we should not set tasks which measure these abilities. Look at the following tasks which, though invented, are based on others taken from well known tests.

1. Write the conversation you have with a friend about the holiday you plan to have together.
2. You spend a year abroad. While you are there, you are asked to talk to a group of young people about life in your country. Write down what you would say to them.
3. 'Envy is the sin which most harms the sinner.' Discuss.
4. Discuss the advantages and disadvantages of being born into a wealthy family.

The first task seems to make demands on creativity, imagination, and indeed on script-writing ability. Success at the second would seem to depend to at least some extent on the ability to give talks. It is in fact hard to imagine either of the tasks being derived from a careful specification of writing tasks. The third and fourth tasks clearly favour candidates who have, or can instantly create, an ordered set of arguments on any topic which they meet. A clear indication that not only language ability is being tested is the fact that many educated native speakers (including me) would not be confident of completely satisfying the examiners. Francis Bacon might have done well, if his answers were not thought too brief.

Another ability that at times interferes with the accurate measurement of writing ability is that of reading. While it is perfectly acceptable to expect the candidate to be able to read simple instructions, care has to be taken to ensure these can be fully understood by everyone whose ability is of sufficiently high standard otherwise to perform adequately on the writing task. Nor should the instructions be too long. Part (b) of the following item may be thought to suffer from both these faults.

Answer **ONE** of the following questions in **about** 250 **words**:

Either (a) You've been asked to contribute an article to an international magazine, which is running a series called "A Good Read". Write, for the magazine, a review of a book you like.

Or (b) You have recently heard that each year the Axtel Corporation offers the opportunity for a small number of people to spend between three and six months working in one of their offices in Australia, New Zealand, the United States, or Britain. The aim of the scheme is to promote international understanding, and to foster an awareness of different working methods.

Candidates for the scheme are asked to write an initial letter of application, briefly outlining their general background and, more importantly, giving the reasons why they feel they would benefit from the scheme. In addition, they should indicate in which country they would like to work. On the basis of this letter they may be invited for interview and offered a post.

Write the letter of application.

One way of reducing dependence on the candidates' ability to read is to make use of illustrations. The following is from the Assessment and Qualification Alliance, and was intended principally for science students.

The diagram below shows three types of bee.

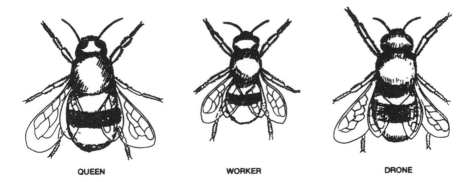

QUEEN   WORKER   DRONE

Compare and contrast the three bees.

Write about three-quarters of a page.

A series of pictures can be used to elicit a narrative.

Look at these pictures and then tell the story. Begin, 'Something very exciting happened to my mother yesterday'.

This may take the form of a quite realistic transfer of information from graphic form to continuous prose.

Average annual earnings of four working groups: 1980–2000

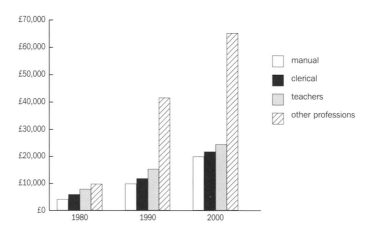

Using the data in the above chart, write a paragraph in which you discuss the relative annual incomes of the four groups over the period 1980–2000.

Restrict candidates

This echoes the general point made in Chapter 5. The question above about envy, for example, could result in very different answers from the same person on different occasions. There are so many significantly different ways of developing a response to the stimulus. Writing tasks should be well defined: candidates should know just what is required of them, and they should not be allowed to go too far astray. A useful device is to provide information in the form of notes (or pictures, as above).

The following example – slightly modified – was used in the test I was concerned with, mentioned earlier in the chapter.

> Compare the benefits of a university education in English with that of one in Arabic. Use all of the points given below and come to a conclusion. You should write about one page.
>
> a) Arabic
> 1. Easier for students
> 2. Easier for most teachers
> 3. Saves a year in most cases
>
> b) English
> 1. Books and scientific sources mostly in English.
> 2. English international language – more and better job opportunities.
> 3. Learning second language part of education/culture.

Care has to be taken when notes are given not to provide students with too much of what they need in order to carry out the task. Full sentences are generally to be avoided, particularly where they can be incorporated into the composition with little or no change.

One last thing to say about tasks is that they should not only fit well with the specifications, but they should also be made as authentic as possible. When thinking of authenticity, it is important to take into account the nature of the candidates and their relationship with the people to or for whom the task requires them to write. A task which may be authentic for one set of candidates may be quite inauthentic for another. For example, it would be quite normal in some situations for language teachers to write to their supervisor for advice, while in other situations it would be unthinkable.

Ensure valid and reliable scoring

Set tasks which can be reliably scored

A number of the suggestions made to obtain a representative performance will also facilitate reliable scoring.

Set as many tasks as possible

The more scores for each candidate, the more reliable should be the total score.

Restrict candidates

The greater the restrictions imposed on the candidates, the more directly comparable will be the performances of different candidates.

Give no choice of tasks

Making the candidates perform all tasks also makes comparisons between candidates easier.

Ensure long enough samples

The samples of writing that are elicited have to be long enough for judgements to be made reliably. This is particularly important where diagnostic information is sought. For example, in order to obtain reliable information on students' organisational ability in writing, the pieces have to be long enough for organisation to reveal itself. Given a fixed period of time for the test, there is an almost inevitable tension between the need for length and the need to have as many samples as possible.

Create appropriate scales for scoring

One expects to find the scales used in rating performance in the specifications under the heading 'criterial levels of performance'. There are two basic approaches to scoring: holistic and analytic.

Holistic scoring

Holistic scoring (sometimes referred to as 'impressionistic' scoring) involves the assignment of a single score to a piece of writing on the basis of an overall impression of it. This kind of scoring has the advantage of being very rapid. Experienced scorers can judge a one-page piece of writing in just a couple of minutes or even less (scorers of the TOEFL Test of Written English apparently have just one and a half minutes for each scoring of a composition). This means that it is possible for each piece of work to be scored more than once, which is fortunate, since it is also necessary! Harris (1968) refers to research in which, when each student wrote one 20-minute composition – scored only once – the reliability coefficient was only 0.25. If well conceived and well organised, holistic scoring in which each student's work is scored by four different trained scorers can result in high scorer reliability. There is nothing magical about the number 'four'; it is simply that research has quite consistently shown acceptably high scorer reliability when writing is scored four times.

I expressed above a reservation about the need for such scoring to be well conceived. Not every scoring system will give equally valid and reliable results in every situation. The system has to be appropriate to the level of the candidates and the purpose of the test. Look at the following scoring system used in the English-medium university already referred to in this chapter.

NS	Native speaker standard
NS-	Close to native speaker standard
MA	Clearly more than adequate
MA-	Possibly more than adequate
A	ADEQUATE FOR STUDY AT THIS UNIVERSITY
D	Doubtful
NA	Clearly not adequate
FBA	Far below adequate

This scale worked perfectly well in the situation for which it was designed. The purpose of the writing component of the test was to determine whether a student's writing ability was adequate for study in English in that university. The standards set were based on an examination of undergraduate students' written work and their teachers' judgements as to the acceptability of the English therein. With students writing two compositions, each independently scored twice, using the above scale, scorer reliability was 0.9. This is about as high as one is likely to achieve in ordinary circumstances (i.e. not in some kind of experiment or research where practicality is of no importance). It was designed for a specific purpose and obviously it would be of little use in most other circumstances. Testers have to be prepared to modify existing scales to suit their own purposes. Look now at the following, which is a component of the TOEFL (Educational Testing Services).

TEST OF WRITTEN ENGLISH

Scoring guide

Readers will assign scores based on the following scoring guide. Though examinees are asked to write on a specific topic, parts of the topic may be treated by implication. Readers should focus on what the examinee does well.

[6] Demonstrates clear competence in writing on both the rhetorical and syntactic levels, though it may have occasional errors.

A paper in this category

- effectively addresses the writing task
- is well organized and well developed
- uses clearly appropriate details to support a thesis or illustrate ideas
- displays consistent facility in the use of language
- demonstrates syntactic variety and appropriate word choice

[5] Demonstrates competence in writing on both the rhetorical and syntactic levels, though it will probably have occasional errors

A paper in this category

- may address some parts of the task more effectively than others
- is generally well organized and developed
- uses details to support a thesis or illustrate an idea
- displays facility in the use of language
- demonstrates some syntactic variety and range of vocabulary

[4] Demonstrates minimal competence in writing on both the rhetorical and syntactic levels.

A paper in this category

- addresses the writing topic adequately but may slight parts of the task
- is adequately organized and developed
- uses some details to support a thesis or illustrate an idea
- demonstrates adequate but possibly inconsistent facility with syntax and usage
- may contain some errors that occasionally obscure meaning

[3] Demonstrates some developing competence in writing, but it remains flawed on either the rhetorical or syntactic level, or both.

A paper in this category may reveal one or more of the following weaknesses:

- inadequate organization or development
- inappropriate or insufficient details to support or illustrate generalizations
- a noticeably inappropriate choice of words or word forms
- an accumulation of errors in sentence structure and/or usage

[2] Suggests incompetence in writing.

A paper in this category is seriously flawed by one or more of the following weaknesses:

- serious disorganization or underdevelopment
- little or no detail, or irrelevant specifics
- serious and frequent errors in sentence structure or usage
- serious problems with focus

[1] Demonstrates incompetence in writing.

A paper in this category

- may be incoherent
- may be undeveloped
- may contain severe and persistent writing errors

Though similar, this scale is different in two ways. First, because scores on the Test of Written English are used by many institutions, not just one, the headings are more general. Second, it provides some indication of the linguistic features of written work at each of the six levels. This may be useful both to the scorers and to the test score users.

If these indications become too detailed, however, a problem arises. Look at the following, which is part of the ACTFL (American Council for the Teaching of Foreign Languages) descriptors for writing, and represents an attempt to provide external criteria against which foreign language learning in schools and colleges can be assessed[3]. The full scale has 10 points, from Novice-Low to Superior.

ADVANCED LOW — Writers at the Advanced-Low level are able to meet basic work and/or academic writing needs, produce routine social correspondence, write about familiar topics by means of narratives and descriptions of a factual nature, and write cohesive summaries. Advanced-Low writing reflects the ability to combine and link sentences into texts of paragraph length and structure. Their accounts, while adequate, may not be substantive. Writers at the Advanced-Low level demonstrate an ability to write with a limited number of cohesive devices, and may resort to much redundancy, and awkward repetition. Use of dependent clauses is present and structurally coherent, while it often reflects the writer's native language or patterns. Writing at the Advanced-Low level may resemble native language patterns of oral discourse. More often than not, the vocabulary, grammar, and style are essentially reflective of informal writing. Writers demonstrate sustained control of simple target-language sentence structures and partial control of more complex structures. While attempting to perform functions at the Superior level, their writing will deteriorate significantly. Writing at the Advanced-Low level is understood by natives not used to the writing of non-natives.

INTERMEDIATE HIGH — Writers at the Intermediate-High level are able to meet all practical writing needs such as taking rather detailed notes on familiar topics, writing uncomplicated letters, summaries, and essays related to work, school experiences, and topics of current, general interest. They can also write simple descriptions and narrations of paragraph length on everyday events and situations in different time frames, although with some

---

inaccuracies and inconsistencies. Intermediate-High writers connect sentences into paragraphs using basic cohesive elements, but with some breakdown in one or more features of the Advanced level. They are often successful in their use of paraphrase and elaboration. In those languages that use verbal markers to indicate tense and aspect, forms are not consistently accurate. The vocabulary, grammar, and style of Intermediate-High writers are essentially reflective of the spoken language. Their writing, even with numerous but not significant errors, is generally comprehensible to natives not used to the writing of non-natives.

INTERMEDIATE MID — Writers at the Intermediate-Mid level are able to meet a number of practical writing needs. They can write short, simple letters, essays, and descriptions in loosely connected text that are based on personal preferences, daily routines, common events, and other topics related to personal experiences and immediate surroundings. Most writing is framed in present time, with inconsistent references to other time frames. There is some evidence (although minimal) of the use of grammatical and stylistic cohesive elements – object pronouns, relative pronouns, adverbs of time, coordinating conjunctions, and subordinate clauses. The writing style is reflective of the grammar and lexicon of spoken language. Writers at the Intermediate-Mid level show evidence of the control of the syntax in non-complex sentences and in basic verb forms, such as declensions or conjugations. Writing is best defined as a collection of discrete sentences, since there is little evidence of deliberate organization. Intermediate-mid writers can be readily understood by natives used to the writing of non-natives.

INTERMEDIATE LOW — Writers at the Intermediate-Low level are able to meet some limited practical writing needs. They can create statements and formulate questions based on familiar material. Most sentences are recombinations of learned vocabulary and structures. These are short and simple conversational-style sentences with basic subject-verb-object word order. They are written mostly in present time with occasional and often incorrect uses of past or future time. Writing tends to be a collection of simple sentences loosely strung together, often with repetitive structure. Vocabulary is limited to common objects and routine activities, adequate to express elementary needs. Writing is somewhat mechanistic and topics are limited to highly predictable content areas

> and personal information tied to limited language experience. There may be basic errors in grammar, word choice, punctuation, spelling, and in the formation and use of nonalphabetic symbols. Their writing is understood by natives used to the writing of non-natives.

The descriptions imply a pattern of development common to all language learners. They assume that a particular level of grammatical ability will always be associated with a particular level of lexical ability. This is, to say the least, highly questionable, and the scales have been criticized for not being based on research into the acquisition order of the various elements. Where scales are to be used to measure achievement, this criticism is, I believe, justified. If the different levels are not closely based on research into changes in performance over time, then their use is unlikely to lead to valid measures of achievement.

This is not to say that all scales need to be based on what is known of the way languages are learned. The ILR (Interagency Round Table) Levels are similar in many ways to the ACTFL scales. The difference is that the ILR Levels were designed to assign individuals to a Level in order to determine whether their foreign language ability was sufficient for a particular job. The purpose is purely to measure proficiency, regardless of how it has been achieved. The ILR Levels (for speaking) are illustrated in the next chapter.

An issue which arises when using scales of the ACTFL (and ILR) kind is how to rate someone whose language is described partly by one level and partly by another (or others). What we decide must depend in part on the purpose of the assessment. If we are trying to find out if a person has sufficient language ability for, say, a diplomatic post, we might decide that we have to place them at the lowest level that (partly) describes their language. If the purpose is to measure achievement, we may be more willing to allow strengths in one area to compensate for weaknesses in another.

Analytic scoring

Methods of scoring which require a separate score for each of a number of aspects of a task are said to be analytic. The following scale, devised by John Anderson, is based on an oral ability scale found in Harris (1968).

Grammar

6. Few (if any) noticeable errors of grammar or word order.
5. Some errors of grammar or word order which do not, however, interfere with comprehension.
4. Errors of grammar or word order fairly frequent; occasional re-reading necessary for full comprehension.
3. Errors of grammar or word order frequent; efforts of interpretation sometimes required on reader's part.
2. Errors of grammar or word order very frequent; reader often has to rely on own interpretation.
1. Errors of grammar or word order so severe as to make comprehension virtually impossible.

Vocabulary

6. Use of vocabulary and idiom rarely (if at all) distinguishable from that of educated native writer.
5. Occasionally uses inappropriate terms or relies on circumlocutions; expression of ideas hardly impaired.
4. Uses wrong or inappropriate words fairly frequently; expression of ideas may be limited because of inadequate vocabulary.
3. Limited vocabulary and frequent errors clearly hinder expression of ideas.
2. Vocabulary so limited and so frequently misused that reader must often rely on own interpretation.
1. Vocabulary limitations so extreme as to make comprehension virtually impossible.

Mechanics

6. Few (if any) noticeable lapses in punctuation or spelling.
5. Occasional lapses in punctuation or spelling which do not, however, interfere with comprehension.
4. Errors in punctuation or spelling fairly frequent; occasional re-reading necessary for full comprehension.
3. Frequent errors in spelling or punctuation; lead sometimes to obscurity.
2. Errors in spelling or punctuation so frequent that reader must often rely on own interpretation.
1. Errors in spelling or punctuation so severe as to make comprehension virtually impossible.

Fluency (style and ease of communication)

6. Choice of structures and vocabulary consistently appropriate; like that of educated native writer.
5. Occasional lack of consistency in choice of structures and vocabulary which does not, however, impair overall ease of communication.
4. 'Patchy', with some structures or vocabulary items noticeably inappropriate to general style.
3. Structures or vocabulary items sometimes not only inappropriate but also misused; little sense of ease of communication.
2. Communication often impaired by completely inappropriate or misused structures or vocabulary items.
1. A 'hotch-potch' of half-learned misused structures and vocabulary items rendering communication almost impossible.

Form (organisation)

6. Highly organised; clear progression of ideas well linked; like educated native writer.
5. Material well organised; links could occasionally be clearer but communication not impaired.
4. Some lack of organisation; re-reading required for clarification of ideas.
3. Little or no attempt at connectivity, though reader can deduce some organisation.
2. Individual ideas may be clear, but very difficult to deduce connection between them.
1. Lack of organisation so severe that communication is seriously impaired.

SCORE:
Gramm: ___ + Voc: ___ + Mech ___ + Fluency ___ + Form = ____

(TOTAL)

There are a number of advantages to analytic scoring. First, it disposes of the problem of uneven development of subskills in individuals. Secondly, scorers are compelled to consider aspects of performance which they might otherwise ignore. And thirdly, the very fact that the scorer has to give a number of scores will tend to make the scoring more reliable. While it is doubtful that scorers can judge each of the aspects independently of the others (there is what is called a 'halo effect'), the mere fact of having (in this case) five 'shots' at assessing the student's performance should lead to greater reliability.

In Anderson's scheme, each of the components is given equal weight. In other schemes (such as that of Jacobs et al. (1981), below), the relative importance of the different aspects, as perceived by the tester (with or without statistical support), is reflected in weightings attached to the various components. Grammatical accuracy, for example, might be given greater weight than accuracy of spelling. A candidate's total score is the sum of the weighted scores.

The main disadvantage of the analytic method is the time that it takes. Even with practice, scoring will take longer than with the holistic method. Particular circumstances will determine whether the analytic method or the holistic method will be the more economical way of obtaining the required level of scorer reliability.

A second disadvantage is that concentration on the different aspects may divert attention from the overall effect of the piece of writing. Inasmuch as the whole is often greater than the sum of its parts, a composite score may be very reliable but not valid. Indeed the aspects that are scored separately (the 'parts'), presumably based on the theory of linguistic performance that most appeals to the author of any particular analytic framework, may not in fact represent the complete, 'correct' set of such aspects. To guard against this, an additional, impressionistic score on each composition is sometimes required of scorers, with significant discrepancies between this and the analytic total being investigated.

It is worth noting a potential problem in Anderson's scale. This arises from the conjunction of frequency of error and the effect of errors on communication. It is not necessarily the case that the two are highly correlated. A small number of grammatical errors of one kind could have a much more serious effect on communication than a large number of another kind. This problem is not restricted to analytic scales, of course; it is just as difficult an issue in more holistic scales. Research in the area of error analysis, particularly the study of error gravity, offers insights to those wishing to pursue the matter further.

An analytic scale widely used at college level in North America is that of Jacobs et al. (1981), reproduced on p. 104. As can be seen, it has five components, 'content' being given the greatest weight and 'mechanics' the least. The weightings reflect the perceived importance of the different components in writing at college level. They would not necessarily be appropriate for testing the writing at a more elementary level, where control of mechanics might be considered more important. Note also that, except in the case of mechanics, a *range* of scores is associated with

ESL COMPOSITION PROFILE			
STUDENT		DATE	TOPIC

	SCORE	LEVEL	CRITERIA	COMMENTS
CONTENT		30-27	EXCELLENT TO VERY GOOD: knowledgeable • substantive • thorough development of thesis • relevant to assigned topic	
		26-22	GOOD TO AVERAGE: some knowledge of subject • adequate range • limited development of thesis • mostly relevant to topic, but lacks detail	
		21-17	FAIR TO POOR: limited knowledge of subject • little substance • inadequate development of topic	
		16-13	VERY POOR: does not show knowledge of subject • non-substantive • not pertinent • OR not enough to evaluate	
ORGANIZATION		20-18	EXCELLENT TO VERY GOOD: fluent expression • ideas clearly stated/supported • succinct • well-organized • logical sequencing • cohesive	
		17-14	GOOD TO AVERAGE: somewhat choppy • loosely organized but main ideas stand out • limited support • logical but incomplete sequencing	
		13-10	FAIR TO POOR: non-fluent • ideas confused or disconnected • lacks logical sequencing and development	
		9-7	VERY POOR: does not communicate • no organization • OR not enough to evaluate	
VOCABULARY		20-18	EXCELLENT TO VERY GOOD: sophisticated range • effective word/idiom choice and usage • word form mastery • appropriate register	
		17-14	GOOD TO AVERAGE: adequate range • occasional errors of word/idiom form, choice, usage *but meaning not obscured*	
		13-10	FAIR TO POOR: limited range • frequent errors of word/idiom form, choice, usage • *meaning confused or obscured*	
		9-7	VERY POOR: essentially translation • little knowledge of English vocabulary, idioms, word form • OR not enough to evaluate	
LANGUAGE USE		25-22	EXCELLENT TO VERY GOOD: effective complex constructions • few errors of agreement, tense, number, word order/function, articles, pronouns, prepositions	
		21-18	GOOD TO AVERAGE: effective but simple constructions • minor problems in complex constructions • several errors of agreement, tense, number, word order/function, articles, pronouns, prepositions *but meaning seldom obscured*	
		17-11	FAIR TO POOR: major problems in simple/complex constructions • frequent errors of negation, agreement, tense, number, word order/function, articles, pronouns, prepositions and/or fragments, run-ons, deletions • *meaning confused or obscured*	
		10-5	VERY POOR: virtually no mastery of sentence construction rules • dominated by errors • does not communicate • OR not enough to evaluate	
MECHANICS		5	EXCELLENT TO VERY GOOD: demonstrates mastery of conventions • few errors of spelling, punctuation, capitalization, paragraphing	
		4	GOOD TO AVERAGE: occasional errors of spelling, punctuation, capitalization, paragraphing *but meaning not obscured*	
		3	FAIR TO POOR: frequent errors of spelling. punctuation, capitalization, paragraphing • poor handwriting • *meaning confused or obscured*	
		2	VERY POOR: no mastery of conventions • dominated by errors of spelling, punctuation, capitalization, paragraphing • handwriting illegible • OR not enough to evaluate	

TOTAL SCORE	READER	COMMENTS

Figure 1. Jacobs et al.'s (1981) Scoring profile

each descriptor, allowing the scorer to vary the score assigned in accordance with how well the performance fits the descriptor.

The choice between holistic and analytic scoring depends in part on the purpose of the testing. If diagnostic information is required directly from the ratings given, then analytic scoring is essential[4].

The choice also depends on the circumstances of scoring. If it is being carried out by a small, well-knit group at a single site, then holistic scoring, which is likely to be more economical of time, may be the most appropriate. But if scoring is being conducted by a heterogeneous, possibly less well trained group, or in a number of different places analytic scoring is probably called for. Whichever is used, if high accuracy is sought, multiple scoring is desirable.

STEPS IN CONSTRUCTING A RATING SCALE

Constructing a valid rating scale is no easy matter. What follows is a practical guide to scale construction, assuming that it will not be possible to carry out extensive empirical research or use advanced statistical methods. It can also be used for the construction of oral rating scales.

1. Ask: What is the purpose of the testing?
   - How many distinctions in ability have to be made?
   - How will the 'scores' be reported?
   - What are the components of the ability which you want to measure?
   - Is it intended to provide feedback? If so, how detailed must it be?

2. In the light of the answers to the previous questions, decide:
   - whether scoring should be analytic or holistic, or both;
   - how many components the scale should have;
   - how many separate levels the scale should have.

3. Search for existing scales that are similar to what you need or that can contribute to the construction of your scale.

4. Modify existing scales to suit your purpose.

5. Trial the scale you have constructed and make whatever modifications prove necessary. If possible, retrial the scale before calibrating it.

Any scale which is used, whether holistic or analytic, should reflect the particular purpose of the test and the form that the reported scores on it will take. Because valid scales are not easy to construct, it is eminently reasonable to begin by reviewing existing scales and choosing those that are closest to one's needs. It should go without saying, however, that the chosen scales will almost certainly need to be adapted for the situation in which they are to be used.

Finally in this section, it is also worth pointing out that since scales are in effect telling candidates 'These are the criteria by which we will judge you', their potential for backwash is considerable, provided that candidates are made aware of them.

Calibrate the scale to be used

Any scale which is to be used should first be calibrated. As said in the previous chapter, this means collecting samples of performance collected under test conditions, and covering the full range of the scales. Members of the testing team (or another set of experts) then look at these samples and assign each of them to a point (or points in the case of an analytic scale) on the relevant scale. The assigned samples provide reference points for all future uses of the scale, as well as being essential training materials.

Select and train scorers

Not everyone is equally good at rating written work, even with training. Ideally, trainee scorers should be native speakers (or be near-native) speakers of the language being tested. They should be sensitive to language, have had experience of teaching writing and marking written work. It is also helpful if they have had training in testing.

I would recommend that training be carried out in three stages, each to be held on a separate day. If possible, the training should take place on three consecutive days. A possible outline for training follows.

Training Stage 1 Background and Overview

- Background and rationale.
- Trainees are given a copy of the writing handbook and taken through its contents.
- Examples of writing are given, one at a time, with one at each level. Participants compare relevant descriptors with the pieces of work. There is discussion about each piece of work and how it should be rated. The trainer will have an agreed completed rating sheet for each piece of work.
- All pieces of work should be on the same topic, for all stages of the training.
- There should be at least one case where quite different pieces of work are assigned to the same level. For example, one may be strong in

grammar and vocabulary but not very well organised, while the other is well structured and coherent but contains significantly more grammatical errors.

- Trainees are asked to study the handbook and the sample compositions before the second stage of training.

Training Stage 2

- Queries arising from the handbook are answered.
- A set of calibrated pieces of work is given to each trainee. (All levels should be covered, with extra examples being in the middle of the range.) Trainees are asked to complete a rating sheet independently, assigning each piece of work to a level.
- A discussion follows the assignment of all pieces of work to levels. The trainer has an agreed completed rating sheet for each piece of work. This cannot be challenged.
- All completed rating sheets are kept as a record of the trainees' performance.

Training Stage 3 Assessment

- As stage 2, except that there is no discussion.
- An agreed level of accuracy is required for someone to become a rater. Those who do not achieve it do not become raters.

Follow acceptable scoring procedures

It is assumed that scorers have already been trained. Once the test is completed, a search should be made to identify 'benchmark' scripts that typify key levels of ability on each writing task (in the case of the English medium university referred to above, these were 'adequate' and 'not adequate'; another test might require examples at all levels). Copies of these should then be presented to the scorers for an initial scoring. Only when there is agreement on these benchmark scripts should scoring begin. Each task of each student should be scored independently by two or more scorers (as many scorers as possible should be involved in the assessment of each student's work), the scores being recorded on separate sheets. A third, senior member of the team should collate scores and identify discrepancies in scores awarded to the same piece of writing. Where these are small, the two scores can be averaged; where they are larger, senior members of the team will decide the score. It is also worth looking for large discrepancies between an individual's performance on different tasks. These may accurately reflect their performance, but they may also be the result of inaccurate scoring.

It is important that scoring should take place in a quiet, well-lit environment. Scorers should not be allowed to become too tired. While holistic scoring can be very rapid, it is nevertheless extremely demanding if concentration is maintained.

Multiple scoring should ensure scorer reliability, even if not all scorers are using quite the same standard. Nevertheless, once scoring is completed, it is useful to carry out simple statistical analyses to discover if anyone's scoring is unacceptably aberrant. One might find, for example, that one person is rating higher (or lower) than the others. This can be brought to their attention. If someone's rating is markedly wayward, but not in one direction, it may be wise not to ask them to rate work in future.

Feedback

There will be many situations in which feedback to the candidates on their performance will be useful. The provisional content of a feedback pro forma can be decided during calibration. Here, for example, is a list of the elements that were thought worthy of inclusion at calibration sessions I attended recently.

In addition to feedback on linguistic features (e.g. grammar; vocabulary, limited or used inappropriately), the following elements should be included on the feedback pro forma:

Non-writing-specific:

- incomplete performance of the task in terms of:
    1. topic: not all parts addressed
          very superficial treatment
    2. operations called for (e.g. compare and contrast)
- pointless repetition

Writing-specific:

- misuse of quotation marks
- inappropriate underlining
- capitalization
- style conventions
- failure to split overlong sentences
- inappropriate use of sentence fragments
- handwriting

Reader activities

1. Following the advice given in this chapter, construct two writing tasks appropriate to a group of students with whom you are familiar. Carry out the tasks yourself. If possible, get the students to do them as well. Do any of the students produce writing different in any significant way from what you hoped to elicit? If so, can you see why? Would you wish to change the tasks in any way?
2. This activity is best carried out with colleagues. Score the following three short compositions on how to increase tourism, using each of the scales presented in the chapter. Which do you find easiest to use, and why? How closely do you and your colleagues agree on the scores you assign? Can you explain any large differences? Do the different scales place the compositions in the same order? If not, can you see why not? Which of the scales would you recommend in what circumstances?

1. Nowadays a lot of countries tend to develop their tourism's incomes, and therefore trourism called the factory without chemny. Turkey, which undoubtedly needs forign money, trys to increase the number of foreign tourists coming to Turkey. What are likely to do in order to increase this number.

At first, much more and better advertising should do in foreign countries and the information offices should open to inform the people to decide to come Turkey. Secondly, improve facilities, which are hotels, transportation and communecation. Increase the number of hotels, similarly the number of public transportation which, improve the lines of communication. Thirdly which is important as two others is training of personnel. This is also a basic need of tourism, because the tourist will want to see in front of him a skilled guides or a skilled hotel managers. The new school will open in order to train skilled personnel and as well as theoric knowledges, practice must be given them.

The countries which are made available these three basic need for tourists have already improved their tourism's incomes. Spain is a case in point or Greec. Although Turkey needs this income; it didn't do any real attempts to achive it. In fact all of them should have already been done, till today. However it is late, it can be begin without loosing any time.

2. A nation can't make improvements, if it doesn't let the minds of their people breathe and expand to understand more

about life than what is at the end of the street, this improvement can be made by means of tourism.

There are several ways to attract more people to our country. First of all, advertisements and information take an important place. These advertisements and information should be based on the qualities of that place without exaggeration. The more time passes and the more information tourists gather about one country, the more assured they can be that it will be a good experience. People travel one place to another in order to spend their holiday, to see different cultures or to attend conferences. All of these necessitate facilities. It is important to make some points clear. Hotel, transportation and communication facilities are a case in point. To some extent, we can minimize the difficulties by means of money. Furthermore, this situation does not only depend on the financial situation, but also behaviors towards the tourists. Especially, a developing country should kept in mind the challenge of the future rather than the mistakes of the past, in order to achive this, the ways of training of personnel may be found. The most important problem faced by many of countries is whether the decisions that must be made are within the capabilities of their education system. Educating guides and hotel managers are becoming more and more important.

As a result, it should once more be said that, we may increase the number of foreign tourists coming to Turkey by taking some measures. Advertisement, information, improving facilities and training personnel may be effective, but also all people should be encouraged to contribute this event.

3. Tourism is now becoming a major industry troughout the world. For many countries their tourist trade is an essential source of their revenue.

All countries have their aim particular atractions for tourists and this must be kept in mind when advertising Turkey abroad. For example Turkey, which wants to increase the number of foreign tourists coming must advertise its culture and sunshine.

Improving facilities like hotels, transportation and communication play important role on this matter more Hotels can be built and avaliable ones can be kept clean and tidy. New and modern transportation systems must be given to foreign tourists and one more, the communication system must work regularly to please these people.

Tourists don't want to be led around like sheep. They want to explore for themselves and avoid the places which are pact out with many other tourist. Because of that there must be their trained guides on their towns through anywhere and on the other hand hotel managers must be well trained. They must keep being kind to foreign tourist and must know English as well.

If we make tourists feel comfortable im these facts, tourism will increase and we will benefit from it.

(Hughes et al. 1987 145–7)

3. This activity is also best carried out with colleagues. Construct a holistic writing scale and an analytic writing scale appropriate for use with the group of students you have already identified. If possible, score the students' efforts on the two tasks (Activity 1), using both methods. Look at differences between scorers and between methods, as in the previous activity. What changes would you make in the scales? Which of the two scales would be most useful for your purposes?

Further reading

Weigle (2002) is a thorough treatment of the assessment of writing. It includes chapters on portfolio assessment and on the future of writing assessment (including the use of computers as raters). Jacobs et al. (1981), from which one of the scales presented in this chapter was taken, is also recommended. Hamp-Lyons (1991) is a collection of papers on the assessment of writing in academic contexts. Jennings et al. (1999) found that allowing a choice of topic did not make a difference to test takers' scores (but one should be wary about extrapolating from one study in one situation). Hamp-Lyons (1995) points to problems with holistic scoring. North and Schneider (1998) report on the development of a language proficiency scale. Council of Europe (2001) contains a number of scales (not only of writing ability) which are potentially useful to test constructors needing to create their own, as well as an annotated bibliography on language proficiency scaling. (Weigle 1994) reports the effects of training on raters of ESL compositions. Greenberg (1986) reports on the development of the TOEFL writing test. At the time I am writing this, the TOEFL website provides 100 practice TWE composition prompts which can be downloaded. The complete ACTFL and ILR scales can be found on the Internet (see the book's website). For a discussion of the relationship between the frequency and the gravity of errors, see James (1998). Godshalk et al. (1966) describes the development of an indirect test of writing ability.

1. We will also assume that the writing of elementary students is not to be tested. Whatever writing skills are required of them can be assessed informally. There seems little point in constructing, for example, a formal test of the ability to form characters or transcribe simple sentences.
2. Referred to as 'functions' in the Handbook.
3. There is more than one version of the ACTFL scales to be found on the Internet.
4. Where there is holistic scoring, a checklist may be used for raters to indicate particular strengths and weaknesses (see the box on p.108).

10 Testing oral ability

The assumption is made in this chapter that the objective of teaching spoken language is the development of the ability to interact successfully in that language, and that this involves comprehension as well as production. It is also assumed that at the earliest stages of learning formal testing of this ability will not be called for, informal observation providing any diagnostic information that is needed.

The basic problem in testing oral ability is essentially the same as for testing writing.

1. We want to set tasks that form a representative sample of the population of oral tasks that we expect candidates to be able to perform.
2. The tasks should elicit behaviour which truly represents the candidates' ability.
3. The samples of behaviour can and will be scored validly and reliably.

Following the pattern of the previous chapter, we shall deal with each of these in turn.

Representative tasks

Specify all possible content

We will begin by looking at the specified content of the Cambridge CCSE Test of Oral Interaction, covering all four levels at which a certificate is awarded.

Operations[1]

Expressing: likes, dislikes, preferences, agreement/disagreement, requirements, opinions, comment, attitude, confirmation, complaints, reasons, justifications, comparisons

Directing: instructing, persuading, advising, prioritising

Describing: actions, events, objects, people, processes

Eliciting: information, directions, clarification, help
Narration: sequence of events
Reporting: description, comment, decisions and choices

Types of text Discussion

Addressees 'Interlocutor' (teacher from candidate's school) and one fellow candidate

Topics Unspecified

Dialect, Accent and Style also unspecified

It can be seen that the content specifications are similar to those for the Test of Writing. They may be compared with those for a test with which I have been concerned. The categorisation of the operations (here referred to as skills) is based on Bygate (1987).

Skills

Informational skills
Candidates should be able to:
- provide personal information
- provide non-personal information
- describe sequence of events (narrate)
- give instructions
- make comparisons
- give explanations
- present an argument
- provide required information
- express need
- express requirements
- elicit help
- seek permission
- apologise
- elaborate an idea
- express opinions
- justify opinions
- complain
- speculate
- analyse
- make excuses
- paraphrase
- summarise (what they have said)
- make suggestions

- express preferences
- draw conclusions
- make comments
- indicate attitude

Interactional skills
Candidates should be able to:
- express purpose
- recognise other speakers' purpose
- express agreement
- express disagreement
- elicit opinions
- elicit information
- question assertions made by other speakers
- modify statements or comments
- justify or support statements or opinions of other speakers
- attempt to persuade others
- repair breakdowns in interaction
- check that they understand or have been understood correctly
- establish common ground
- elicit clarification
- respond to requests for clarification
- correct themselves or others
- indicate understanding (or failure to understand)
- indicate uncertainty

Skills in managing interactions
Candidates should be able to:
- initiate interactions
- change the topic of an interaction
- share the responsibility for the development of an interaction
- take their turn in an interaction
- give turns to other speakers
- come to a decision
- end an interaction

Types of text
- Presentation (monologue)
- Discussion
- Conversation
- Service encounter
- Interview

Other speakers (addressees)
- may be of equal or higher status
- may be known or unknown

Topics Topics which are familiar and interesting to the candidates

Dialect Standard British English or Standard American English

Accent RP, Standard American

Style Formal and informal

Vocabulary range Non-technical except as the result of preparation for a presentation

Rate of speech Will vary according to task

It can be seen that this second set of content specifications is rather fuller than the first. What is more, splitting the skills into three categories (informational, interactional, and management), as it does, should help in creating tasks which will elicit a representative sample of each. In my view, the greater the detail in the specification of content, the more valid the test is likely to be. Readers may wish to select elements from the two sets of specifications for their own purposes.

Include a representative sample of the specified content when setting tasks

Any one oral test should sample from the full specified range. The reasons for doing this are the same as those given in the previous chapter. Let us look at the materials for a recent Level 4 CCSE test. The test has two sections. In the first section a candidate talks with a teacher from their own institution. In the second they talk with a fellow student, and after some time the teacher joins in their discussion[2].

It is interesting to try to predict which of the functions listed in the specifications would be elicited by these tasks. You might want to attempt to do this before reading any further. Looking at them myself, I thought that in performing the tasks the speakers were quite likely to express opinions, likes and dislikes, preferences, reasons, justifications. They might also describe, narrate or report, depending perhaps on the nature of the justification they provide for their opinions and preferences. It came as a surprise to me therefore to read in the Examiners' Report for this test that the aim of the first task was to elicit 'describing, explaining and justifying', and that of the second was to elicit 'exchanging opinions and justifying'. But it does allow me to make two related

Section I

1   You have 5 minutes to read the task and **think** about what you want to say.

2   If there is anything which you don't understand, please ask the teacher who is with you.

3   You can make a few notes if you want to. The examiner will not look at them.

4   After this 5 minute preparation time, you will go into the exam room and talk about the subject with a teacher. The examiner will listen.

TASK 3

What makes a good friend?

You are going to talk to the teacher about what you value in your friends.

Look at the suggestions below:

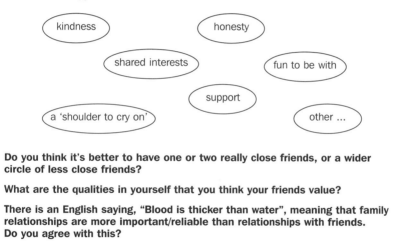

Do you think it's better to have one or two really close friends, or a wider circle of less close friends?

What are the qualities in yourself that you think your friends value?

There is an English saying, "Blood is thicker than water", meaning that family relationships are more important/reliable than relationships with friends. Do you agree with this?

points. The first is that, unless the tasks are extremely restrictive (which they are not in the CCSE test), it is not possible to predict all the operations which will be performed in an interactive oral test. The second point is that, even where quite specific tasks are set, as in the present case, the 'interlocutor' can have a considerable influence on the content of an oral test. Interviewers therefore need to be well trained and always aware of the need to elicit a representative sample of the operations listed in the specifications.

Section II

1   You have 5 minutes to read the task and **think** about what you want to say.

2   If there is anything which you don't understand, please ask the teacher who is with you. **DON'T start talking with your partner yet.**

3   You can make a few notes if you want to. The examiner will not look at them.

4   After this 5 minute preparation time, you will go into the exam room with your partner.

5   The teacher will start your discussion with you and will then leave the room. He or she will join your conversation later for a further 5 minutes. The examiner will listen.

TASK 1

Whether you have a mobile phone or not, many people have opinions about them.

Look at the statements below. Tick (✓) the ones <u>you</u> agree with.

☐   "I hate it when phones ring at the theatre or cinema."

☐   "If you have a mobile phone you never feel alone."

☐   "It's really dangerous to drive and phone at the same time."

☐   "I feel safer with a mobile phone."

☐   "I hate them – people look stupid walking around talking on the phone!"

Exchange your ideas about mobile phones with your partner. Talk about the reasons why people have them. What advantages do they have over conventional phones? Are there any disadvantages?

When the teacher returns, tell him/her about your discussion. S/he will then ask you what limits (if any) should be put on when and where mobile phones can be used.

In what ways, for better or worse, is technology changing how we communicate with each other? What about future developments?

Elicit a valid sample of oral ability

Choose appropriate techniques

Three general formats are presented here: interview; interaction with fellow candidates; responses to audio- or video-recorded stimuli.

Format 1 Interview

Perhaps the most common format for the testing of oral interaction is the interview. In its traditional form, however, it has at least one potentially serious drawback. The relationship between the tester and the candidate is usually such that the candidate speaks as to a superior and is unwilling to take the initiative. As a result, only one style of speech is elicited, and many functions (such as asking for information) are not represented in the candidate's performance. It is possible, however, to get round this problem by introducing a variety of elicitation techniques into the interview situation.

Useful techniques are:

Questions and requests for information
Yes/No questions should generally be avoided, except perhaps at the very beginning of the interview, while the candidate is still warming up. Performance of various operations (of the kind listed in the two sets of specifications above) can be elicited through requests of the kind:

'Can you explain to me how/why ...?' and

'Can you tell me what you think of ...?'

Requests for elaboration: such as *What exactly do you mean?, Can you explain that in a little more detail?, What would be a good example of that? Tell me more.*

Appearing not to understand: This is most appropriate where the interviewer really isn't sure of what the candidate means but can also be used simply in order to see if the candidate can cope with being misunderstood. The interviewer may say, for example, *I'm sorry, but I don't quite follow you.*

Invitation to ask questions: *Is there anything you'd like to ask me?*

Interruption: To see how the candidate deals with this.

Abrupt change of topic: To see how the candidate deals with this.

Pictures
Single pictures are particularly useful for eliciting descriptions. Series of pictures (or video sequences) form a natural basis for narration (the series of pictures on page 92 for example).

Role play
Candidates can be asked to assume a role in a particular situation. This allows the ready elicitation of other language functions. There can be a series of brief items, such as:

> A friend invites you to a party on an evening when you want to stay at home and watch the last episode of a television serial. Thank the friend (played by the tester) and refuse politely.

Or there can be a more protracted exchange:

> You want your mother (played by the tester) to increase your pocket money. She is resistant to the idea. Try to make her change her mind.

> You want to fly from London to Paris on 13 March, returning a week later. Get all the information that you need in order to choose your flights from the travel agent (played by the tester).

In my experience, however, where the aim is to elicit 'natural' language and an attempt has been made to get the candidates to forget, to some extent at least, that they are being tested, role play can destroy this illusion. I have found that some candidates, rather than responding to the situation as if it were one they were actually facing, will resort to uttering half remembered snatches of exchanges once learned by rote.

Interpreting
It is not intended that candidates should be able to act as interpreters (unless that is specified). However, simple interpreting tasks can test both production and comprehension in a controlled way. If there are two testers, one of the testers acts as a monolingual speaker of the candidate's native language, the other as a monolingual speaker of the language being tested. Situations of the following kind can be set up:

> The native language speaker wants to invite a foreign visitor to his or her home for a meal. The candidate has to convey the invitation and act as an interpreter for the subsequent exchange.

Comprehension can be assessed when the candidate attempts to convey what the visitor is saying, and indeed unless some such device is used, it is difficult to obtain sufficient information on candidates' powers of comprehension. Production is tested when the candidate tries to convey the meaning of what the native speaker says.

Prepared monologue

In the first edition of this book I said that I did not recommend prepared monologues as a means of assessing candidates' oral ability. This was because I knew that the technique was frequently misused. What I should have said is that it should only be used where the ability to make prepared presentations is something that the candidates will need. Thus it could be appropriate in a proficiency test for teaching assistants, or in an achievement test where the ability to make presentations is an objective of the course.

Reading aloud

This is another technique the use of which I discouraged in the first edition, pointing out that there are significant differences amongst native speakers in the ability to read aloud, and that interference between the reading and the speaking skills was inevitable. But, if that ability is needed or its development has been a course objective, use of the technique may be justified.

Format 2 Interaction with fellow candidates

An advantage of having candidates interacting with each other is that it should elicit language that is appropriate to exchanges between equals, which may well be called for in the test specifications. It may also elicit better performance, inasmuch as the candidates may feel more confident than when dealing with a dominant, seemingly omniscient interviewer.

There is a problem, however. The performance of one candidate is likely to be affected by that of the others. For example, an assertive and insensitive candidate may dominate and not allow another candidate to show what he or she can do. If interaction with fellow candidates is to take place, the pairs should be carefully matched whenever possible. In general, I would advise against having more than two candidates interacting, as with larger numbers the chance of a diffident candidate failing to show their ability increases.

Possible techniques are:

Discussion

An obvious technique is to set a task which demands discussion between the two candidates, as in the Test of Oral Interaction above. Tasks may require the candidates to go beyond discussion and, for example, take a decision.

Role play

Role play can be carried out by two candidates with the tester as an observer. For some roles this may be more natural than if the tester were involved. It may, for example, be difficult to imagine the tester as 'a friend'. However, I believe that the doubts about role play expressed above still apply.

Format 3 Responses to audio- or video-recordings

Uniformity of elicitation procedures can be achieved through presenting all candidates with the same computer generated or audio-/video-recorded stimuli (to which the candidates themselves respond into a microphone). This format, often described as 'semi-direct', ought to promote reliability. It can also be economical where a language laboratory is available, since large numbers of candidates can be tested at the same time. The obvious disadvantage of this format is its inflexibility: there is no way of following up candidates' responses.

A good source of techniques is the ARELS (Association of Recognised English Language Schools) Examination in Spoken English and Comprehension. These include:

Described situations
For example:

> You are walking through town one day and you meet two friends who you were sure had gone to live in the USA. What do you say?

Remarks in isolation to respond to
For example:

> The candidate hears, 'I'm afraid I haven't managed to fix that cassette player of yours yet. Sorry.'
>
> or 'There's a good film on TV tonight.'

Simulated conversation
For example:

> The candidate is given information about a play which they are supposed to want to see, but not by themselves. The candidate is told to talk to a friend, Ann, on the telephone, and ask her to go to the theatre and answer her questions. The candidate hears:
>
> Ann: Hello. What can I do for you?

Ann: Hold on a moment. What's the name of the play, and who's it by?

Ann: Never heard of it. When's it on exactly?

Ann: Sorry to mention it, but I hope it isn't too expensive.

Ann: Well which night do you want to go, and how much would you like to pay?

Ann: OK. That's all right. It'll make a nice evening out. 'Bye.

Note that although what Ann says is scripted, the style of speech is appropriately informal. For all of the above, an indication is given to candidates of the time available (for example ten seconds) in which to respond. Note, too, that there is room for confusion towards the end of the exchange if the candidate does not say that there are different priced tickets. This is something to be avoided.

The Test of Spoken English (TSE), developed by Educational Testing Services, uses the same elicitation techniques that are found in interviews. In the sample test found in the Standard-setting Kit:

Candidates see a simple town plan and are asked for (a) recommendation for a visit to one of the buildings, with reasons; (b) directions to the movie theatre; (c) a summary of a favourite movie and their reasons for liking it.

Candidates are given a series of pictures in which a man sits on a recently painted park bench and asked to (a) narrate the story (b) say how the accident could have been avoided (c) imagine that the accident has happened to them and they must persuade the dry cleaners to clean their suit the same day (d) state the advantages and disadvantages of newspapers and television as sources of news (the man in the pictures reads a newspaper on the park bench!).

Candidates are asked to talk about the desirability or otherwise of keeping animals in zoos, define a key term in their field of study, describe the information given in a graph and discuss its implications.

Candidates are given printed information about a trip which has had some handwritten amendments made to it. They must make a presentation to the group of people who are going on the trip, explaining the changes.

Candidates are told how long they have to study the information they are given and how long they are expected to speak for.

123

Both the ARELS test and the TSE provide useful models for anyone interested in developing tape mediated speaking tests. Notice, however, that the TWE does not make any real attempt to assess interactive skills.

Plan and structure the testing carefully

1. Make the oral test as long as is feasible. It is unlikely that much reliable information can be obtained in less than about 15 minutes, while 30 minutes can probably provide all the information necessary for most purposes. As part of a placement test, however, a five- or ten-minute interview should be sufficient to prevent gross errors in assigning students to classes.

2. Plan the test carefully. While one of the advantages of individual oral testing is the way in which procedures can be adapted in response to a candidate's performance, the tester should nevertheless have some pattern to follow. It is a mistake to begin, for example, an interview with no more than a general idea of the course that it might take. Simple plans of the kind illustrated below can be made and consulted unobtrusively during the interview

---

INTRO: Name, etc.
How did you get here today? traffic problems?

School: position, class sizes, children
Typical school day; school holidays
3 pieces of advice to new teachers
Examinations and tests
Tell me about typical errors in English
How do you teach ... present perfect v. past tense
        future time reference
        conditionals

What if... you hadn't become a teacher
     ... you were offered promotion

INTERPRETING: How do I get onto the Internet?
          How do I find out about the cheapest flights to Europe?

NEWSPAPER: (look at the headlines)

EXPLAIN IDIOMS: For example, 'Once in a blue moon' or 'See the light'

---

3. Give the candidate as many 'fresh starts' as possible. This means a number of things. First, if possible and if appropriate, more than one format should be used. Secondly, again if possible, it is desirable for

candidates to interact with more than one tester. Thirdly, within a format there should be as many separate 'items' as possible. Particularly if a candidate gets into difficulty, not too much time should be spent on one particular function or topic. At the same time, candidates should not be discouraged from making a second attempt to express what they want to say, possibly in different words.

4. Use a second tester for interviews. Because of the difficulty of conducting an interview and of keeping track of the candidate's performance, it is very helpful to have a second tester present. This person can not only give more attention to how the candidate is performing but can also elicit performance which they think is necessary in order to come to a reliable judgement. The interpretation task suggested earlier needs the co-operation of a second tester.

5. Set only tasks and topics that would be expected to cause candidates no difficulty in their own language.

6. Carry out the interview in a quiet room with good acoustics.

7. Put candidates at their ease so that they can show what they are capable of. Individual oral tests will always be particularly stressful for candidates. It is important to be pleasant and reassuring throughout, showing interest in what the candidate says through both verbal and non-verbal signals. It is especially important to make the initial stages of the test well within the capacities of all reasonable candidates. Interviews, for example, can begin with straightforward requests for personal (but not too personal) details, remarks about the weather, and so on.

Testers should avoid constantly reminding candidates that they are being assessed. In particular they should not be seen to make notes on the candidates' performance during the interview or other activity. For the same reason, transitions between topics and between techniques should be made as natural as possible. The interview should be ended at a level at which the candidate clearly feels comfortable, thus leaving him or her with a sense of accomplishment.

8. Collect enough relevant information. If the purpose of the test is to determine whether a candidate can perform at a certain predetermined level, then, after an initial easy introduction, the test should be carried out at that level. If it becomes apparent that a candidate is clearly very weak and has no chance of reaching the criterion level, then an interview should be brought gently to a close, since nothing will be learned from subjecting her or him to a longer ordeal. Where, on the other hand, the purpose of the test is to see what level the candidate is at, in an interview the tester has to begin by guessing what this level is on the basis of early responses. The

interview is then conducted at that level, either providing confirmatory evidence or revealing that the initial guess is inaccurate. In the latter case the level is shifted up or down until it becomes clear what the candidate's level is. A second tester, whose main role is to assess the candidate's performance, can elicit responses at a different level if it is suspected that the principal interviewer may be mistaken.

9. Do not talk too much. There is an unfortunate tendency for interviewers to talk too much, not giving enough talking time to candidates. Avoid the temptation to make lengthy or repeated explanations of something that the candidate has misunderstood.

10. Select interviewers carefully and train them. Successful interviewing is by no means easy and not everyone has great aptitude for it. Interviewers need to be sympathetic and flexible characters, with a good command of the language themselves. But even the most apt need training. What follows is the outline of a possible four-stage training programme for interviewers, where interviewing is carried out as recommended above, with two interviewers.

Stage 1 Background and overview
- Trainees are given background on the interview.
- Trainees are given a copy of the handbook and taken through its contents.
- The structure of the interview is described.
- A video of a typical interview is shown.
- Trainees are asked to study the handbook before the second stage of the training.

Stage 2 Assigning candidates to levels
- Queries arising from reading the handbook are answered.
- A set of calibrated videos is shown.
- After each video, trainees are asked to write down the levels to which they assign the candidate according to the level descriptions and the analytic scale, and to complete a questionnaire on the task. A discussion follows.
- All papers completed by trainees during this stage are kept as a record of their performance.

Stage 3 Conducting interviews
- Pairs of trainees conduct interviews, which are videoed.
- The other trainees watch the interview on a monitor in another room.
- After each interview, all trainees assign the candidate to a level and complete a questionnaire. These are then discussed.
- Each trainee will complete 6 interviews.

Stage 4 Assessment

- Procedures will be as in Stage 3, except that the performance of trainees will not be watched by other trainees. Nor will there be any discussion after each interview.

Ensure valid and reliable scoring

Create appropriate scales for scoring

As was said for tests of writing in the previous chapter, rating scales may be holistic or analytic. The advantages and disadvantages of the two approaches have already been discussed in the previous chapter. We begin by looking at the degree of skill that Level 3 candidates for the CCSE Test of Oral Interaction are required to show. These will have been applied to candidates performing the tasks presented above.

ACCURACY	Pronunciation must be clearly intelligible even if some influences from L1 remain. Grammatical/lexical accuracy is high though grammatical errors which do not impede communication are acceptable.
APPROPRIACY	The use of language must be generally appropriate to function and to context. The intention of the speaker must be clear and unambiguous.
RANGE	A wide range of language must be available to the candidate. Any specific items which cause difficulties can be smoothly substituted or avoided.
FLEXIBILITY	There must be consistent evidence of the ability to 'turn-take' in a conversation and to adapt to new topics or changes of direction.
SIZE	Must be capable of making lengthy and complex contributions where appropriate. Should be able to expand and develop ideas with minimal help from the Interlocutor.

Notice that certain elements in these descriptions of degree of skill (such as 'ability to turn-take') could be placed in the content section of the specifications. As long as such elements are taken into account in constructing the tasks (and they are in the CCSE test) this would not seem to be a problem. The CCSE differs from the ILR descriptors below in that the CCSE does specify functions separately.

The ILR speaking levels go from 0 (zero) to 5 (native speaker like), with a plus indicating a level intermediate between two 'whole number' levels. Levels 2, 2+ and 3 follow.

Speaking 2 (Limited Working Proficiency)

Able to satisfy routine social demands and limited work requirements. Can handle routine work-related interactions that are limited in scope. In more complex and sophisticated work-related tasks, language usage generally disturbs the native speaker. Can handle with confidence, but not with facility, most normal, high-frequency social conversational situations including extensive, but casual conversations about current events, as well as work, family, and autobiographical information. The individual can get the gist of most everyday conversations but has some difficulty understanding native speakers in situations that require specialized or sophisticated knowledge. The individual's utterances are minimally cohesive. Linguistic structure is usually not very elaborate and not thoroughly controlled; errors are frequent. Vocabulary use is appropriate for high-frequency utterances, but unusual or imprecise elsewhere.

Examples: While these interactions will vary widely from individual to individual, the individual can typically ask and answer predictable questions in the workplace and give straightforward instructions to subordinates. Additionally, the individual can participate in personal and accommodation-type interactions with elaboration and facility; that is, can give and understand complicated, detailed, and extensive directions and make non-routine changes in travel and accommodation arrangements. Simple structures and basic grammatical relations are typically controlled; however, there are areas of weakness. In the commonly taught languages, these may be simple markings such as plurals, articles, linking words, and negatives or more complex structures such as tense/aspect usage, case morphology, passive constructions, word order, and embedding.

Speaking 2+ (Limited Working Proficiency, Plus)

Able to satisfy most work requirements with language usage that is often, but not always, acceptable and effective. The individual shows considerable ability to communicate effectively on topics relating to particular interests and special fields of competence.

Often shows a high degree of fluency and ease of speech, yet when under tension or pressure, the ability to use the language effectively may deteriorate. Comprehension of normal native speech is typically nearly complete. The individual may miss cultural and local references and may require a native speaker to adjust to his/her limitations in some ways. Native speakers often perceive the individual's speech to contain awkward or inaccurate phrasing of ideas, mistaken time, space, and person references, or to be in some way inappropriate, if not strictly incorrect.

Examples: Typically the individual can participate in most social, formal, and informal interactions; but limitations either in range of contexts, types of tasks, or level of accuracy hinder effectiveness. The individual may be ill at ease with the use of the language either in social interaction or in speaking at length in professional contexts. He/she is generally strong in either structural precision or vocabulary, but not in both. Weakness or unevenness in one of the foregoing, or in pronunciation, occasionally results in miscommunication. Normally controls, but cannot always easily produce, general vocabulary. Discourse is often incohesive.

Speaking 3 (General Professional Proficiency)

Able to speak the language with sufficient structural accuracy and vocabulary to participate effectively in most formal and informal conversations on practical, social, and professional topics. Nevertheless, the individual's limitations generally restrict the professional contexts of language use to matters of shared knowledge and/or international convention. Discourse is cohesive. The individual uses the language acceptably, but with some noticeable imperfections; yet, errors virtually never interfere with understanding and rarely disturb the native speaker. The individual can effectively combine structure and vocabulary to convey his/her meaning accurately. The individual speaks readily and fills pauses suitably. In face-to-face conversation with natives speaking the standard dialect at a normal rate of speech, comprehension is quite complete. Although cultural references, proverbs, and the implications of nuances and idiom may not be fully understood, the individual can easily repair the conversation. Pronunciation may be obviously foreign. Individual sounds are accurate; but stress, intonation, and pitch control may be faulty.

> *Examples:* Can typically discuss particular interests and special fields of competence with reasonable ease. Can use the language as part of normal professional duties such as answering objections, clarifying points, justifying decisions, understanding the essence of challenges, stating and defending policy, conducting meetings, delivering briefings, or other extended and elaborate informative monologues. Can reliably elicit information and informed opinion from native speakers. Structural inaccuracy is rarely the major cause of misunderstanding. Use of structural devices is flexible and elaborate. Without searching for words or phrases, individual uses the language clearly and relatively naturally to elaborate concepts freely and make ideas easily understandable to native speakers. Errors occur in low-frequency and highly complex structures.

It was said that holistic and analytic scales can be used as a check on each other. An example of this in oral testing is the American FSI (Foreign Service Institute) interview procedure[3], which requires the two testers concerned in each interview both to assign candidates to a level holistically and to rate them on a six-point scale for each of the following: accent, grammar, vocabulary, fluency, comprehension. These ratings are then weighted and totalled. The resultant score is then looked up in a table which converts scores into the holistically described levels. The converted score should give the same level as the one to which the candidate was first assigned. If not, the testers will have to reconsider whether their first assignments were correct. The weightings and the conversion tables are based on research which revealed a very high level of agreement between holistic and analytic scoring. Having used this system myself when testing bank staff, I can attest to its efficacy. For the reader's interest I reproduce the rating scales and the weighting table. It must be remembered, however, that these were developed for a particular purpose and should not be expected to work well in a significantly different situation without modification. It is perhaps also worth mentioning that the use of a native-speaker standard against which to judge performance has recently come in for criticism in some language testing circles.

Proficiency Descriptions

Accent
1. Pronunciation frequently unintelligible.
2. Frequent gross errors and a very heavy accent make understanding difficult, require frequent repetition.
3. "Foreign accent" requires concentrated listening, and mispronunciations lead to occasional misunderstanding and apparent errors in grammar or vocabulary.
4. Marked "foreign accent" and occasional mispronunciations which do not interfere with understanding.
5. No conspicuous mispronunciations, but would not be taken for a native speaker.
6. Native pronunciation, with no trace of "foreign accent."

Grammar
1. Grammar almost entirely inaccurate except in stock phrases.
2. Constant errors showing control of very few major patterns and frequently preventing communication.
3. Frequent errors showing some major patterns uncontrolled and causing occasional irritation and misunderstanding.
4. Occasional errors showing imperfect control of some patterns but no weakness that causes misunderstanding.
5. Few errors, with no patterns of failure.
6. No more than two errors during the interview.

Vocabulary
1. Vocabulary inadequate for even the simplest conversation.
2. Vocabulary limited to basic personal and survival areas (time, food, transportation, family, etc.).
3. Choice of words sometimes inaccurate, limitations of vocabulary prevent discussion of some common professional and social topics.
4. Professional vocabulary adequate to discuss special interests; general vocabulary permits discussion of any non-technical subject with some circumlocutions.
5. Professional vocabulary broad and precise; general vocabulary adequate to cope with complex practical problems and varied social situations.
6. Vocabulary apparently as accurate and extensive as that of an educated native speaker.

Fluency

1. Speech is so halting and fragmentary that conversation is virtually impossible.
2. Speech is very slow and uneven except for short or routine sentences.
3. Speech is frequently hesitant and jerky; sentences may be left uncompleted.
4. Speech is occasionally hesitant, with some unevenness caused by rephrasing and groping for words.
5. Speech is effortless and smooth, but perceptively non-native in speed and evenness.
6. Speech on all professional and general topics as effortless and smooth as a native speaker's.

Comprehension

1. Understands too little for the simplest type of conversation.
2. Understands only slow, very simple speech on common social and touristic topics; requires constant repetition and rephrasing.
3. Understands careful, somewhat simplified speech when engaged in a dialogue, but may require considerable repetition and rephrasing.
4. Understands quite well normal educated speech when engaged in a dialogue, but requires occasional repetition or rephrasing.
5. Understands everything in normal educated conversation except for very colloquial or low-frequency items, or exceptionally rapid or slurred speech.
6. Understands everything in both formal and colloquial speech to be expected of an educated native speaker.

WEIGHTING TABLE

	1	2	3	4	5	6	(A)
Accent	0	1	2	2	3	4	_____
Grammar	6	12	18	24	30	36	_____
Vocabulary	4	8	12	16	20	24	_____
Fluency	2	4	6	8	10	12	_____
Comprehension	4	8	12	15	19	23	_____
						Total	_____

Note the relative weightings for the various components.

> The total of the weighted scores is then looked up in the follow-
> ing table, which converts it into a rating on a scale 0–4+.
>
> ## CONVERSION TABLE
>
> | Score | Rating | Score | Rating | Score | Rating |
> |-------|--------|-------|--------|-------|--------|
> | 16–25 | 0+ | 43–52 | 2 | 73–82 | 3+ |
> | 26–32 | 1 | 53–62 | 2+ | 83–92 | 4 |
> | 33–42 | 1+ | 63–72 | 3 | 93–99 | 4+ |

(Adams and Frith 1979: 35–8)

Where analytic scales of this kind are used to the exclusion of holistic
scales, the question arises (as with the testing of writing) as to what
pattern of scores (for an individual candidate) should be regarded as
satisfactory. This is really the same problem (though in a more obvious
form) as the failure of individuals to fit holistic descriptions. Once again
it is a matter of agreeing, on the basis of experience, what failures to
reach the expected standard on particular parameters are acceptable.

The advice on creating rating scales given in the previous chapter is
equally relevant here:

Calibrate the scale to be used

Generally the same procedures are followed in calibrating speaking
scales as were described for writing scales, with the obvious difference
that video-recordings are used rather than pieces of written work.

Train scorers (as opposed to interviewers)

The training of interviewers has already been outlined. Where raters are
used to score interviews without acting as interviewers themselves, or
are involved in the rating of responses to audio- or video-recorded
stimuli, the same methods can be used as for the training of raters of
written work.

Follow acceptable scoring procedures

Again, the advice that one would want to offer here is very much the
same as has already been given in the previous chapter. Perhaps the only
addition to be made is that great care must be taken to ignore personal
qualities of the candidates that are irrelevant to an assessment of their

language ability. I remember well the occasion when raters quite seriously underestimated the ability of one young woman who had dyed her hair blonde. In an oral test it can be difficult to separate such features as pleasantness, prettiness, or the cut of someone's dress, from their language ability – but one must try!

Conclusion

The accurate measurement of oral ability is not easy. It takes considerable time and effort, including training, to obtain valid and reliable results. Nevertheless, where a test is high stakes, or backwash is an important consideration, the investment of such time and effort may be considered necessary. Readers are reminded that the appropriateness of content, of rating scales levels, and of elicitation techniques used in oral testing will depend upon the needs of individual institutions or organisations.

Reader activities

These activities are best carried out with colleagues.
1. For a group of students that you are familiar with, prepare a holistic rating scale (five bands) appropriate to their range of ability. From your knowledge of the students, place each of them on this scale.
2. Choose three methods of elicitation (for example role play, group discussion, interview). Design a test in which each of these methods is used for five to ten minutes.
3. Administer the test to a sample of the students you first had in mind.
4. Note problems in administration and scoring. How would you avoid them?
5. For each student who takes the test, compare scores on the different tasks. Do different scores represent real differences of ability between tasks? How do the scores compare with your original ratings of the students?

Further reading

Two books devoted to oral testing and assessment are Luoma (2003) and Underhill (1987). Fulcher (1996a) investigates task design in relation to the group oral. Chahloub-Deville (1995) and Fulcher (1996b) address issues in rating scale construction, the latter with particular reference to fluency. Kormos (1999) provides evidence that role play can be a useful testing technique, especially when one wants to assess the ability to manage interactions. Lazaraton (1996) examines the kinds of linguistic and interactional support which interlocutors may give to candidates. Douglas (1994) shows how the same rating may be assigned to qualitatively different performances in an oral test. Lumley and McNamara (1995) report on a study into rater bias in oral testing. Wigglesworth (1993) shows how bias in raters can be detected and how raters can improve when their bias is brought to their attention. Shohamy et al. (1986) report on the development of a new national oral test which appears to show desirable psychometric qualities and to have beneficial backwash. Bachman and Savignon (1986) is an early critique of the ACTFL oral interview, to which Lowe (1986) responds. Salaberry (2000) is also critical of it and proposes changes. Shohamy (1994) discusses the validity of direct versus semi-direct oral tests. Powers et al. (1999) report on the validation of the TSE. Luoma (2001) reviews the TSE. The Cambridge CCSE handbook and past papers are a good source of ideas for tasks (address to be found on page 73). Modern 'communicative' textbooks are another source of ideas for tasks. Information on the ARELS examinations (and past papers with recordings) can be obtained from ARELS Examinations Trust, 113 Banbury Road, Oxford, OX2 6JX.

1. Referred to as 'functions' in the handbook.
2. Three tasks are offered for each section but a student only performs one of them. The institution decides which task is most appropriate for each student. As can be seen, only one task for each section is reproduced here.
3. I understand that the FSI no longer tests oral ability in the way that it did. However, I have found the methods described in their 'Testing Kit', which also includes both holistic and analytic scales, very useful when testing the language ability of professional people in various situations.

11 Testing reading

This chapter begins by considering how we should specify what candidates can be expected to do, and then goes on to make suggestions for setting appropriate test tasks.

Specifying what the candidate should be able to do

Operations

The testing of reading ability seems deceptively straightforward when it is compared to, say, the testing of oral ability. You take a passage, ask some questions about it, and there you are. But while it is true that you can very quickly construct a reading test, it may not be a very good test, and it may not measure what you want it to measure.

The basic problem is that the exercise of receptive skills does not necessarily, or usually, manifest itself directly in overt behaviour. When people write and speak, we see and hear; when they read and listen, there will often be nothing to observe. The challenge for the language tester is to set tasks which will not only cause the candidate to exercise reading (or listening) skills, but will also result in behaviour that will demonstrate the successful use of those skills. There are two parts to this problem. First, there is uncertainty about the skills which may be involved in reading and which, for various reasons, language testers are interested in measuring; many have been hypothesised but few have been unequivocally demonstrated to exist. Second, even if we believe in the existence of a particular skill, it is still difficult to know whether an item has succeeded in measuring it.

The proper response to this problem is not to resort to the simplistic approach to the testing of reading outlined in the first paragraph, while we wait for confirmation that the skills we think exist actually do. We believe these skills exist because we are readers ourselves and are aware of at least some of them. We know that, depending on our purpose in reading and the kind of text we are dealing with, we may read in quite different ways. On one occasion we may read slowly and carefully, word by word, to follow, say, a philosophical argument. Another time we may flit from page to page, pausing only a few seconds on each, to get the gist of something. At yet another time we may look quickly down a column of text, searching for a particular piece of information. There is little doubt that accomplished readers are skilled in adapting the way they read according to purpose and text. This being so, I see no difficulty in including these different kinds of reading in the specifications of a test.

If we reflect on our reading, we become conscious of other skills we have. Few of us will know the meaning of every word we ever meet, yet we can often infer the meaning of a word from its context. Similarly, as we read, we are continually making inferences about people, things and events. If, for example, we read that someone has spent an evening in a pub and that he then staggers home, we may infer that he staggers because of what has he drunk (I realise that he could have been an innocent foot- baller who had been kicked on the ankle in a match and then gone to the pub to drink lemonade, but I didn't say that all our inferences were correct).

It would not be helpful to continue giving examples of the reading skills we know we have. The point is that we do know they exist. The fact that not all of them have had their existence confirmed by research is not a reason to exclude them from our specifications, and thereby from our tests. The question is: Will it be useful to include them in our test? The answer might be thought to depend at least to some extent on the purpose of the test. If it is a diagnostic test which attempts to iden- tify in detail the strengths and weaknesses in learners' reading abilities, the answer is certainly yes. If it is an achievement test, where the devel- opment of these skills is an objective of the course, the answer must again be yes. If it is a placement test, where a rough and ready indica- tion of reading ability is enough, or a proficiency test where an 'overall' measure of reading ability is sufficient, one might expect the answer to be no. But the answer 'no' invites a further question. If we are not going to test these skills, what *are* we going to test? Each of the questions that were referred to in the first paragraph must be testing *something*. If our items are going to test *something*, surely on grounds of validity, in a test of overall ability, we should try to test a sample of all the skills that are involved in reading and are relevant to our purpose. This is what I would recommend.

Of course the weasel words in the previous sentence are 'relevant to our purpose'. For beginners, there may be an argument for including in a diagnostic test items which test the ability to distinguish between letters (e.g. between *b* and *d*). But normally these will be tested indirectly through higher level items. The same is true for grammar and vocabulary. They are both tested indirectly in every reading test, but the place for grammar and vocabulary items is, I would say, in grammar and vocabulary tests. For that reason I will not discuss them further in this chapter.

To be consistent with our general framework for specifications, we will refer to the skills that readers perform when reading a text as 'operations'. In the boxes that follow are checklists (not meant to be exhaustive) which it is thought the reader of this book may find useful. Note the distinction, based on differences of purpose, between expeditious (quick and efficient) reading and slow and careful reading. There has been a tendency in the past for expeditious reading to be given less prominence in tests than it deserves. The backwash effect of this is that many students have not been trained to read quickly and efficiently. This is a considerable disadvantage when, for example, they study overseas and are expected to read extensively in very limited periods of time. Another example of harmful backwash!

Expeditious reading operations

Skimming
The candidate can:
- obtain main ideas and discourse topic quickly and efficiently;
- establish quickly the structure of a text;
- decide the relevance of a text (or part of a text) to their needs.

Search reading
The candidate can quickly find information on a predetermined topic.

Scanning
The candidate can quickly find:
- specific words or phrases;
- figures, percentages;
- specific items in an index;
- specific names in a bibliography or a set of references.

Note that any serious testing of expeditious reading will require candidates to respond to items without having time to read the full contents of a passage.

Careful reading operations

- identify pronominal reference;
- identify discourse markers;
- interpret complex sentences;
- interpret topic sentences;
- outline logical organisation of a text;
- outline the development of an argument;
- distinguish general statements from examples;
- identify explicitly stated main ideas;
- identify implicitly stated main ideas;
- recognise writer's intention;
- recognise the attitudes and emotions of the writer;
- identify addressee or audience for a text;
- identify what kind of text is involved (e.g. editorial, diary, etc.);
- distinguish fact from opinion;
- distinguish hypothesis from fact;
- distinguish fact from rumour or hearsay.

Make inferences:
- infer the meaning of an unknown word from context.
- make propositional informational inferences, answering questions beginning with *who, when, what*.
- make propositional explanatory inferences concerned with motivation, cause, consequence and enablement, answering questions beginning with *why, how*).
- make pragmatic inferences.

The different kinds of inference described above deserve comment. Propositional inferences are those which do not depend on information from outside the text. For example, if John is Mary's brother, we can infer that Mary is John's sister (if it is also clear from the text that Mary is female). Another example: If we read the following, we can infer that Harry was working at her studies, not at the fish and chip shop. *Harry worked as hard as she had ever done in her life. When the exam results came out, nobody was surprised that she came top of the class.*

Pragmatic inferences are those where we have to combine information from the text with knowledge from outside the text. We may read, for example: *It took them twenty minutes by road to get from Reading to Heathrow airport.* In order to infer that they travelled very quickly, we have to know that Reading and Heathrow airport are not close by each other. The fact that many readers will not know this allows us to make the point that where the ability to make pragmatic inferences is to be tested, the knowledge that is needed from outside the text must be knowledge which all the candidates can be assumed to have[1].

Texts

Texts that candidates are expected to be able to deal with can be specified along a number of parameters: type, form, graphic features, topic, style, intended readership, length, readability or difficulty, range of vocabulary and grammatical structure.

Text types include: text books, handouts, articles (in newspapers, journals or magazines), poems/verse, encyclopaedia entries, dictionary entries, leaflets, letters, forms, diary, maps or plans, advertisements, postcards, timetables, novels (extracts) and short stories, reviews, manuals, computer Help systems, notices and signs.

Text forms include: description, exposition, argumentation, instruction, narration. (These can be broken down further if it is thought appropriate: e.g. expository texts could include outlines, summaries, etc.)

Graphic features include: tables, charts, diagrams, cartoons, illustrations.

Topics may be listed or defined in a general way (such as non-technical, non-specialist) or in relation to a set of candidates whose background is known (such as familiar to the students).

Style may be specified in terms of formality.

Intended readership can be quite specific (e.g. native speaking science undergraduate students) or more general (e.g. young native speakers).

Length is usually expressed in number of words. The specified length will normally vary according to the level of the candidates and whether one is testing expeditious or careful reading (although a single long text could be used for both).

Readability is an objective, but not necessarily very valid, measure of the difficulty of a text. Where this is not used, intuition may be relied on.

Range of vocabulary may be indicated by a complete list of words (as for the Cambridge tests for young learners), by reference either to a word list or to indications of frequency in a learners' dictionary. Range may be expressed more generally (e.g. non-technical, except where explained in the text).

Range of grammar may be a list of structures, or a reference to those to be found in a course book or (possibly parts of) a grammar of the language.

The reason for specifying texts in such detail is that we want the texts included in a test to be representative of the texts candidates should be able to read successfully. This is partly a matter of content validity but also relates to backwash. The appearance in the test of only a limited range of texts will encourage the reading of a narrow range by potential candidates.

It is worth mentioning authenticity at this point. Whether or not authentic texts (intended for native speakers) are to be used will depend at least in part on what the items based on them are intended to measure.

Speed

Reading speed may be expressed in words per minute. Different speeds will be expected for careful and expeditious reading. In the case of the latter, the candidate is, of course, not expected to read all of the words. The expected speed of reading will combine with the number and difficulty of items to determine the amount of time needed for the test, or part of it.

Criterial level of performance

In norm-referenced testing our interest is in seeing how candidates perform by comparison with each other. There is no need to specify criterial levels of performance before tests are constructed, or even before they are administered. This book, however, encourages a broadly criterion-referenced approach to language testing. In the case of the testing of writing, as we saw in the previous chapter, it is possible to describe levels of writing ability that candidates have to attain. While this would not satisfy everyone's definition of criterion-referencing, it is very much in the spirit of that form of testing, and would promise to bring the benefits claimed for criterion-referenced testing.

Setting criterial levels for receptive skills is more problematical. Traditional passmarks expressed in percentages (40 per cent? 50 per cent? 60 per cent?) are hardly helpful, since there seems no way of providing a direct interpretation of such a score. To my mind, the best way to proceed is to use the test tasks themselves to define the level. All of the items (and so the tasks that they require the candidate to perform) should be within the capabilities of anyone to whom we are prepared to give a pass. In other words, in order to pass, a candidate should be expected, in principle, to score 100 per cent. But since we know that human performance is not so reliable, we can set the actual cutting point rather lower, say at the 80 per cent level. In order to distinguish between candidates of different levels of ability, more than one test may be required (see page 55).

As part of the development (and validation) of a reading test, one might wish to compare performance on the test with the rating of candidates' reading ability using scales like those of ACTFL or the ILR. This would be most appropriate where performance in the productive skills are being assessed according to those scales and some equivalence between tests of the different skills is being sought.

Setting the tasks

Selecting texts

Successful choice of texts depends ultimately on experience, judgement, and a certain amount of common sense. Clearly these are not qualities that a handbook can provide; practice is necessary. It is never the less possible to offer useful advice. While the points may seem rather obvious, they are often overlooked.

1. Keep specifications constantly in mind and try to select as representative a sample as possible. Do not repeatedly select texts of a particular kind simply because they are readily available.
2. Choose texts of appropriate length. Expeditious reading tests may call for passages of up to 2,000 words or more. Detailed reading can be tested using passages of just a few sentences.
3. In order to obtain both content validity and acceptable reliability, include as many passages as possible in a test, thereby giving candidates a good number of fresh starts. Considerations of practicality will inevitably impose constraints on this, especially where scanning or skimming is to be tested.
4. In order to test search reading, look for passages which contain plenty of discrete pieces of information.
5. For scanning, find texts which have the specified elements that have to be scanned for.
6. To test the ability to quickly establish the structure of a text, make sure that the text has a clearly recognizable structure (It's surprising how many texts lack this quality).
7. Choose texts that will interest candidates but which will not over-excite or disturb them. A text about cancer, for example, is almost certainly going to be distressing to some candidates.
8. Avoid texts made up of information that may be part of candidates' general knowledge. It may be difficult not to write items to which correct responses are available to some candidates without reading the passage. On a reading test I encountered once, I was able to

answer 8 out of 11 items without reading the text on which they were based. The topic of the text was rust in cars, an area in which I had had extensive experience.

9. Assuming that it is only reading ability that is being tested, do not choose texts that are too culturally laden.
10. Do not use texts that students have already read (or even close approximations to them). This happens surprisingly often.

Writing items

The aim must be to write items that will measure the ability in which we are interested, that will elicit reliable behaviour from candidates, and that will permit highly reliable scoring. Since the act of reading does not in itself demonstrate its successful performance, we need to set tasks that will involve candidates in providing evidence of successful reading.

Possible techniques

It is important that the techniques used should interfere as little as possible with the reading itself, and that they should not add a significantly difficult task on top of reading. This is one reason for being wary of requiring candidates to write answers, particularly in the language of the text. They may read perfectly well but difficulties in writing may prevent them demonstrating this. Possible solutions to this problem include:

Multiple choice

The candidate provides evidence of successful reading by making a mark against one out of a number of alternatives. The superficial attraction of this technique is outweighed in institutional testing by the various problems enumerated in Chapter 8. This is true whether the alternative responses are written or take the form of illustrations, as in the following:

> Choose the picture (A, B, C, or D) that the following sentence describes: The man with a dog was attacked in the street by a woman.

It has already been pointed out that True/False items, which are to be found in many tests, are simply a variety of multiple choice, with only one distractor and a 50 per cent probability of choosing the correct response by chance! Having a 'not applicable' or 'we don't know' category adds a second 'distractor' and reduces the likelihood of guessing correctly to $33\frac{1}{3}$ per cent.

Short answer

The best short answer questions are those with a unique correct response, for example:

> In which city do the people described in the 'Urban Villagers' live?

to which there is only one possible correct response, e.g. *Bombay*.

The response may be a single word or something slightly longer (e.g. *China and Japan*; *American women*).

The short answer technique works well for testing the ability to identify referents. An example (based on the newspaper article about smoking, on page 150) is:

> What does the word 'it' (line 26) refer to? _____

Care has to be taken that the precise referent is to be found in the text. It may be necessary on occasion to change the text slightly for this condition to be met.

The technique also works well for testing the ability to predict the meaning of unknown words from context. An example (also based on the smoking article) is:

> Find a single word in the passage (between lines 1 and 26) which has the same meaning as 'making of laws'. (The word in the passage may have an ending like -s, -tion, -ing, -ed, etc.)

The short answer technique can be used to test the ability to make various distinctions, such as that between fact and opinion. For example:

> Basing your answers on the text, mark each of the following sentences as FACT or OPINION by writing F or O in the correct space on your answer sheet. You must get all three correct to obtain credit.
>
> 1. Farm owners are deliberately neglecting their land.
> 2. The majority of young men who move to the cities are successful.
> 3. There are already enough farms under government control.

Because of the requirement that all three responses are correct, guessing has a limited effect in such items.

Scanning can be tested with the short answer technique:

> Which town listed in Table 4 has the largest population? _____
>
> According to the index, on which page will you learn about Nabokov's interest in butterflies? ___

The short answer technique can also be used to write items related to the structure of a text. For example:

> There are five sections in the paper. In which section do the writers deal with:
>
> (a) choice of language in relation to national unity [Section .....]
> (b) the effects of a colonial language on local culture [Section .....]
> (c) the choice of a colonial language by people in their fight for liberation [Section .....]
> (d) practical difficulties in using local languages for education [Section .....]
> (e) the relationship between power and language [Section .....]

Again, guessing is possible here, but the probabilities are lower than with straightforward multiple choice.

A similar example (with the text) is[2]:

> In what order does the writer do the following in her article reproduced below? To answer this, put the number 1 in the answer column next to the one that appears first, and so on. If an idea does not appear in the article, write N/A (not applicable) in the answer column.

> a) She gives some of the history of migraine.
> b) She recommends specific drugs.
> c) She recommends a herbal cure.
> d) She describes migraine attacks.
> e) She gives general advice to migraine sufferers.

SUNDAY PLUS

ONE-SIDED HEADACHE

SUE LIMB begins an occasional series by sufferers from particular ailments

LIVING WITH ILLNESS
MIGRAINE

Migraine first visited me when I was 20, and for years afterwards it hung about my life like a blackmailer, only kept at bay by constant sacrifices on my part. Its tyranny was considerable. Many innocent everyday experiences would trigger an attack: stuffy rooms, fluorescent light, minute amounts of alcohol, staying up late, lying in at the weekend, having to wait for meals, loud noises, smoke-filled rooms, the sun, and watching TV for more than two hours.

Work, social life and holidays were all equally disrupted. Naturally, all these prohibitions made me very tense and angry, but anger and tension were dangerous luxuries to a woman with my volatile chemistry.

At its worst, migraine was incapacitating me three times a week, for hours on end. I was losing more than half my life. I had to change my life-style radically — giving up my job and becoming self-employed — before the headaches would retreat. Nowadays, I can sometimes go for 3 or 4 months without an attack, as long as I keep my immediate environment as cool, dark and peaceful as possible. Sometimes I think I should live in a cave, or lurk under a stone like a toad.

Migraine is rather like a possessive parent or lover who cannot bear to see its victim enjoying ordinary life. Indeed, my loved ones have sometimes in their turn felt jealous at the way in which migraine sweeps me off my feet and away from all company, keeping me in a darkened room where it feasts off me for days on end.

❝Tyrant blackmailer, kidnapper, bore❞

Migraine sufferers often feel a deep sense of guilt, for migraine is a bore as well as a tyrant and kidnapper. It destroys social plans and devastates work-schedules. Despite its destructive power, however, the ignorant still dismiss it as the product of a fevered (and probably female) imagination: a bit like the vapours. But if you've ever felt it, or seen someone live through it, you know: migraine is the hardest, blackest and most terrifying of everyday pains.

Eyes shrink to the size of currants, the face turns deathly pale, the tongue feels like an old gardening glove, the entire body seems to age about 70 years, so only a palsied shuffle to the bathroom is possible. Daylight is agonising, a thirst rages, and the vomiting comes almost as a relief, since in the paroxysm of nausea the pain recedes for a few blissful seconds. Above all, the constant feeling of a dagger striking through the eyeball and twisting into the brain can make the sufferer long for death. When at last (sometimes three days later) the pain begins to ebb, and one can slowly creep back into life, it's like being reborn.

Migraine is the focus of many myths. It is emphatically not a recent ailment, or a response to the stresses of modern life. It has been with us always. Its very name derives from the ancient Greek for *half the skull* — migraine is always a one-sided headache. The Egyptians had a god for it: no doubt he was more often cursed than hymned. Some suggest that migraine sufferers are intellectual types, or particularly conscientious personalities. There is little basis for any of this. Migraine affects 7 to 18 per cent of the population, impartially; the eggheads and the emptyheaded alike.

Anxiety, of course, can cause migraine. And fear of an attack can itself be a cause of massive anxiety. Caught in this Catch 22 situation, some sufferers no longer dare make any plans, so reluctant are they to let down their family or friends yet again. This incapacitating fear (Mellontophobia) shows the far-reaching damage migraine is doing to the lives of six million adults in Great Britain alone.

The best thing these sufferers can do is to join the British Migraine Association without delay. This excellent, lively and informal organisation produces leaflets and a newsletter, and organises fund-raising activities to sponsor research. It keeps its members informed about the latest sophisticated drugs available, and also (most importantly) swaps members' hints about herbal treatment and self-help techniques.

There are several drugs available on prescription for the control of migraine, but perhaps the most exciting recent development in research involves a modest hedgerow plant, native to the British Isles and used for centuries by wise women for a variety of ailments. It is feverfew (Chrysanthemum Parthenium).

In 1979, Dr E. Stewart Johnson, Research Director of the City of London Migraine Clinic, saw three patients who had been using feverfew as a preventative, and soon afterwards he became involved in its clinical trials. Dr Johnson's work is still progressing, but early results hint at spectacular success. 70 per cent of subjects claim their attacks are less frequent and not so severe: 33 per cent seem completely migraine-free. A few experience unpleasant side-effects (mostly mouth-ulcers: feverfew is a very bitter herb), and it is not recommended for pregnant women. But for the rest of us, three vile-tasting feverfew leaves a day have become indispensable.

Ten years ago I was taking Librium to reduce stress and Ergotamine to treat the actual migraine pain. They were powerful drugs, which left me feeling doped and poisoned, and they didn't always cure the headache, either. Nowadays, I eat my three leaves, feel good, and probably never get the headache in the first place.

Acupuncture has also helped, partly by improving my general sense of well-being, but during a migraine the pain can be immediately dulled and eventually dispersed by needles placed on special points in the feet or temples. Finger pressure on these points can help too, in the absence of an acupuncturist. Locally applied heat (a hot water bottle or acupuncturist's moxa stick a bit like a cigar—is very soothing).

But above all the best thing I've done about my migraine is learn to relax all the muscles surrounding the eye. The natural response to severe pain is to tense up the muscles, making the pain worse. Deliberately relaxing these muscles instead is a demanding discipline and requires undisturbed concentration, but the effect is dramatic. Immediately the pain becomes less acute.

Migraine is a formidable adversary: tyrant, blackmailer, kidnapper, bore; but after many years' struggle I really feel I've got it on the run. And though I'm a great admirer of the best of Western orthodox medicine, it's pleasing that my migraines have finally started to slink away when faced not with a futuristic superpill, but with the gentle healing practices of the East and the Past.

The British Migraine Association, 178a High Road, Byfleet, Weybridge, Surrey KT14 7ED. Tel: Byfleet 52468.
The City of London Migraine Clinic, 22 Charterhouse Square, London, EC1M 6DX will treat sufferes caught away from home with a severe attack.

It should be noted that the scoring of 'sequencing' items of this kind can be problematical. If a candidate puts one element of the text out of sequence, it may cause others to be displaced and require complex decision making on the part of the scorers.

One should be wary of writing short answer items where correct responses are not limited to a unique answer. Thus:

> According to the author, what does the increase in divorce rates show about people's expectations of marriage and marriage partners?

might call for an answer like:

> (They/Expectations) are greater (than in the past).

The danger is of course that a student who has the answer in his or her head after reading the relevant part of the passage may not be able to express it well (equally, the scorer may not be able to tell from the response that the student has arrived at the correct answer).

Gap filling

This technique is particularly useful in testing reading. It can be used any time that the required response is so complex that it may cause writing (and scoring) problems. If one wanted to know whether the candidate had grasped the main idea(s) of the following paragraph, for instance, the item might be:

> Complete the following, which is based on the paragraph below.
>
> 'Many universities in Europe used to insist that their students speak and write only _____ . Now many of them accept _____ as an alternative, but not a _____ of the two.'

Until recently, many European universities and colleges not only taught EngEng but actually required it from their students; i.e. other varieties of standard English were not allowed. This was the result of a conscious decision, often, that some norm needed to be established and that confusion would arise if teachers offered conflicting models. Lately, however, many universities have come to relax this requirement, recognising that their students are as likely (if not more likely) to encounter NAmEng as EngEng, especially since some European students study for a time in North America. Many universities therefore now permit students to speak and write either EngEng or NAmEng, so long as they are consistent. (Trudgill and Hannah 2002:2)

A possible weakness in this particular item is that the candidate has to provide one word (mixture or combination) which is not in the passage. In practice, however, it worked well.

Gap filling can be used to test the ability to recognise detail presented to support a main idea:

To support his claim that the Mafia is taking over Russia, the author points out that the sale of _____ _____ in Moscow has increased by _____ per cent over the last two years.

Gap filling can also be used for scanning items:

According to Figure 1, _____ per cent of faculty members agree with the new rules.

Gap filling is also the basis for what has been called 'summary cloze'. In this technique, a reading passage is summarised by the tester, and then gaps are left in the summary for completion by the candidate. This is really an extension of the gap filling technique and shares its qualities. It permits the setting of several reliable but relevant items on a relatively short passage. Here is an example:

THE GOVERNMENT'S first formal acknowledgement that inhaling other people's tobacco smoke can cause lung cancer led to calls yesterday for legislation to make non-smoking the norm in offices, factories and public places. 5

The Government's Independent Scientific Committee on Smoking and Health concluded that passive smoking was consistent with an increase in lung cancer of between 10 and 30 per cent in non-smokers. While the home was probably an important source of tobacco smoke exposure particularly for the young, "work and indoor leisure environments with their greater time occupancy may be more important for adults", the committee said. 10 15

The Department of Health said the findings were consistent with 200 to 300 lung cancer deaths a year in non-smokers and some deaths from other smoking-related diseases such as bronchitis. The risk had been estimated at about 100 times greater than the risk of lung cancer from inhaling asbestos over 20 years in the amounts in which it is usually found in buildings. 20 25

The findings are to be used by the Health Education Council to drive home the message that passive smoking is accepted as causing lung cancer. The Government should encourage proprietors of all public places to provide for clean air in all enclosed spaces, the council said, and legislation should not be ruled out. 30 35

Action on Smoking and Health went further, saying legislation was essential to make non-smoking the norm in public places. "In no other area of similar risk to the public does the Government rely on voluntary measures," David Simpson, the director of ASH said. 40

The Department of Health said concern over passive smoking had risen in part through better insulation and draught proofing. But ministers believed the best way to discourage smoking was by persuasion rather than legislation. 45

The committee's statement came in an interim report. Its full findings are due later this year. 50

Norman Fowler, the Secretary of State for Social Services, said it would be for the new Health Education Authority, which will replace the Health Education Council at the end of the month, to take account of the committee's work. 55

The Independent Scientific Committee on Smoking and Health has just issued an interim report. It says that _____ smoking (that is, breathing in other people's _____ smoke) is consistent with an increase in _____ of between 10 and 30 per cent amongst people who do not _____. The risk of getting the disease in this way is reckoned to be very much greater than that of getting it through breathing in typical amounts of _____ over long periods of time. Children might be subjected to significant amounts of tobacco smoke at _____, but for _____ places of work and indoor leisure might be more important.

In response to the report, the Health Education Council (which is soon to be _____ by the Health Education Authority) said that the Government should encourage owners of _____ places to ensure that the _____ in all enclosed spaces is clean. Action on Smoking and Health said that _____ was necessary. However, it is known that government ministers would prefer to use _____.

Information transfer

One way of minimising demands on candidates' writing ability is to require them to show successful completion of a reading task by supplying simple information in a table, following a route on a map, labelling a picture, and so on.

A cart is the simplest type of wheeled vehicle. The following terms are used in describing the parts of one type of cart.

Read the definitions and choose 11 suitable words from the list of 16 to label the parts numbered on the figure below. The first one is done for you. Write the labels on the table below the figure.

axle: a horizontal arm on which wheels turn.

dirtboard: a curved plate of wood or metal projecting from the beam to which the axle is fixed; protects the space between the end of the axle and the hub of the wheel.

exbed: a beam running the width of the cart to which the axle is fixed.

felloe: a section of the wooden rim on the wheel of the cart.

forehead: a plank forming the upper portion of the front end of a cart; usually with a curved top.

longboard: a plank of wood running parallel to the cart sides to form the floor of the cart.

rail:	a plank running across the front or back end of a cart.
rave:	a horizontal beam forming part of the side wall of the cart.
shaft:	one of a pair of wooden boards between which the horse is harnessed to pull the cart.
shutter:	a piece of stout wood stretching across the bottom of a cart; joins the sides and supports the floorboards.
sole:	a short extension of the lower timbers of the cart frame which projects behind the cart on each side.
standard:	a vertical bar of wood which is part of the frame for the side of the cart.
stock:	a hub made of elm wood into which wooden bars or spokes are fixed.
strake:	an iron tyre made in sections and nailed to the rim of wheel to protect it.
strouter:	a curved wooden support to strengthen the cart sides; often elegantly carved.
topboard:	a board with a curved top nailed to the top rave of the cart.

A CART

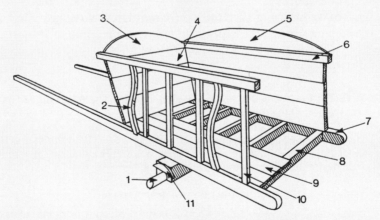

1	axle	7	
2		8	
3		9	
4		10	
5		11	
6			

Relatively few techniques have been presented in this section. This is because, in my view, few basic techniques are needed, and non-professional testers will benefit from concentrating on developing their skills within a limited range, always allowing for the possibility of modifying these techniques for particular purposes and in particular circumstances. Many professional testers appear to have got by with just one – multiple choice! The more usual varieties of cloze and the C-Test technique (see Chapter 14) have been omitted because, while they obviously involve reading to quite a high degree, it is not clear that reading ability is all that they measure. This makes it all the harder to interpret scores on such tests in terms of criterial levels of performance.

Which language for items and responses?

The wording of reading test items is not meant to cause candidates any difficulties of comprehension. It should always be well within their capabilities, and less demanding than the text itself. In the same way, responses should make minimal demands on writing ability. Where candidates share a single native language, this can be used both for items and for responses. There is a danger, however, that items may provide some candidates with more information about the content of the text than they would have obtained from items in the foreign language.

Procedures for writing items

The starting point for writing items is a careful reading of the text, having the specified operations in mind. One should be asking oneself what a competent reader should derive from the text. Where relevant, a note should be taken of main points, interesting pieces of information, stages of argument, examples, and so on. The next step is to decide what tasks it is reasonable to expect candidates to be able to perform in relation to these. It is only then that draft items should be written. Paragraph numbers and line numbers should be added to the text if items need to make reference to these. The text and items should be presented to colleagues for moderation. Items and even the text may need modification. A moderation checklist follows:

	YES	NO
1. Is the English of text and item grammatically correct?		
2. Is the English natural and acceptable?		
3. Is the item in accordance with specified parameters?		
4. Is specified reading sub-skill necessary in order to respond correctly?		
5. (a) Multiple choice: Is there just one correct response? (b) Gap filling and summary cloze: Are there just one or two correct responses for each gap? (c) Short answer: Is answer within productive abilities? Can it be scored validly and reliably? (d) Unique answer: Is there just one clear answer?		
6. Multiple choice: Are all the distractors likely to distract?		
7. Is the item economical?		
8. Is the key complete and correct?		

Practical advice on item writing

1. In a scanning test, present items in the order in which the answers can be found in the text. Not to do this introduces too much random variation and so lowers the test's reliability.
2. Do not write items for which the correct response can be found without understanding the text (unless that is an ability that you are testing!). Such items usually involve simply matching a string of words in the question with the same string in the text. Thus (around line 45 in the smoking passage, on page 150):

> What body said that concern over passive smoking had arisen in part through better insulation and draught proofing?

Better might be:

> What body has claimed that worries about passive smoking are partly due to improvements in buildings?

Items that demand simple arithmetic can be useful here. We may learn in one sentence that before 1985 there had only been three hospital operations of a particular kind; in another sentence, that there have been 45 since. An item can ask how many such operations there have been to date, according to the article.

3. Do not include items that some candidates are likely to be able to answer from general knowledge without reading the text. For example:
   Inhaling smoke from other people's cigarettes can cause ....
   It is not necessary, however, to choose such esoteric topics as characterised the Joint Matriculation Board's Test in English (Overseas). These included coracles, the Ruen, and the people of Willington.

4. Make the items independent of each other; do not make a correct response on one item depend on another item being responded to correctly.
   In the following example, taken from a test handbook, the candidate who does not respond correctly to the first item is unlikely to be able to respond to the following two parts (the second of which uses the YES/NO technique). For such a candidate, (b) and (c) might as well not be there.

   > (a) Which soup is made for slimmers?
   > (b) Name one thing which surprised the author about this soup.
   > (c) Did the writer like the taste?

   However, complete independence is just about impossible in items that are related to the structure of a text (for example, in the Migraine passage above).

5. Be prepared to make *minor* changes to the text to improve an item. If you do this and are not a native speaker, ask a native speaker to look at the changed text.

A note on scoring

General advice on obtaining reliable scoring has already been given in Chapter 5. It is worth adding here, however, that in a reading test (or a listening test), errors of grammar, spelling or punctuation should not be penalised, provided that it is clear that the candidate has successfully performed the reading task which the item set. The function of a reading test is to test reading ability. To test productive skills at the same time (which is what happens when grammar, etc. are taken into account) simply makes the measurement of reading ability less valid.

Reader activities

1. Following the procedures and advice given in the chapter, construct a 12-item reading test based on the passage about New Zealand Youth Hostels on page 157.
    (The passage was used in the Oxford Examination in English as a Foreign Language, Preliminary Level, in 1987.)
    (a) For each item, make a note of the skill(s) (including sub-skills) you believe it is testing. If possible, have colleagues take the test and provide critical comment. Try to improve the test. Again, if possible, administer the test to an appropriate group of students. Score the tests. Interview a few students as to how they arrived at correct responses. Did they use the particular sub-skills that you predicted they would?
    (b) Compare your questions with the ones in Appendix 3. Can you explain the differences in content and technique? Are there any items in the appendix that you might want to change? Why? How?
2. Do the sequencing item that is based on the Migraine text. Do you have any difficulties? If possible, get a number of students of appropriate ability to do the item, and then score their responses. Do you have any problems in scoring?
3. Write a set of short answer items with unique correct responses to replace the sequencing items that appear with the Migraine text.
4. The following is part of an exercise designed to help students learn to cope with 'complicated sentences'. How successful would this form of exercise be as part of a reading test? What precisely would it test? Would you want to change the exercise in any way? If so, why and how? Could you make it non-multiple choice? If so, how?

    > The intention of other people concerned, such as the Minister of Defence, to influence the government leaders to adapt their policy to fit in with the demands of the right wing, cannot be ignored.

    > What is the subject of 'cannot be ignored'?
    > a. the intention
    > b. other people concerned
    > c. the Minister of Defence
    > d. the demands of the right wing.

(Swan 1975)

NEW ZEALAND YOUTH HOSTELS

Where in New Zealand could you find a night's accommodation for only $10 NZ, and share dinner with a friendly crowd from around the world?

In any one of New Zealand's 60 plus youth hostels!

Meeting people is a highlight of any trip, and the communal hostel atmosphere is just the place to meet with fellow travellers. On a typical night you'll find Australians, Canadians, British, Americans, Germans, Danes, and Japanese, and, of course, some New Zealanders at a hostel. Many are making the trip of a lifetime after study, while others are on their third or fourth holiday in New Zealand.

Still others, like Don and Jean Cameron from South Australia, are on a "retirement" holiday, three months motorcycling the South Island. I met up with Don and Jean last summer at the Queenstown hostel. "Our friends thought we were mad" laughed Jean, "but we find the hostels very comfortable, and we've met so many interesting people that we'll have to make a world trip next year just to see them all!"

SPECTACULAR

The Queenstown hostel is tucked onto the shoreline of Lake Wakatipu, with spectacular views across to the rugged Remarkable Mountains. This busy tourist town is the centre for both leisurely and adventurous activities – from a cruise on the historic steamer Earnslaw and visit to a working sheep-station, to fast and furious white water rafting on the Kawarau and Shotover Rivers.

Further north, at Mt Cook, the Youth Hostel Association's biggest ever project is under way. The present hostel, usually bulging at the seams, is being replaced with a large specially designed hostel, which will soon be opening.

As New Zealand's tallest mountain, Mt Cook is a major tourist attraction, but you don't need to be a climber to enjoy the park. Rangers can suggest a wide range of walks that open up the alpine world – massive glacier moraines, icy streams, and tiny alpine plants.

WAFFLES

Across the Southern Alps, Westland National Park offers a quite different experience. The Franz Josef and Fox glaciers, centre-pieces of this spectacular area, plunge down from the main divide through Westland's luxuriant forest to only a few hundred metres above sea level.

A short car ride from the Franz Josef glacier is one of New Zealand's nicest hostels. The manager is renowned for cooking up the best ever waffles and ice cream as an after-dinner treat. They're guaranteed to put back the calories you took off walking up to the glacier lookout, or on a forest or lakeside ramble.

The South Island mountains and lakes are a favourite of mine, but whatever your holiday plans you'll find youth hostels there. Prefer a lazy-beach stay with sun-bathing, swimming, sailing, or scuba diving? With a coastline of 10,000 km, the choice is yours!

The Bay of Islands (north of Auckland) has long been a mecca for all of the sea sports. Two hostels serve the Bay – one at the historic township of Kerikeri, the other on the Whangaroa Harbour. A boat charter company offers Kerikeri hostellers a special discount – a whole day out on a sailing boat for around $30 NZ per person.

Whangaroa's sheltered harbour, sub-tropical bush, and a comfortable hostel with superb harbour view make for a perfect break. After a lazy day on a cruise, and trying our hand at fishing, a group of us headed down to the local hotel for a freshly caught seafood dinner – some of the ones that didn't get away.

If the world of bubbling hot pools and soaring geysers is more your scene, then a stop in Rotorua is a must. The Rotorua hostel is right in the middle of town, just an easy walk to Whakarewarewa Thermal Reserve and the hot pools. For longer trips hire a bicycle from the hostel, or use any of the wide range of bus tours to see the area.

The hostel network hasn't forgotten the major cities. Auckland has an inner-city and a suburban hostel, as well as two island hideaways. Wellington, the capital and transport centre of the country, has an inner city hostel; while Christchurch boasts a stately home hostel as well as a downtown base. Dunedin, the Scottish city of the south, has one of the grandest of all – with small bedrooms and three living rooms.

Whether you're in New Zealand for a short stop-over, or here for several months, hostels will stretch your travel funds much further. Hostels aren't luxury hotels, but they do provide simple, comfortable accommodation with good kitchen, laundry and bathroom facilities. Kitchens are well equipped, all you need supply is the food. Many hostels have a small shop too, selling meal-sized portions of food.

For further information about New Zealand youth hostels, write to Youth Hostel Association National Office, PO Box 436, Christchurch, New Zealand.

The following exercise is meant to improve the learner's ability to 'develop a mental schema of a text'. Subject it to the same considerations as the previous exercise type.

B I told you a bit of a lie

Reading comprehension; vocabulary; grammar (conditionals).

1 Read the text. Don't take more than five minutes. You can use a dictionary or ask the teacher for help (but try to guess the meaning of a word first).

clearing up crimes like petty theft and burglary.

Parachutist, 81, wins place of honour at jump

Even experts were a little surprised when a man of 62 turned up at a parachute training school and said he was interested in learning to become a parachutist.

They agreed to put him through the course, but only after giving him a series of tests to prove that he was fit enough.

Mr Archie Macfarlane completed the course successfully, surprising everyone with his agility and toughness.

A few weeks later, when he was ready for his first jump, he confessed to the chief instructor: "I told you a bit of a lie. I'm really 75."

That was six years ago and yesterday Archie Macfarlane made his 18th jump. He was given the place of honour – first out of the plane – at a weekend meeting for parachutists over 40 years old.

Archie's interest in parachuting is just one of the hobbies that his wife has to worry about. He also enjoys motorcycling and mountaineering.

Last year he fell while climbing on Snowdon, and had to be rescued by helicopter.

His daughter said: "Sometimes I think he ought to give it all up. But as my mother says, so long as he's happy, it's better than being miserable. He tried hang-gliding once and said he thought it was a bit too easy."

Now Archie is thinking of taking up water-skiing.

(adapted from a press report)

2 Here are three summaries of the text. Which do you think is the best?

1. Archie Macfarlane started parachuting when he was 75, and he has done 18 parachute jumps over the last six years. Recently he was given the place of honour at a parachutists' meeting. When he started parachuting, he told a lie about his age. His wife and daughter are worried about him.

2. Archie Macfarlane is an unusual person. Although he is an old man, he is interested in very tough sporting activities like parachuting, mountaineering and water-skiing. His wife and daughter are worried, but think it's best for him to do things that make him happy.

3. When Archie Macfarlane first learnt parachute jumping, he pretended that he was only 62. In fact, he is much older than that, and he is really becoming too old to take part in outdoor sporting activities. His wife and daughter wish that he would stop motorcycling, mountaineering and hang-gliding.

(Swan and Walter 1988)

Further reading

For a very full treatment of the testing of reading, I recommend Alderson (2000). Urquhart and Weir (1998) discuss testing in the contexts of theories of reading and the teaching of reading. Issues in the testing of reading sub-skills are addressed in Weir et al (1993), Weir and Porter (1995), Alderson (1990a, 1990b, 1995) and Lumley (1993, 1995). Alderson et al (2000) explore sequencing as a test technique. Riley and Lee (1996) look at recall and summary protocols as measures of reading comprehension. Freedle and Kostin (1999) investigate the variables that affect the difficulty of reading items. Shohamy (1984) reports on research that explored the effect of writing items in the candidates' native language. Weir et al (2002) describe the development of the specifications of a reading test in China. Allan (1992) reports on the development of a scale to measure test-wiseness of people taking reading tests. This demonstrates how items that are faulty in a number of specified ways can permit some students (more than others) to work out the correct response without necessarily having the language knowledge that is supposedly being tested. The article includes the complete set of items used.

1. It has to be admitted that the distinction between propositional and prag-matic inferences is not watertight. In a sense *all* inferences are pragmatic: even being able to infer, say, that a man born in 1941 will have his seventieth birthday in 2111 (if he lives that long) depends on knowledge of arithmetic, it could be argued. However, the distinction remains useful when we are constructing reading test items. Competent readers integrate information from the text into their knowledge of the world.
2. This item is from one of the RSA tests that eventually became the CCSE. CCSE has now been replaced by CELS.

12 Testing listening

It may seem rather odd to test listening separately from speaking, since the two skills are typically exercised together in oral interaction. However, there are occasions, such as listening to the radio, listening to lectures, or listening to railway station announcements, when no speaking is called for. Also, as far as testing is concerned, there may be situations where the testing of oral ability is considered, for one reason or another, impractical, but where a test of listening is included for its backwash effect on the development of oral skills. Listening may also be tested for diagnostic purposes.

Because it is a receptive skill, the testing of listening parallels in most ways the testing of reading. This chapter will therefore spend little time on issues common to the testing of the two skills and will concentrate more on matters that are particular to listening. The reader who plans to construct a listening test is advised to read both this and the previous chapter.

The special problems in constructing listening tests arise out of the transient nature of the spoken language. Listeners cannot usually move backwards and forwards over what is being said in the way that they can a written text. The one apparent exception to this, when a tape-recording is put at the listener's disposal, does not represent a typical listening task for most people. Ways of dealing with these problems are discussed later in the chapter.

Specifying what the candidate should be able to do

As with the other skills, the specifications for reading tests should say what it is that candidates should be able to do.

Content

Operations

Some operations may be classified as *global*, inasmuch as they depend on an overall grasp of what is listened to. They include the ability to:

- obtain the gist;
- follow an argument;
- recognise the attitude of the speaker.

Other operations may be classified in the same way as were oral skills in Chapter 10. In writing specifications, it is worth adding to each operation whether what is to be understood is explicitly stated or only implied.

Informational:
- obtain factual information;
- follow instructions (including directions);
- understand requests for information;
- understand expressions of need;
- understand requests for help;
- understand requests for permission;
- understand apologies;
- follow sequence of events (narration);
- recognise and understand opinions;
- follow justification of opinions;
- understand comparisons;
- recognise and understand suggestions;
- recognise and understand comments;
- recognise and understand excuses;
- recognise and understand expressions of preferences;
- recognise and understand complaints;
- recognise and understand speculation.

Interactional:
- understand greetings and introductions;
- understand expressions of agreement;
- understand expressions of disagreement;
- recognise speaker's purpose;
- recognise indications of uncertainty;
- understand requests for clarification;
- recognise requests for clarification;
- recognise requests for opinion;
- recognise indications of understanding;

- recognise indications of failure to understand;
- recognise and understand corrections by speaker (of self and others);
- recognise and understand modifications of statements and comments;
- recognise speaker's desire that listener indicate understanding;
- recognise when speaker justifies or supports statements, etc. of other speaker(s);
- recognise when speaker questions assertions made by other speakers;
- recognise attempts to persuade others.

It may also be thought worthwhile testing lower level listening skills in a diagnostic test, since problems with these tend to persist longer than they do in reading. These might include:

- discriminate between vowel phonemes;
- discriminate between consonant phonemes;
- interpret intonation patterns (recognition of sarcasm, questions in declarative form, etc., interpretation of sentence stress).

Texts

For reasons of content validity and backwash, texts should be specified as fully as possible.

Text type might be first specified as monologue, dialogue, or multi-participant, and further specified: conversation, announcement, talk or lecture, instructions, directions, etc.

Text forms include: description, exposition, argumentation, instruction, narration.

Length may be expressed in seconds or minutes. The extent of short utterances or exchanges may be specified in terms of the number of turns taken.

Speed of speech may be expressed as words per minute (wpm) or syllables per second (sps). Reported average speeds for samples of British English are:

	wpm	sps
Radio monologues	160	4.17
Conversations	210	4.33
Interviews	190	4.17
Lectures to non-native speakers	140	3.17

(Tauroza and Allison, 1990)

Dialects may include standard or non-standard varieties.

Accents may be regional or non-regional.

If authenticity is called for, the speech should contain such natural features as assimilation and elision (which tend to increase with speed of delivery) and hesitation phenomena (pauses, fillers, etc.).

Intended audience, style, topics, range of grammar and vocabulary may be indicated.

Setting criterial levels of performance

The remarks made in the chapter on testing reading apply equally here. If the test is set at an appropriate level, then, as with reading, a near perfect set of responses may be required for a 'pass'. ACTFL, ILR or other scales may be used to validate the criterial levels that are set.

Setting the tasks

Selecting samples of speech (texts)

Passages must be chosen with the test specifications in mind. If we are interested in how candidates can cope with language intended for native speakers, then ideally we should use samples of authentic speech. These can usually be readily found. Possible sources are the radio, television, spoken-word cassettes, teaching materials, the Internet and and our own recordings of native speakers. If, on the other hand, we want to know whether candidates can understand language that may be addressed to them as non-native speakers, these too can be obtained from teaching materials and recordings of native speakers that we can make ourselves. In some cases the indifferent quality of the recording may necessitate re-recording. It seems to me, although not everyone would agree, that a poor recording introduces difficulties additional to the ones that we want to create, and so reduces the validity of the test. It may also introduce unreliability, since the performance of individuals may be affected by the recording faults in different degrees from occasion to occasion. If details of what is said on the recording interfere with the writing of good items, testers should feel able to edit the recording, or to make a fresh recording from the amended transcript. In some cases, a recording may be used simply as the basis for a 'live' presentation.

If recordings are made especially for the test, then care must be taken to make them as natural as possible. There is typically a fair amount of redundancy in spoken language: people are likely to paraphrase what they have already said (*'What I mean to say is . . .'*), and to remove this redundancy is to make the listening task unnatural. In particular, we should avoid passages originally intended for reading, like the following, which appeared as an example of a listening comprehension passage for a well-known test:

> *She found herself in a corridor which was unfamiliar, but after trying one or two doors discovered her way back to the stone-flagged hall which opened onto the balcony. She listened for sounds of pursuit but heard none. The hall was spacious, devoid of decoration: no flowers, no pictures.*

This is an extreme example, but test writers should be wary of trying to create spoken English out of their imagination: it is better to base the passage on a genuine recording, or a transcript of one. If an authentic text is altered, it is wise to check with native speakers that it still sounds natural. If a recording is made, care should be taken to ensure that it fits with the specifications in terms of speed of delivery, style, etc.

Suitable passages may be of various lengths, depending on what is being tested. A passage lasting ten minutes or more might be needed to test the ability to follow an academic lecture, while twenty seconds could be sufficient to give a set of directions.

Writing items

For extended listening, such as a lecture, a useful first step is to listen to the passage and note down what it is that candidates should be able to get from the passage. We can then attempt to write items that check whether or not they have got what they should be able to get. This note-making procedure will not normally be necessary for shorter passages, which will have been chosen (or constructed) to test particular abilities.

In testing extended listening, it is essential to keep items sufficiently far apart in the passage. If two items are close to each other, candidates may miss the second of them through no fault of their own, and the effect of this on subsequent items can be disastrous, with candidates listening for 'answers' that have already passed. Since a single faulty item can have such an effect, it is particularly important to trial extended listening tests, even if only on colleagues aware of the potential problems.

Candidates should be warned by key words that appear both in the item and in the passage that the information called for is about to be heard. For example, an item may ask about 'the second point that the speaker makes' and candidates will hear 'My second point is . . .'.

The wording does not have to be identical, but candidates should be given fair warning in the passage. It would be wrong, for instance, to ask about 'what the speaker regards as her most important point' when the speaker makes the point and only afterwards refers to it as the most important. Less obvious examples should be revealed through trialling.

Other than in exceptional circumstances (such as when the candidates are required to take notes on a lecture without knowing what the items will be, see below), candidates should be given sufficient time at the outset to familiarise themselves with the items. As was suggested for reading in the previous chapter, there seems no sound reason not to write items and accept responses in the native language of the candidates. This will in fact often be what would happen in the real world, when a fellow native speaker asks for information that we have to listen for in the foreign language.

Possible techniques

Multiple choice
The advantages and disadvantages of using multiple choice in extended listening tests are similar to those identified for reading tests in the previous chapter. In addition, however, there is the problem of the candidates having to hold in their heads four or more alternatives while listening to the passage and, after responding to one item, of taking in and retaining the alternatives for the next item. If multiple choice is to be used, then the alternatives must be kept short and simple. The alternatives in the following, which appeared in a sample listening test of a well-known examination, are probably too complex.

> When stopped by the police, how is the motorist advised to behave?
>
> a. He should say nothing until he has seen his lawyer.
> b. He should give only what additional information the law requires.
> c. He should say only what the law requires.
> d. He should in no circumstances say anything.

Better examples would be:
(Understanding request for help)

> I don't suppose you could show me where this goes, could you?
> Response:
> a. No, I don't suppose so.

b. Of course I can.
c. I suppose it won't go.
d. Not at all.

(Recognising and understanding suggestions)

I've been thinking. Why don't we call Charlie and ask for his opinion?

Response:
a. Why is this his opinion?
b. What is the point of that?
c. You think it's his opinion?
d. Do you think Charlie has called?

Multiple choice can work well for testing lower level skills, such as phoneme discrimination.

The candidate hears *bat*
and chooses between pat   mat   fat   bat

Short answer
This technique can work well, provided that the question is short and straightforward, and the correct, preferably unique, response is obvious.

Gap filling
This technique can work well where a short answer question with a unique answer is not possible.

Woman: Do you think you can give me a hand with this?

Man: I'd love to help but I've got to go round to my mother's in a minute.

The woman asks the man if he can _____ her but he has to visit his _____ .

Information transfer
This technique is as useful in testing listening as it is in testing reading, since it makes minimal demands on productive skills. It can involve such activities as the labelling of diagrams or pictures, completing forms, making diary entries, or showing routes on a map. The following example, which is taken from the ARELS examination, is one of a series of related tasks in which the candidate 'visits' a friend who has been involved in a motor accident. The friend has hurt his hand, and the candidate (listening to a tape-recording) has to help Tom write his report of the accident. Time allowed for each piece of writing is indicated.

In this question you must write your answers. Tom also has to draw a sketch map of the accident. He has drawn the streets, but he can't write in the names. He asks you to fill in the details. Look at the sketch map in your book. Listen to Tom and write on the map what he tells you.

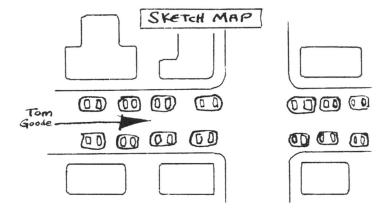

Tom: This is a rough map of where the accident happened. There's the main road going across with the cars parked on both sides of it – that's Queen Street. You'd better write the name on it – Queen Street. (five seconds) And the smaller road going across it is called Green Road. Write Green Road on the smaller road. (five seconds) Now, I was riding along Queen Street where the arrow is and the little boy ran into the road from my right, from between the two buildings on the right. The building on the corner is the Star Cinema – just write Star on the corner building. (five seconds) And the one next to it is the Post Office. Write P.O. on that building next to the cinema. (five seconds) Well the boy ran out between those two buildings, and into the road. Can you put an arrow in where the boy came from, like I did for me and the bike, but for the boy? (five seconds) When he ran out I turned left away from him and hit one of the parked cars. It was the second car back from the crossroads on the left. Put a cross on the second car back. (three seconds) It was quite funny really. It was parked right outside the police station. A policeman heard the bang and came out at once. You'd better write Police on the police station there on the corner. (five seconds) I think that's all we need. Thanks very much.

Note taking

Where the ability to take notes while listening to, say, a lecture is in question, this activity can be quite realistically replicated in the testing situation. Candidates take notes during the talk, and only after the talk is finished do they see the items to which they have to respond. When constructing such a test, it is essential to use a passage from which notes can be taken successfully. This will only become clear when the task is first attempted by test writers. I believe it is better to have items (which can be scored easily) rather than attempt to score the notes, which is not a task that is likely to be performed reliably. Items should be written that are perfectly straightforward for someone who has taken appropriate notes.

It is essential when including note taking as part of a listening test that careful moderation and, if possible, trialling should take place. Otherwise, items are likely to be included that even highly competent speakers of the language do not respond to correctly. It should go without saying that, since this is a testing task which might otherwise be unfamiliar, potential candidates should be made aware of its existence and, if possible, be provided with practice materials. If this is not done, then the performance of many candidates will lead us to underestimate their ability.

Partial dictation

While dictation may not be a particularly authentic listening activity (although in lectures at university, for instance, there is often a certain amount of dictation), it can be useful as a testing technique. As well as providing a 'rough and ready' measure of listening ability, it can also be used diagnostically to test students' ability to cope with particular difficulties (such as weak forms in English).

Because a traditional dictation is so difficult to score reliably, it is recommended that partial dictation is used, where part of what the candidates hear is already written down for them. It takes the following form:

The candidate sees:

> It was a perfect day. The sun _____ in a clear blue sky and Diana felt that all was _____ with the world. It wasn't just the weather that made her feel this way. It was also the fact that her husband had _____ agreed to a divorce. More than that, he had agreed to let her keep the house and to pay her a small fortune every month. Life _____ be better.

The tester reads:

> It was a perfect day. The sun shone in a clear blue sky and Diana felt that all was right with the world. It wasn't just the weather

that made her feel this way. It was also the fact that her husband
had finally agreed to a divorce. More than that, he had agreed
to let her keep the house and to pay her a small fortune every
month. Life couldn't be better.

Since it is listening that is meant to be tested, correct spelling should
probably not be required for a response to be scored as correct. However, it is not enough for candidates simply to attempt a representation
of the sounds that they hear, without making sense of those sounds.
To be scored as correct, a response has to provide strong evidence of
the candidate's having heard and recognised the missing word, even if
they cannot spell it. It has to be admitted that this can cause scoring
problems.

The gaps may be longer than one word:

It was a perfect day. The sun shone ………………...…………
and Diana felt that all was well with the world.

While this has the advantage of requiring the candidate to do more than
listen for a single word, it does make the scoring (even) less straightforward.

Transcription

Candidates may be asked to transcribe numbers or words which are
spelled letter by letter. The numbers may make up a telephone number.
The letters should make up a name or a word which the candidates
should not already be able to spell. The skill that items of this kind test
belong directly to the 'real world'. In the trialling of a test I was involved
with recently, it was surprising how many teachers of English were
unable to perform such tasks satisfactorily. A reliable and, I believe,
valid way of scoring transcription is to require the response to an item
to be entirely correct for a point to be awarded.

Moderating the items

The moderation of listening items is essential. Ideally it should be
carried out using the already prepared recordings or with the item
writer reading the text as it is meant to be spoken in the test. The
moderators begin by 'taking' the test and then analyse their items and
their reactions to them. The moderation checklist given on page 154 for
reading items needs only minor modifications in order to be used for
moderating listening items.

Presenting the texts (live or recorded?)

The great advantage of using recordings when administering a listening test is that there is uniformity in what is presented to the candidates. This is fine if the recording is to be listened to in a well-maintained language laboratory or in a room with good acoustic qualities and with suitable equipment (the recording should be equally clear in all parts of the room). If these conditions do not obtain, then a live presentation is to be preferred. If presentations are to be live, then greatest uniformity (and so reliability) will be achieved if there is just a single speaker for each (part of a) test. If the test is being administered at the same time in a number of rooms, more than one speaker will be called for. In either case, a recording should be made of the presentation, with which speakers can be trained, so that the intended emphases, timing, etc. will be observed with consistency. Needless to say, speakers should have a good command of the language of the test and be generally highly reliable, responsible and trustworthy individuals.

Scoring the listening test

It is probably worth mentioning again that in scoring a test of a receptive skill there is no reason to deduct points for errors of grammar or spelling, provided that it is clear that the correct response was intended.

Reader activities

1. Choose an extended recording of spoken language that would be appropriate for a group of students with whom you are familiar (you may get this from published materials, or you may record a native speaker or something on the radio). Play a five-minute stretch to yourself and take notes. On the basis of the notes, construct eight short-answer items. Ask colleagues to take the test and comment on it. Amend the test as necessary, and administer it to the group of students you had in mind, if possible. Analyse the results. Go through the test item by item with the students and ask for their comments. How far, and how well, is each item testing what you thought it would test?
2. Design short items that attempt to discover whether candidates can recognise: sarcasm, surprise, boredom, elation. Try these on colleagues and students as above.

3. Design a test that requires candidates to draw (or complete) simple pictures. Decide exactly what the test is measuring. Think what other things could be measured using this or similar techniques. Administer the test and see if the students agree with you about what is being measured.

Further reading

Buck (2001) is a thorough study of the assessment of listening. Freedle and Kostin (1999) investigate the importance of the text in TOEFL minitalk items. Sherman (1997) examines the effects of candidates previewing listening test items. Buck and Tatsuoka (1998) analyse performance on short-answer items. Hale and Courtney (1994) look at the effects of note taking on performance on TOEFL listening items. Buck (1991) uses introspection in the validation of a listening test. Shohamy and Inbar (1991) look at the effects of texts and question type. Arnold (2000) shows how performance on a listening test can be improved by reducing stress in those who take it. Examples of recordings in English that might be used as the basis of listening tests are Crystal and Davy (1975); Hughes and Trudgill (1996), if regional British accents are relevant.

13 Testing grammar and vocabulary

Testing grammar

Why test grammar?

Can one justify the separate testing of grammar? There was a time when this would have seemed a very odd question. Control of grammatical structures was seen as the very core of language ability and it would have been unthinkable not to test it. But times have changed. As far as proficiency tests are concerned, there has been a shift towards the view that since it is language skills that are usually of interest, then it is these which should be tested directly, not the abilities that seem to underlie them. For one thing, it is argued, there is more to any skill than the sum of its parts; one cannot accurately predict mastery of the skill by measuring control of what we believe to be the abilities that underlie it. For another, as has been argued earlier in this book, the backwash effect of tests that measure mastery of skills directly may be thought preferable to that of tests that might encourage the learning of grammatical structures in isolation, with no apparent need to use them. Considerations of this kind have resulted in the absence of any grammar component in some well-known proficiency tests.

But probably most proficiency tests that are administered on a large scale still retain a grammar section. One reason for this must be the ease with which large numbers of items can be administered and scored within a short period of time. Related to that, and at least as important, is the question of content validity. If we decide to test writing ability directly, then we are severely limited in the number of topics, styles of writing, and what we earlier referred to as 'operations' that we can cover in any one version of the test. We cannot be completely confident that the sample chosen is truly representative of all possibilities. Neither can we be sure, of course, that a (proficiency) grammar test includes a good sample of all possible grammatical elements. But the very fact that there can be so many items does put the grammar test at an advantage.

Even if one has doubts about testing grammar in a proficiency test, there is often good cause to include a grammar component in the achievement, placement and diagnostic tests of teaching institutions. It seems unlikely that there are many institutions, however 'communicative' their approach, that do not teach some grammar in some guise or other. Wherever the teaching of grammar is thought necessary, then consideration should be given to the advisability of including a grammar component in achievement tests. If this is done, however, it would seem prudent, from the point of view of backwash, not to give such components too much prominence in relation to tests of skills, the development of which will normally constitute the primary objectives of language courses.

Whether or not grammar has an important place in an institution's teaching, it has to be accepted that grammatical ability, or rather the lack of it, sets limits to what can be achieved in the way of skills performance. The successful writing of academic assignments, for example, must depend to some extent on command of more than the most elementary grammatical structures. It would seem to follow from this that in order to place students in the most appropriate class for the development of such skills, knowledge of a student's grammatical ability would be very useful information. There appears to be room for a grammar component in at least some placement tests.

It would be very useful to have diagnostic tests of grammar which could tell us – for individual learners and groups – what gaps exist in their grammatical repertoire. Such tests could inform not only teachers but also learners, so that they could take responsibility for filling the existing gaps themselves. For this reason, it would be important for the tests to be linked in some way or other to learning materials. There is reason to believe that we may be on the point of having computer based tests of grammar that will be able to provide such information.

Writing specifications

For achievement tests where teaching objectives or the syllabus list the grammatical structures to be taught, specification of content should be quite straightforward. When there is no such listing it becomes necessary to infer from textbooks and other teaching materials what structures are being taught. Specifications for a placement test will normally include all of the structures identified in this way, as well as, perhaps, those structures the command of which is taken for granted in even the lowest classes. For proficiency and diagnostic tests, the van Ek and Trim publications referred to in the Further reading section, which are based on a notional-functional approach, are especially useful, as are grammars like the Cobuild English Usage.

Sampling

This will reflect an attempt to give the test content validity by selecting widely from the structures specified. It should also take account of what are regarded for one reason or another as the most important structures. It should not deliberately concentrate on the structures that happen to be easiest to test.

Writing items

Whatever techniques are chosen for testing grammar, it is important for the text of the item to be written in grammatically correct and natural language. It is surprising how often this is not the case. Two examples I have to hand from items written by teachers are:

> We can't work with this class because there isn't enough silence.

and

> I want to see the film. The actors play well.

To avoid unnatural language of this kind, I would recommend using corpus based examples. One readily available source for English is the British National Corpus sampler on CD.

Four techniques are presented for testing grammar: gap filling, paraphrase, completion, and multiple choice. Used with imagination, they should meet just about all our needs. The first three require production on the part of the candidates, while multiple choice, of course, calls only for recognition. This difference may be a factor in choosing one technique rather than another.

Gap filling

Ideally, gap filling items should have just one correct response.

> For example: What was most disturbing _____ that for the first time in his life Henry was on his own. [was]

> Or: The council must do something to improve transport in the city. _____, they will lose the next election. [Otherwise] (Sentence linking can be tested extensively using gap filling)

> Or: He arrived late, _____ was a surprise. [which]

An item with two possible correct responses may be acceptable if the meaning is the same, whichever is used: Thus:

> He displayed the wide, bright smile _____ had charmed so many people before. [which, that]

But an item is probably to be rejected if the different possibilities give different meanings or involve quite different structures, one of which is the one that is supposed to be tested.

> Patient: My baby keeps me awake all night. She won't stop crying.
>
> Doctor: _____ let her cry. She'll stop in the end.
>   [Just, I'd, Well, Then, etc.]

This item may be improved by including the words 'Then' and 'just' so that it cannot fill the gap.

> Doctor: Then _____ just let her cry. She'll stop in the end.

(But if *you* or *I'd* is thought to be a possible correct response, then the item is still not acceptable)

It's worth saying here that if contractions like *I'd* are to be allowed in the gaps (and I would recommend this), the possibility should be made very clear to the candidates and at least one example of it should be given at the beginning of the test.

As was pointed out in Chapter 8, adding to the context can often restrict the number of possible correct responses to a single one. An extension of this is to present a longer passage with several gaps. These may be used to test a set of related structures, such as the articles:

(Candidates are required to write *the*, *a* or *NA* (No Article).)

> In England children go to _____ school from Monday to Friday. _____ school that Mary goes to is very small. She walks there each morning with _____ friend. One morning they saw _____ man throwing _____ stones and _____ pieces of wood at _____ dog. _____ dog was afraid of _____ man.

And so on.

The technique can also be used to test a variety of structures.

(The text is taken from Colin Dexter, *The Secret of Annexe 3*.)

> When the old man died, _____ was probably no great joy _____ heaven; and quite certainly little if any real grief in Charlbury Drive, the pleasantly unpretentious cul-de-sac

_____ semi-detached houses to which he _____
retired.

There can be just a gap, as above, or there can be a prompt for each gap, as in the example below.

Part 5

For questions **56–65**, read the text below. Use the word given in capitals at the end of each line to form a word that fits in the space in the same line. There is an example at the beginning **(0)**. Write your answers **on the separate answer sheet**.

Example: | **0** | **ability** |

COMPUTERS THAT PLAY GAMES

Computers have had the **(0)** ...*ability*... to play chess for many years	**ABLE**
now, and their **(56)** .... in games against the best players in	**PERFORM**
the world has shown steady **(57)** .... However, it will be	**IMPROVE**
years before designers of computer games machines can beat their	
(58) .... challenge yet – the ancient board game called Go.	**BIG**
The playing area is **(59)** .... larger than in chess and there	**CONSIDERABLE**
are far more pieces, so that the **(60)** .... of moves is almost	**COMBINE**
(61) .... The game involves planning so many moves ahead	**END**
that even the **(62)** .... calculations of the fastest modern	**IMPRESS**
computers are **(63)** .... to deal with the problems of the game.	**SUFFICIENT**
In recent **(64)** .... for computer Go machines, the best	**COMPETE**
machine beat all its computer rivals, but lost **(65)** .... to three	**HEAVY**
young schoolchildren, so there is obviously still a lot of work to do!	

UCLES FCE Handbook 1997

Paraphrase

Paraphrase items require the student to write a sentence equivalent in meaning to one that is given. It is helpful to give part of the paraphrase in order to restrict the students to the grammatical structure being tested.

Thus:
1. Testing passive, past continuous form.

> When we arrived, a policeman was questioning the bank clerk.
> When we arrived, the bank clerk ....

2. Testing present perfect with *for*.

> It is six years since I last saw him.
> I ....…………. six years.

Completion

This technique can be used to test a variety of structures. Note how the context in a passage like the following, from the Cambridge First Certificate in English (FCE) Testpack 1, allows the tester to elicit specific structures, in this case interrogative forms[1].

> In the following conversation, the sentences numbered (1) to (6) have been left incomplete. Complete them suitably. Read the whole conversation before you begin to answer the question.
> (Mr Cole wants a job in Mr Gilbert's export business. He has come for an interview.)

Mr Gilbert:	Good morning, Mr Cole. Please come in and sit down. Now let me see. (1) Which school ....?
Mr Cole:	Whitestone College.
Mr Gilbert:	(2) And when ,,?
Mr Cole:	In 1972, at the end of the summer term.
Mr Gilbert:	(3) And since then what ....?
Mr Cole:	I worked in a bank for a year. Then I took my present job, selling cars. But I would like a change now.
Mr Gilbert:	(4) Well, what sort of a job ....?
Mr Cole:	I'd really like to work in your Export Department.
Mr Gilbert:	That might be a little difficult. What are your qualifications? (5) I mean what languages .... besides English?
Mr Cole:	Well, only a little French.
Mr Gilbert:	That would be a big disadvantage, Mr Cole. (6) Could you tell me why ....?
Mr Cole:	Because I'd like to travel and to meet people from other countries.
Mr Gilbert:	I don't think I can help you at present, Mr Cole. Perhaps you ought to try a travel agency.

Multiple choice

Reasons for being careful about using multiple choice were given in Chapter 8. There are times, however, when gap filling will not test what we want it to test (at least, in my experience). Here is an example where we want to test epistemic *could*.
If we have the simple sentence:

<blockquote>They left at seven. They _____ be home by now.</blockquote>

There are obviously too many possibilities for the gap (must, should, may, could, might, will).

We can add context, having someone reply: *Yes, but we can't count on it, can we?* This removes the possibility of *must* and *will* but leaves the other possibilities.

At this point I would think that I could only test the epistemic use of *could* satisfactorily by resorting to multiple choice.

<blockquote>
A: They left at seven. They _____ be home by now.
B: Yes, but we can't count on it, can we?

   a. can   b. could   c. will   d. must
</blockquote>

I would also use multiple choice when testing discontinuous elements.

<blockquote>
A: Poor man, he .... at that for days now.
B: Why doesn't he give up?

   a. was working
   b. has been working
   c. is working
   d. had worked
</blockquote>

(*Why doesn't he give up?* is added to eliminate the possibility of d being correct, which might just be possible despite the presence of *now*.)

Also, all the above non-multiple-choice techniques can be given a multiple choice structure, but the reader who attempts to write such items can often expect to have problems in finding suitable distractors.

Moderation of items is of course essential. The checklist included in Chapter 7 should be helpful in this.

Scoring production grammar tests

Gap filling and multiple choice items should cause no problems. The important thing when scoring other types of item is to be clear about what each item is testing, and to award points for that only. There may be just one element, such as subject-pronoun-verb inversion, and all available points should be awarded for that; nothing should be deducted for non-grammatical errors, or for errors in elements of grammar which are not being tested by the item. For instance, a candidate should not be penalised for a missing third person -*s* when the item is testing relative pronouns; *opend* should be accepted for *opened*, without penalty.

If two elements are being tested in an item, then points may be assigned to each of them (for example present perfect form and *since* with past time reference point). Alternatively, it can be stipulated that both elements have to be correct for any points to be awarded, which makes sense in those cases where getting one element wrong means that the student does not have full control of the structure. For items such as these, to ensure scoring is valid and reliable careful preparation of the scoring key is necessary.

Testing vocabulary

Why test vocabulary?

Similar reasons may be advanced for testing vocabulary in proficiency tests to those used to support the inclusion of a grammar section (though vocabulary has its special sampling problems). However, the arguments for a separate component in other kinds of test may not have the same strength. One suspects that much less time is devoted to the regular, conscious teaching of vocabulary than to the similar teaching of grammar. If there is little teaching of vocabulary, it may be argued that there is little call for achievement tests of vocabulary. At the same time, it *is* to be hoped that vocabulary *learning* is taking place. Achievement tests that measure the extent of this learning (and encourage it) perhaps do have a part to play in institutional testing. For those who believe that systematic teaching of vocabulary is desirable, vocabulary achievement tests are appreciated for their backwash effect.

The usefulness (and indeed the feasibility) of a general diagnostic test of vocabulary is not readily apparent. As far as placement tests are concerned, we would not normally require, or expect, a particular set of lexical items to be a prerequisite for a particular language class. All we would be looking for is some general indication of the adequacy of the student's vocabulary. The learning of specific lexical items in class will rarely depend on previous knowledge of other, specified items. One alternative is to use a published test of vocabulary. The other is to construct one's own vocabulary proficiency test.

Writing specifications

How do we specify the vocabulary for an achievement test? If vocabulary is being consciously taught, then presumably all the items thereby presented to the students should be included in the specifications. To these we can add all the new items that the students have met in other activities (reading, listening, etc.). Words should be grouped according to whether their recognition or their production is required. A subsequent step is to group the items in terms of their relative importance.

We have suggested that a vocabulary placement test will be in essence a proficiency test. The usual way to specify the lexical items that may be tested in a proficiency test is to make reference to one of the published word lists that indicate the frequency with which the words have been found to be used (see Further reading).

Sampling

Words can be grouped according to their frequency and usefulness. From each of these groups, items can be taken at random, with more being selected from the groups containing the more frequent and useful words.

Writing items

Testing recognition ability

This is one testing problem for which multiple choice can be recommended without too many reservations. For one thing, distractors are usually readily available. For another, there seems unlikely to be any serious harmful backwash effect, since guessing the meaning of vocabulary items is something that we would probably wish to encourage. However, the writing of successful items is not without its difficulties.

Items may involve a number of different operations on the part of the candidates:

Recognise synonyms

> Choose the alternative (a, b, c or d) which is closest in meaning to the word on the left of the page.
>
> *gleam*   a. gather   b. shine   c. welcome   d. clean

The writer of this item has probably chosen the first alternative because of the word glean. The fourth may have been chosen because of the similarity of its sound to that of gleam. Whether these distractors would work as intended would only be discovered through trialling.

Note that all of the options are words that the candidates are expected to know. If, for example, *welcome* were replaced by *groyne*, most candidates, recognising that it is the meaning of the stem (gleam) on which they are being tested, would dismiss *groyne* immediately.

On the other hand, the item could have a common word as the stem with four less frequent words as options:

shine   a. malm   b. gleam   c. loam   d. snarl

The drawback to doing this is the problem of what distractors to use. Clearly they should not be too common, otherwise they will not distract. But even if they are not common, if the test taker knows them, they will not distract. This suggests that the first method is preferable.

Note that in both items it is the word *gleam* that is being tested.

Recognise definitions

    loathe means   a. dislike intensely
                  b. become seriously ill
                  c. search carefully
                  d. look very angry

Note that all of the options are of about the same length. It is said that test-takers who are uncertain of which option is correct will tend to choose the one which is noticeably different from the others. If *dislike intensely* is to be used as the definition, then the distractors should be made to resemble it. In this case the writer has included some notion of intensity in all of the options.

Again the difficult word could be one of the options, although the concern expressed above about this technique applies here too.

    One word that means to *dislike intensely* is a. growl
                                        b. screech
                                        c. sneer
                                        d. loathe

Thrasher (Internet) believes that vocabulary is best tested in context and, referring to the first edition of this book, suggests that a better way to test knowledge of *loathe* would be:

Bill is someone I *loathe*.

    a. like very much
    b. dislike intensely
    c. respect
    d. fear

For the moment, I leave it to the reader to consider whether the provision of context makes an improvement.

Recognise appropriate word for context
Context, rather than a definition or a synonym, can be used to test knowledge of a lexical item.

> The strong wind _____ the man's efforts to put up the tent.
>
> a. disabled   b. hampered   c. deranged   d. regaled

Note that the context should not itself contain words that the candidates are unlikely to know.

Having now presented an item testing vocabulary in context myself, I return to Thrasher's suggested improvement. It could be argued that, since learners and language users in general normally meet vocabulary in context, providing context in an item makes the task more authentic and perhaps results in a more valid measure of the candidate's ability. The context may help activate a memory of the word, in the same way as meeting it when reading in a non-test situation. It may also be said that there could be some negative backwash when words are presented in isolation. However, when we test vocabulary *by means of multiple choice*, the range of possible distractors will be wider if words are presented in isolation. In Thrasher's item, I suspect that the difference in length between the first two and the second two options would encourage candidates who don't know the word to choose a or b, thereby increasing the possibility of a correct response by guessing. I have to admit that I know of no systematic research that has compared test performance on vocabulary items with and without context.

Testing production ability

The testing of vocabulary productively is so difficult that it is practically never attempted in proficiency tests. Information on receptive ability is regarded as sufficient. The suggestions presented below are intended only for possible use in achievement tests.

Pictures
The main difficulty in testing productive lexical ability is the need to limit the candidate to the (usually one) lexical item that we have in mind, while using only simple vocabulary ourselves. One way round this is to use pictures.

> Each of the objects drawn below has a letter against it. Write down the names of the objects:
>
> A ....

B ....

C ....

D ....

E ....

F ....

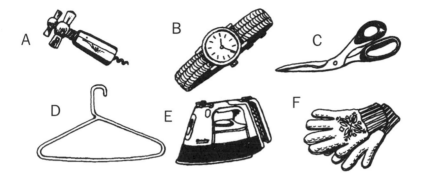

This method of testing vocabulary is obviously restricted to concrete nouns that can be unambiguously drawn.

Definitions

This may work for a range of lexical items:

> A .... is a person who looks after our teeth.
>
> .... is frozen water.
>
> .... is the second month of the year.

But not all items can be identified uniquely from a definition: any definition of say *feeble* would be unlikely to exclude all of its synonyms. Nor can all words be defined entirely in words more common or simpler than themselves.

Gap filling

This can take the form of one or more sentences with a single word missing.

> Because of the snow, the football match was _____ until the following week.

I _____ to have to tell you this, Mrs Jones, but your husband has had an accident.

Too often there is an alternative word to the one we have in mind. Indeed the second item above has at least two acceptable responses (which was not intended when it was written!). This problem can be solved by giving the first letter of the word (possibly more) and even an indication of the number of letters.

I r_____ to have to tell you ...

or I r _ _ _ _ _ to have to tell you.

Again, moderation of items is necessary and the checklist in Chapter 7 can be used, possibly with minor modifications.

Postscript

This chapter should end with a reminder that while grammar and vocabulary contribute to communicative skills, they are rarely to be regarded as ends in themselves. It is essential that tests should not accord them too much importance, and so create a backwash effect that undermines the achievement of the objectives of teaching and learning where these are communicative in nature.

Reader activities

Construct items to test the following:

- Conditional: *If .... had ...., ... would have .... .*
- Comparison of equality.
- Relative pronoun *whose*.
- Past continuous: *... was -ing, when ... .*

Which of the techniques suggested in the chapter suits each structure best? Can you say why?

Can you see anything wrong with the following multiple choice items taken from tests written by teachers (use the checklist given as Table 1 in Chapter 7)? If so, what? Try to improve them.

a) I said to my friend ' _____ be stupid.'

   Isn't   Aren't   Didn't   Don't be

b) What _____ you do, if your car broke down?

   must   did   shall

c) You are too thin. You should eat.......................

    many   more   a few

d) – I'm sorry that the child saw the accident.
   – I don't think it matters. He soon _____ it.

   is forgetting   forgets   will forget   will be forgetting

e) People _____ in their reaction to the same stimulus.

   replace   vary   upset   very

Produce three vocabulary tests by writing three items for each of the following words. One set of items should be multiple choice *without* context; one set should be multiple choice *with* context; the third set should be gap filling. Give each test to a different (but comparable) group of students. Compare performance on items testing the same word. Can differences of performance be attributed to a difference in technique?

beard	sigh	bench	deaf	genial
tickle	weep	greedy	mellow	callow

(If the words are inappropriate for your students, replace them with others.)

Further reading

For a highly detailed taxonomy of notions and functions and their grammatical and lexical realisations, see van Ek and Trim (2001a, b and c). I have also found Collins Cobuild (1992) useful in writing specifications. A thorough study of vocabulary assessment (going beyond testing) is Read (2000). It includes methods of assessing both size (breadth) and quality (depth) of knowledge. Read and Chapelle (2001) proposes a framework for vocabulary assessment. A new book of word frequencies is Leech et al (2001). It gives information for spoken and written varieties of English. West (1953) is a standard word list of high frequency words learners should know. Collins COBUILD English Language Dictionary and the Longman Dictionary of Contemporary English mark words according to their frequency in the language.

---

1. This technique is no longer used in the FCE.

14 Testing overall ability

The previous five chapters have given advice on the testing of different abilities. The assumption has been that we need to obtain separate information on each of these abilities. There are times, however, when we do not need such detailed information, when an estimate of candidates' overall ability is enough.

One way of measuring overall ability is to build a test with a number of components: for example, reading, listening, grammar and vocabulary. Specifications are written for the individual components and these are incorporated into specifications for the entire test, with an indication of the weight that each of the components will be given. The scores on the different components of the test are added together to give an indication of overall ability. This is what happens in many proficiency tests. Even if the scores on the individual components are given, they may be ignored by those who use the test scores.

But building a big test of this kind is hardly economical if we simply want to use test results for making decisions that are not of critical importance and in situations where backwash is not a consideration. One obvious example of this is placement testing in language schools. Typically, all that is asked of language school placement tests is that they assign people to a level in that school. If people are misplaced by the test, they can usually easily be moved to a more appropriate class; provided that not too many such moves are called for, this is not a problem. And since people do not normally prepare for placement tests, there is no need to worry about possible backwash. In these circumstances, it turns out that there are fairly straightforward and economical ways of estimating overall ability.

Before looking at techniques for doing this, however, it is worthwhile giving a little thought to the concept itself. The notion of overall ability is directly related to the commonsense idea that someone can be good (quite good, or poor) at a language. It makes sense to say that someone is good at a language because performance in one skill is usually a reasonable predictor of performance in another. If we hear someone speaking a language fluently and correctly, we can predict that they will also write the language well. On some occasions, of course, we may be wrong in our prediction, but usually we will be right. This is hardly surprising, since, despite their differences, speaking and writing share a great many features, most obviously elements of grammar and vocabulary. It is essentially this sharing of features that allows us to measure overall ability economically.

One last thing to say before looking at techniques is that some of them are based on the idea of *reduced redundancy*. When we listen to someone or read something, there is more information available to us than we actually need in order to interpret what is said or written. There is redundancy. Native speakers of a language can cope well when this redundancy is reduced. They can, for example, understand what someone is saying even though there are noises in the environment that prevent them from hearing every sound that is made. Similarly, they can make out the meaning of the text of a newspaper that has been left outside in the rain, causing the print to become blurred. Because non-native speakers generally find it more difficult to cope with reduced redundancy, the deliberate reduction of redundancy has been used as a means of estimating foreign language ability. Learners' overall ability has been estimated by measuring how well they can restore a reduced text to its original form.

Varieties of cloze procedure

In its original form, the cloze procedure reduces redundancy by deleting a number of words in a passage, leaving blanks, and requiring the person taking the test to attempt to replace the original words. After a short unmutilated 'lead-in', it is usually about every seventh word that is deleted. The following example, which the reader might wish to attempt, was used in research into cloze in the United States (put only one word in each space). The answers are at the end of this chapter.

What is a college?

Confusion exists concerning the real purposes, aims, and goals of a college. What are these? What should a college be?

Some believe that the chief function 1._____ even a liberal arts college is 2._____ vocational one. I feel that the 3._____ function of a college, while important, 4._____ nonetheless secondary. Others profess that the 5._____ purpose of a college is to 6._____ paragons of moral, mental, and spiritual 7._____ – Bernard McFaddens with halos. If they 8._____ that the college should include students 9._____ the highest moral, ethical, and religious 10._____ by precept and example, I 11._____ willing to accept the thesis.

I 12._____ in attention to both social amenities 13._____ regulations, but I prefer to see 14._____ colleges get down to more basic 15._____ and ethical considerations instead of standing in loco parentis 16._____ four years when 17._____ student is attempting in his youthful 18._____ awkward ways, to grow up. It 19._____ been said that it was not 20._____ duty to prolong adolescences. We are 21._____ adept at it.

There are those 22._____ maintain that the chief purpose of 23._____ college is to develop "responsible citizens." 24._____ is good if responsible citizenship is 25._____ by-product of all the factors which 26._____ to make up a college education 27._____ life itself. The difficulty arises from 28._____ confusion about the meaning of responsible 29._____. I know of one college which 30._____ mainly to produce, in a kind 31._____ academic assembly line, outstanding exponents of 32._____ system of free enterprise.

Likewise, I 33._____ to praise the kind of education 34._____ extols one kind of economic system 35._____ the exclusion of the good portions 36._____ other kinds of economic systems. It 37._____ to me therefore, that a college 38._____ represent a combination of all 39._____ above aims, and should be something 40._____ besides – first and foremost an educational 41._____, the center of which is the 42._____ exchange between teachers and students.

I 43._____ read entirely too many statements such 44._____ this one on admissions application papers: "45._____ want a college education because I 46._____ that this will help to support 47._____ and my family." I suspect that 48._____ job as a bricklayer would help this 49._____ to support himself and his family 50._____ better than a college education.

(Oller and Conrad 1971)

Some of the blanks you will have completed with confidence and ease. Others, even if you are a native speaker of English, you will have found difficult, perhaps impossible. In some cases you may have supplied a word which, although different from the original, you may think just as good or even better. All of these possible outcomes are discussed in the following pages.

There was a time when the cloze procedure seemed to be presented almost as a language testing panacea. An integrative method, it was thought by many to draw on the candidate's ability to process lengthy passages of language: in order to replace the missing word in a blank, it was necessary to go beyond the immediate context. In predicting the missing word, candidates made use of the abilities that underlay all their language performance. The cloze procedure therefore provided a measure of those underlying abilities, its content validity deriving from the fact that the deletion of every nth word meant that a representative sample of the linguistic features of the text was obtained. (It would not be useful to present the full details of the argument in a book of this kind. The interested reader is referred to the Further reading section at the end of the chapter.) Support for this view came in the form of relatively high correlations between scores on cloze passages and total scores on much longer, more complex tests, such as the University of California at Los Angeles (UCLA) English as a Second Language Placement Test (ESLPE), as well as with the individual components of such tests (such as reading and listening).

The cloze procedure seemed very attractive as a measure of overall ability. Cloze tests were easy to construct, administer and score. Reports of early research seemed to suggest that it mattered little which passage was chosen or which words were deleted; the result would be a reliable and valid test of candidates' underlying language abilities. Unfortunately, cloze could not deliver all that was promised on its behalf. For one thing, it turned out that different passages gave different results, as did the deletion of different sets of words in the same passage. A close examination of the context that was needed in order to fill a blank successfully (and studies of what context people actually used) showed that it rarely extended far from the gap. Another matter for concern was the fact that intelligent and educated native speakers varied quite considerably in their ability to predict the missing words. What is more, some of them did less well than many non-native speakers. The validity of the procedure was thus brought into question.

Selected deletion cloze

There seems to be fairly general agreement now that the cloze procedure cannot be depended upon automatically to produce reliable and useful tests. There is need for careful selection of texts and some pre-testing. The fact that deletion of every nth word almost always produces problematical items (for example, impossible to predict the missing word), points to the advisability of a careful selection of words to delete, from the outset. The following is an in-house cloze passage, for students at university entrance level, in which this has been done. Again the reader is invited to try to complete the gaps.

> Choose the best word to fill each of the numbered blanks in the passage below. Write your answers in the space provided in the right hand margin. Write only ONE word for each blank.

Ecology

Water, soil and the earth's green mantle of plants
make up the world that supports the animal life of the
earth. Although modern man seldom remembers the
fact, he could not exist without the plants that harness
the sun's energy and manufacture the basic food-stuffs

he depends (1) _____ for life. Our attitude   (1) _____
(2) _____ plants is a singularly narrow   (2) _____
(3) _____. If we see any immediate utility   (3) _____
in (4) _____ plant we foster it.   (4) _____
(5) _____ for any reason we find its presence   (5) _____
undesirable, (6) _____ merely a matter of   (6) _____
indifference, we may condemn (7) _____ to   (7) _____
destruction. Besides the various plants (8) _____   (8) _____
are poisonous to man or to (9) _____ livestock,   (9) _____
or crowd out food plants, many are marked
(10) _____ destruction merely because,   (10) _____
according to our narrow view, they happen to
(11) _____ in the wrong place at the   (11) _____
(12) _____ time. Many others are destroyed   (12) _____
merely (13) _____ they happen to be associates   (13) _____
of the unwanted plants.

The earth's vegetation is (14) _____ of a web   (14) _____
of life in which there are intimate and essential
relations between plants and the earth, between
plants and (15) _____ plants, between plants   (15) _____
and animals. Sometimes we have no (16) _____   (16) _____
but to disturb (17) _____ relationships, but   (17) _____
we should (18) _____ so thoughtfully, with full   (18) _____
awareness that (19) _____ we do may   (19) _____
(20) _____ consequences remote in time and   (20) _____
place.

The deletions in the above passage were chosen to provide 'interesting' items. Most of them we might be inclined to regard as testing 'grammar', but to respond to them successfully more than grammatical ability is needed; processing of various features of context is usually necessary. Another feature is that native speakers of the same general academic ability as the students for whom the test was intended could be expected to provide acceptable responses to all of the items. The acceptable responses are themselves limited in number. Scores on cloze passages of this kind in the Cambridge Proficiency Examination have correlated very highly with performance on the test as a whole. If cloze is to be used to measure overall ability, it is this kind which I would recommend. General advice on the construction of such tests is given below.

Conversational cloze

The two passages used to create cloze tests above are both quite formal prose. If we want our measure of overall ability to reflect (and hopefully predict) oral as well as written ability, we can use passages which represent spoken language. The next passage is based on a tape-recording of a conversation. As this type of material is very culturally bound, probably only a non-native speaker who has been in Britain for some time could understand it fully. It is a good example of informal family conversation, where sentences are left unfinished and topics run into each other. (Again the reader is invited to attempt to predict the missing words. Note that things like *John's*, *I'm*, etc. count as one word. Only one word per space.)

Family reunion
Mother: I love that dress, Mum.
Grandmother: Oh, it's M and S.
Mother: Is it?
Grandmother: Yes, five pounds.
Mother: My goodness, it's not, Mum.
Grandmother: But it's made of that T-shirt stuff, so I don't think it'll
                      wash very .... (1), you know, they go all ...
Mother: sort .... (2) ... I know the kind, yes ...
Grandmother: Yes.
Mother: I've got some T-shirts of that, and .... (3)
                      shrink upwards and go wide ...
Grandmother: I know, so ...

Mother:	It's a super colour. It .... (4) a terribly expensive one, doesn't it? .... (5) you think so when you saw .... (6)?
Grandmother:	Well, I always know in Marks. .... (7) just go in there and ... and .... (8) it's not there I don't buy it. I know I won't like anything else. I got about three from there ... four from there. Only I wait about...
Girl:	Mummy, can I have a sweetie?
Mother:	What, love?
Grandmother:	Do you know what those are called? ... Oh, I used to love them .... (9) I was a little girl. Liquorice comfits. Do you like liquorice? Does she?
Mother:	.... (10) think she quite likes it. Do .... (11)? We've got some liquorice allsorts actually .... (12) the journey.
Grandmother:	Oh yes.
Mother:	And I said she could have one after.
Grandmother:	Oh, I'm going to have one. No, I'm .... (13). No, it'd make me fat, dear.
Mother:	Listen. Do you want some stew? It's hot now.
Grandmother:	No, no, darling. I don't want anything.
Mother:	Don't you want any? Because .... (14) just put it on the table.
Grandmother:	I've got my Limmits.
Mother:	Are you going .... (15) eat them now with us?
Grandmother:	Yes. .... (16) you going to have yours ... yours now?
Mother:	Well, I've just put mine on the plate, but Arth says he doesn't .... (17) any now.
Grandmother:	Oh yes, go on.
Mother:	So ... so he's going to come down later...
Grandmother:	What are .... (18) going to eat? ... Oh, I like .... (19). Is that a thing that...
Mother:	... you gave me, but I altered it.
Grandmother:	Did .... (20) shorten it?
Mother:	I took the frill .... (21).
Grandmother:	I thought it looked...
Mother:	I altered .... (22) straps and I had to...
Girl:	That's .... (23) you gave me, Granny.... Granny, I'm .... (24) big for that...
Mother:	And so is Jake. It's for a doll ... Do you remember that?
Grandmother:	No.
Mother:	Oh, Mum, you're awful. .... (25) made it.

This 'conversational cloze' passage turned out to be a reasonable predictor of the oral ability of overseas students (as rated by their language teachers) who had already been in Britain for some time. It suggests that we should base cloze tests on passages that reflect the kind of language that is relevant for the overall ability we are interested in.

Advice on creating cloze type passages

1. The chosen passages should be at a level of difficulty appropriate to the people who are to take the test. If there is doubt about the level, a range of passages should be selected for trialling. Indeed it is always advisable to trial a number of passages, as their behaviour is not always predictable.
2. The text should be of a style appropriate to the kind of language ability being tested.
3. After a couple of sentences of uninterrupted text, deletions should be made at about every eighth or tenth word (the so called pseudo-random method of deletion). Individual deletions can then be moved a word or two to left or right, to avoid problems or to create interesting 'items'. One may deliberately make gaps that can only be filled by reference to the extended context.
4. The passage should then be tried out on a good number of comparable native speakers and the range of acceptable responses determined.
5. Clear instructions should be devised. In particular, it should be made clear what is to be regarded as a word (with examples of *isn't*, etc., where appropriate). Students should be assured that no one can possibly replace all the original words exactly. They should be encouraged to begin by reading the passage right through to get an idea of what is being conveyed (the correct responses early in the passage may be determined by later content).
6. The layout of the second test in the chapter (Ecology) facilitates scoring. Scorers are given a card with the acceptable responses written in such a way as to lie opposite the candidates' responses.
7. Anyone who is to take a cloze test should have had several opportunities to become familiar with the technique. The more practice they have had, the more likely it is that their scores will represent their true ability in the language.
8. Cloze test scores are not directly interpretable. In order to be able to interpret them we need to have some other measure against which they can be validated.

Mini-cloze items

One problem with the cloze technique is that, once a passage has been chosen, we are limited as to what features of language can be tested. We can only test the grammatical structures and vocabulary that are to be found in that passage. To get good coverage of the features that we think are relevant, we have to include a number of passages, which is hardly economical. An alternative approach is to construct what may be called *mini-cloze* items. These may take various forms, but one that I have used is an item that represents a brief exchange between two or more people, with just one gap. For example:

> A: What time is it?
> B: _____ a quarter to three.
>
> A: You look tired.
> B: Yes, I stayed _____ really late last night. Had to finish that book.

In this way, we can cover just the structures and vocabulary that we want to, and include whatever features of spoken language are relevant for our purpose. If, for example, we want to base the content of the test on the content of the text books used in language schools, including a representative sample of this is relatively straightforward. The one possible disadvantage by comparison with more normal cloze is that the context that must be taken into account in order to fill a gap correctly is very restricted, but for such purposes as placement testing, this would not seem a serious defect[1].

The C-Test

The C-Test is really a variety of cloze, which its originators claim is superior to the kind of cloze described above. Instead of whole words, it is the second half of every second word that is deleted. An example follows.

> There are usually five men in the crew of a fire engine. One o___ them dri___ the eng___. The lea___ sits bes___ the dri___. The ot___ firemen s___ inside t___ cab o___ the f___ engine. T___ leader kn___ how t___ fight diff___ sorts o___ fires. S___, when t___ firemen arr___ at a fire, it is always the leader who decides how to fight a fire. He tells each fireman what to do.

(Klein-Braley and Raatz 1984)

The supposed advantages of the C-Test over the more traditional cloze procedure are that only exact scoring is necessary (native speakers effectively scoring 100 per cent) and that shorter (and so more) passages are possible. This last point means that a wider range of topics, styles, and levels of ability is possible. The deletion of elements less than the word is also said to result in a representative sample of parts of speech being so affected. By comparison with cloze, a C-Test of 100 items takes little space and not nearly so much time to complete (candidates do not have to read so much text).

Possible disadvantages relate to the puzzle-like nature of the task. It is harder to read than a cloze passage, and correct responses can often be found in the surrounding text. Thus the candidate who adopts the right puzzle-solving strategy may be at an advantage over a candidate of similar foreign language ability. However, research would seem to indicate that the C-Test functions well as a rough measure of overall ability in a foreign language. The advice given above about the development of cloze tests applies equally to the C-Test.

Dictation

In the 1960s it was usual, at least in some parts of the world, to decry dictation testing as hopelessly misguided. After all, since the order of words was given, it did not test word order; since the words themselves were given, it did not test vocabulary; since it was possible to identify words from the context, it did not test aural perception. While it might test punctuation and spelling, there were clearly more economical ways of doing this.

At the end of the decade this orthodoxy was challenged. Research revealed high correlations between scores on dictation tests and scores on much longer and more complex tests (such as the UCLA ESLPE). Examination of performance on dictation tests made it clear that words and word order were not really given; the candidate heard only a stream of sound which had to be decoded into a succession of words, stored, and recreated on paper. The ability to identify words from context was now seen as a very desirable ability, one that distinguished between learners at different levels.

Dictation tests give results similar to those obtained from cloze tests. In predicting overall ability they have the advantage of involving listening ability. That is probably the only advantage. Certainly they are as easy to create. They are relatively easy to administer, though not as easy as the paper-and-pencil cloze. But they are certainly not easy to score. Oller, who was a leading researcher into both cloze and dictation, recommends that the score should be the number of words appearing in their original sequence (misspelled words being regarded as correct as long as no phonological rule is broken). This works quite well when performance is reasonably accurate, but is still time-consuming. With poorer students, scoring becomes very tedious.

Because of this scoring problem, *partial* dictation (see pages 168–169) may be considered as an alternative. In this, part of what is dictated is already printed on the candidate's answer sheet. The candidate has simply to fill in the gaps. It is then clear just where the candidate is up to, and scoring is likely to be more reliable.

When using dictation, the same considerations should guide the choice of passages as with the cloze procedure. The passage has then to be broken down into stretches that will be spoken without a break. These should be fairly long, beyond rote memory, so that the candidates will have to decode, store, and then re-encode what they hear (this was a feature of the dictations used in the research referred to above). It is usual, when administering the dictation, to begin by reading the entire passage straight through. Then the stretches are read out, not too slowly, one after the other with enough time for the candidates to write down what they have heard (Oller recommends that the reader silently spell the stretch twice as a guide to writing time).

Mini-partial-dictation items

As far as coverage is concerned, dictation suffers from the same disadvantage as cloze. The passage determines the limits of what can be tested. For that reason, a series of mini-dialogues (possibly mixed with monologues) of the following kind can be constructed.
The candidate sees:

> A: When can I see you again?
> B: How about .... Thursday?

> And hears: When can I see you again?
>   How about a week on Thursday?

Conclusion

There are times when only a general estimate of people's overall language ability is needed and backwash is not a serious consideration. In such cases, any of the methods (the quick and dirty methods, some would say) described in this chapter may serve the purpose. Because of the considerable recent interest in cloze and its common use as a learning exercise in its usual multi-item format, it may be the most obvious choice. I suspect, however, that the simple gap filling methods referred to above as 'mini-cloze' and 'mini-partial-dictation' will give results at least as good as those of any other method.

Reader activities

1. Complete the three cloze passages in the chapter. Say what you think each item is testing. How much context do you need to arrive at each correct response?
   If there are items for which you cannot provide a satisfactory response, can you explain why?
   Identify items for which there seem to be a number of possible acceptable responses. Can you think of responses that are on the borderline of acceptability? Can you say why they are on the borderline?
2. Choose a passage that is at the right level and on an appropriate topic for a group of students with whom you are familiar. Use it to create tests by:

   - deleting every seventh word after a lead in;
   - doing the same, only starting three words after the first deleted word of the first version.

   Compare the two versions. Are they equivalent?
   Now use one of them to create a cloze test of the kind recommended. Make a C-Test based on the same passage. Make a partial dictation of it too. How do all of them compare?
   If possible administer them to the group of students you had in mind, and compare the results (with each other and with your knowledge of the students).

Further reading

For all issues discussed in this chapter, including dictation, the most accessible source is Oller (1979). The research in which the first cloze passage in the chapter was used is described in Oller and Conrad (1971). Chapelle and Abraham (1990) used one passage but different methods of cloze deletion (including C-Test) and obtained different results with the different methods. Brown (1993) examines the characteristics of 'natural' cloze tests and argues for rational deletion. Farhady and Keramati (1996) propose a 'text-driven' procedure for deleting words in cloze passages. Storey (1997) investigates the processes that candidates go through when taking cloze tests. Examples of the kind of cloze recommended here are to be found in Cambridge Proficiency Examination past papers. Hughes (1981) is an account of the research into conversational cloze. Klein-Braley and Raatz (1984) and Klein-Braley (1985) outline the development of the C-Test. Klein-Braley (1997) is a more recent appraisal of the technique. Jafarpur (1995) reports rather negative results for C-Tests he administered. Lado (1961) provides a critique of dictation as a testing technique, while Lado (1986) carried out further research using the passage employed by Oller and Conrad, to cast doubt on their claims. Garman and Hughes (1983) provide cloze passages for teaching, but they could form the basis for tests (native speaker responses given). Hughes et al (1996, 1998) are placement tests developed for ARELS (Association of Recognised English Language Services) and based on mini-cloze and mini-partial–dictation items (information on the Internet).

Answers to cloze tests

What is a college? The words deleted from the passage are as follows:
1. of; 2. a; 3. vocational; 4. is; 5. chief; 6. produce; 7. stamina; 8. mean; 9. with; 10. standards; 11. am; 12. believe; 13. and; 14. our; 15. moral; 16. for; 17. the; 18. and; 19. has; 20. our; 21. singularly; 22. who; 23. a; 24. This; 25. a; 26. go; 27. and; 28. a; 29. citizenship; 30. aims; 31. of; 32. our; 33. hesitate; 34. which; 35. to; 36. of; 37. seems; 38. should; 39. the; 40. else; 41. experience; 42. intellectual; 43. have; 44. as; 45. I; 46. feel; 47. me; 48. a; 49. student; 50. much.

Ecology. The words deleted from the passage are as follows: 1. on; 2. to; 3. one; 4. a; 5. If; 6. or; 7. it; 8. which/that; 9. his; 10. for; 11. be; 12. wrong; 13. because; 14. part; 15. other; 16. choice/ option; 17. these; 18. do; 19. what; 20. have.

Family reunion. Acceptable responses: 1. well; 2. of; 3. they; 4. looks, seems; 5. Did, Didn't; 6. it; 7. I; 8. if; 9. when; 10. I; 11. you; 12. for; 13. not; 14. I've; 15. to; 16. Are; 17. want; 18. you; 19. that; 20. you; 21. off; 22. the; 23. what, one; 24. too; 25. You.

---

1. The fact that these 'mini-cloze' items are indistinguishable in form from gap filling items presented in the previous chapter has not escaped me either!

15 Tests for young learners

This chapter begins by suggesting a general approach to tests for young learners. It then goes on to consider the particular requirements of such tests. Finally it recommends suitable testing techniques.

General approach

While in some countries, for example Norway, children have been learning foreign languages at primary school for decades, in recent years it is has become an increasingly common phenomenon in many other parts of the world. This chapter considers the particular requirements for the successful testing of young learners and makes suggestions as to how this may best be done. By young learners we have in mind children aged from about five to twelve.

One might ask first why we have to test young language learners at all. This is a good question. Not everyone does it. In Norway, for example, where the learning of English appears to be highly successful, children up to the age of thirteen are not formally tested in the subject. One answer to the question might be that we want to be sure that the teaching programme is effective, that the children are really benefiting from the chance to learn a language at an early age. But this invites a further question: Why is testing rather than assessment by other means necessary? The answer I gave in Chapter 1 was that there was a need for a common yardstick, which tests give, in order to make meaningful comparisons. I have to confess, however, as someone who has spent a lot of his time either testing or advising others on testing, that I feel uneasy at the thought of the damage to children's learning, and their attitude to learning, that might be done by insensitive, inappropriate testing. This uneasiness is not lessened by the knowledge that the aims of early language teaching typically include the development of positive attitudes to language learning and to language. But people do test young learners and this being so, I believe it is worthwhile considering what is the best way to do this.

On a more positive note, it seems to me that if young children are going to be tested, such testing provides an opportunity to develop positive attitudes towards assessment, to help them recognise the value of assessment. In order to take advantage of this opportunity, I would make three general recommendations that, together, amount to an approach to such testing. The first recommendation is that a special effort be made to make testing an integral part of assessment, and assessment an integral part of the teaching programme. All three should be consistent with each other in terms of learning objectives and, as far as possible, the kinds of tasks which the children are expected to perform. Testing will not then be seen as something separate from learning, as a trial that has to be endured.

The second recommendation is that feedback from tests (and feedback from assessment generally) should be immediate and positive. By being immediate its value will be maximised. By telling children not only what their weaknesses are but also what they have done well, the potential demoralising effect of test results is lessened.

The third recommendation is that self assessment by the children be made a part of the teaching programme. This will help them to develop the habit of monitoring their own progress. It should also allow them to take pleasure in what they are achieving. To improve their ability to assess themselves, they should be encouraged to compare their own assessments with those of their teacher. On the following page is an example of test material produced by the Norwegian Ministry of Education for 11–12 year olds (Hasselgren 1999). Pupils complete this form after doing an assessment task on reading.

These three recommendations and their intended outcomes may seem somewhat idealistic, but before rejecting them one has to consider the alternative; by default, this is to instil negative attitudes towards tests and, through them, to language learning.

Particular demands

Although we want children to take tests in a relaxed setting, this does not mean that we should relax our own standards for test development. We still need to make sure that our tests are valid and reliable[1]. And the need to seek positive backwash is more important than ever. It would not be appropriate to recapitulate here the advice given earlier on how to make tests valid and reliable, and have a beneficial backwash. It is worth saying, however, that crucial elements are the writing of full specifications and the choice of appropriate test techniques.

EPISODE 1   Try to answer these questions. Put crosses.

Did you ...	yes	mostly	so-so	not really	no
understand what to do?	◯	◯	◯	◯	◯
understand the texts?	◯	◯	◯	◯	◯
have enough time?	◯	◯	◯	◯	◯
do the tasks well?	◯	◯	◯	◯	◯
like the tasks?	◯	◯	◯	◯	◯
manage to guess what new words meant?	◯	◯	◯	◯	◯

Were any texts difficult to understand?

◯ no   ◯ yes (write the numbers)

_____
_____
_____
_____

What have you learnt?

_____
_____
_____
_____

Before considering specific techniques, let us ask what it is about young learners that might require their test to have special features.

1. Young children have a relatively short attention span. For this reason tests should not be long. Individual tasks should be brief and varied. If necessary, what would for other learners have been a single test can be broken down into two or more tests.
2. Children enjoy stories and play. If we want them to become engaged in tests, the tasks should reflect this. Games can include versions of the kind of word games to be found in comics and puzzle books.
3. Children respond well to pictures, attractive typography, and colour[2]. Tests should include these features if possible. With computers,

colour printers and inexpensive scanners generally available, there is usually no reason why they can't be included. It goes without saying that the content of all pictures used should be unambiguous for all the children who may take the test. This might involve testers in checking that children with different cultural backgrounds are familiar with the conventions (such as the different kinds of bubble for speech and for thought) that are used in the test pictures. Pictures may be included even where they are not necessary to complete a task.

4. First language and cognitive abilities are still developing. Tasks should be ones that the children being tested could be expected to handle comfortably in their own language.
5. Since children learn through social interaction, it is appropriate to include tasks that involve interaction between two or more children. This assumes, of course, that similar tasks are used when they are learning the language.
6. If teaching and learning involve tasks which are 'integrated' (in the sense that two or more skills are involved in its completion), similar tasks may have a place in tests. However, these are not so suitable where diagnostic information about separate skills is being sought.

One final recommendation is that every effort be made to create the conditions that allow the children to perform at their best. This means, I think, that they should be tested by sympathetic teachers whom they know and in surroundings with which they are familiar. It is particularly important with children to make sure at the outset that they understand what they have to do. It is also important to include easy tasks at the beginning of a test in order to give them the confidence to tackle the more difficult ones.

Recommended techniques[3]

In what follows I have concentrated on techniques that seem particularly suited to young learners. This does not mean that techniques presented in previous chapters will never be appropriate. The older the children are, the more likely they are to respond well to techniques used with teenagers or adults. Whatever techniques are used with young learners, it is essential that the children have plenty of opportunities to practise with them before they meet them in tests. Ideally, the techniques should be used in learning exercises as well as in testing.

Techniques to test listening

Placing objects or identifying people

The children see a picture with objects placed outside its frame. They have to draw lines to show where the objects are to be placed.

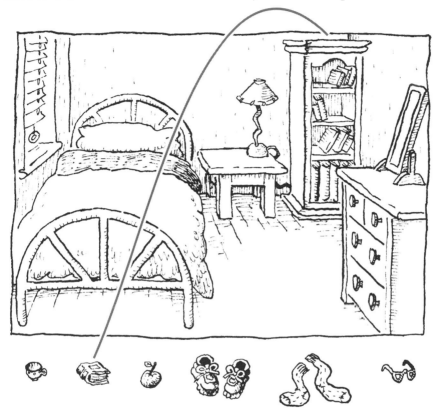

The children hear:

> A: Look at the picture. Listen to the example. Listen and look[4].
> B: Put the book on top of the bookcase.
> C: Pardon?
> B: Put the book on top of the bookcase.
> A: This is an example. Can you see the line? Now you listen and draw a line.
> B: Put the socks on the bed.
> C: Where?
> B: Put the socks on the bed.

An alternative is to have a drawing of children involved in a variety of activities. Outside the picture are the names of a number of children. The children hear something like:

> A: I'm looking for Mary.
> B: Mary? She's painting a picture over there.
> A: Is that her in the corner?
> B: Yes.

They have to draw a line from the word 'Mary' to the representation of her in the picture.

Multiple choice pictures

The children see four pictures, under each of which there is an empty box. They have to tick the box beneath the appropriate picture. For example there may be pictures of four fruits. What the children hear may be as simple as:

> It's an apple.

Or it could be a brief dialogue:

> A: Did you say Harry was eating an orange?
> B: No, it was an apple.

Colour and draw on existing line drawing

The following example is taken from a Cambridge Young Learners sample paper. The children see:

Listen and colour and draw. There is one example.

They hear:

> A: Look at the fish under the ducks.
> B: I can see it. Can I colour it?
>
> A: Yes, colour it red.
> B: The fish under the ducks – colour it red.

and:

> A: Now draw a fish.
> B: Where?
> A: Draw a fish between the boat and the box.
> B: OK. Between the boat and the box.
> A: And colour it green. Colour the fish green.

Information transfer

This will usually involve some simple reading and writing. For example, there may be a chart:

Name: John Thomson

John's best friend: ....

Sports: football and ....

Where John plays football: at ....

How many goals he scored last week: ....

The children may hear an interview with John (or a talk by or about John), in which they can find the information they need to complete the chart. The interview or talk should include sufficient redundancy and include pauses during which answers can be put in the chart. It may be appropriate for the interview or talk to be repeated.

Techniques to test reading

Multiple choice

Reading can be tested by multiple choice in the usual way or, probably better when possible, with pictures. The following example of the latter is taken from EVA materials[5].

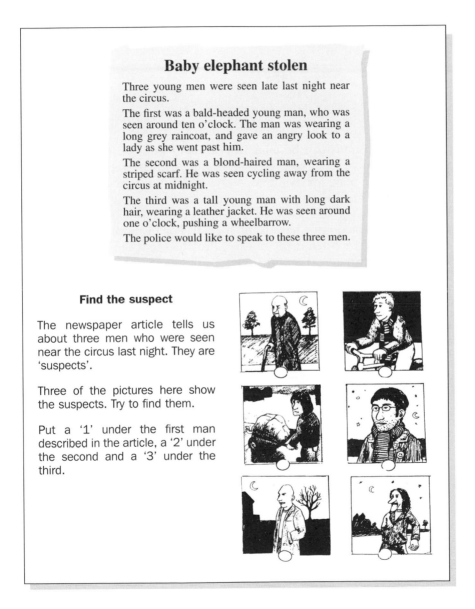

Baby elephant stolen

Three young men were seen late last night near the circus.

The first was a bald-headed young man, who was seen around ten o'clock. The man was wearing a long grey raincoat, and gave an angry look to a lady as she went past him.

The second was a blond-haired man, wearing a striped scarf. He was seen cycling away from the circus at midnight.

The third was a tall young man with long dark hair, wearing a leather jacket. He was seen around one o'clock, pushing a wheelbarrow.

The police would like to speak to these three men.

Find the suspect

The newspaper article tells us about three men who were seen near the circus last night. They are 'suspects'.

Three of the pictures here show the suspects. Try to find them.

Put a '1' under the first man described in the article, a '2' under the second and a '3' under the third.

Multiple choice can also be used in the context of a conversation, interview, or discussion (transcribed as if in, say, a school magazine). The children have to choose the most appropriate response to something that is said. Thus, for example:

> The pop star Billy Wild returns to his old school and is asked questions by members of a class.
>
> Mary: Whose lessons did you like best when you were here, Billy?
>
> Billy Wild: a. Mr Brown's
> b. Football
> c. History
> d. History and geography

And so on.

Simple definitions can be made the basis of multiple choice items in which the chances of correct responses being made by guessing are much reduced. There may, for example, be ten definitions and a set of fifteen words (which include ten to which the definitions apply). The children have to identify the correct word and copy it alongside its definition.

The definitions do not have to be formal. For instance, *wood* may be defined 'Doors are often made of this'. Provided that the presentation of such items is attractive (the words may be different colours, for example, and dotted about the page), such items need not be as grim as they may first sound.

Before leaving the testing of reading, it is worth saying that the short answer technique (Chapter 11) can also be used successfully, provided that the words for the correct responses can be found in the text.

Techniques to test writing

Anagram with picture

To test vocabulary and spelling, children can be presented with a 'puzzle'. There is a series of pictures, and opposite each picture is an anagram of the word the picture represents.

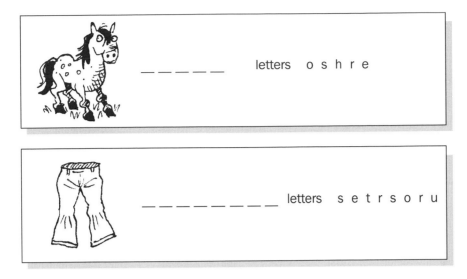

letters o s h r e

_ _ _ _ _

letters s e t r s o r u

_ _ _ _ _ _ _ _

Cartoon story

A series of cartoons tell a simple story.

The instructions are:

> Look at the pictures. See what happens. The girl in the pictures
> is called Sally. Sally writes a letter to her friend David. She tells
> him what happened.

Here is her letter. Write what she says to David.

Dear David
_____
_____
_____
_____
_____
_____
_____

Best wishes
Sally

Gap filling with pictures

This technique may test reading as much as writing. A passage (perhaps a story) is presented in which there are blanks where words are missing. Above each blank there is a pictorial representation of the missing word.

I live in a small [picture] by the sea. Every day I go for

a swim. One day, when I came back after a swim I saw a big

[picture] . In its mouth was a big [picture] .

. . . and so on. Drawings need not be restricted to objects but can also represent actions.

Techniques for testing oral ability

The same general advice for oral testing given in Chapter 10 applies equally to the testing of young learners. What is worth emphasising, perhaps, is the need for a long enough warm-up period for the children to become relaxed. In the case of the youngest children, it may be helpful to introduce toys and dolls from the outset.

Useful techniques include:

- Asking straightforward questions about the child and their family.
- Giving the child a card with a scene on it (a 'scene card'), and then asking them to point out people, say what colour something is, what someone is doing, etc.
- Giving the child small cards, each with an object drawn on it, and asking the child to place each of these 'object cards' in a particular location on a larger scene card. For example, the child may be handed a small card with a picture of a cup on it and be asked to put the cup on the table (which appears on the scene card).
- Giving the child two pictures that are very similar but which differ in obvious ways (for example, one picture might contain a house with three windows and a red door, with a man in the garden; while the other might have a house with four windows, a green door and a woman in the garden). The child is asked to say what the differences are.
- The child is given a short series of pictures that tell a story. The tester begins the story and asks the child to complete it.
- Sets of pictures are presented. In each set there is one picture which does not 'belong'. There may, for example, be three pictures of articles of clothing and one of a bed. The child is asked to identify the odd one out and explain why it is different from the others.

Where we want to see how well children can interact with their peers, useful techniques are:

- If the two children belong to the same class, each can say a specified number of things about another classmate, at the end of which the other child has to guess who is being described.
- There are four different picture postcards. Each child is given three of them, such that they have two cards in common and one which is different. By asking and answering questions in turn, they have to discover which pictures they have in common. All the pictures should have some common features, or the task may end too quickly without much language being used.
- There are two pictures (A and B) which are different but which contain a number of objects that are identical. One child is given picture A, the other picture B. The first child has to describe an object in their picture and the other has to say whether it is to be found in

their picture. The second child then describes something in *their* picture, and the other responds. This continues until they have found a specified number of objects which are in both pictures.

● The children can each be given a card with information on it. In both cases the information is incomplete. The task is for them to ask questions of each other so that they end up with all the information. Examples would be diaries with missing appointments, or timetables with missing classes.

Reader activities

Look at the following activities taken from *Primary Colours* (Hicks and Littlejohn, 2002). These were not originally devised as testing tasks.

What changes, if any, would you make to them in order to create *test* tasks that will be reliable and valid?

Find seven more things. Draw lines.

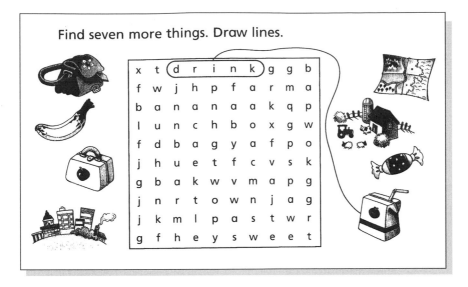

Join the parts. Write the words.

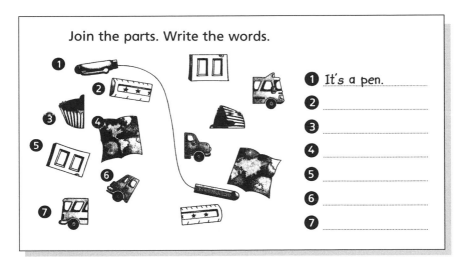

1. It's a pen.
2.
3.
4.
5.
6.
7.

Further reading

Cameron (2001) is a book on teaching language to young learners, which has a chapter on assessment. Rea-Dickens and Rixon (1997) discuss the assessment of young learners of English as a foreign language. Carpenter et al (1995) describe an oral interview procedure for assessing Japanese as a second language. *Language Testing* Volume 17

Number 2 (2000) is a special issue on assessing young language learners. Contributions include a general introduction to the area by Rea-Dickens; an account of how foreign language attainment is assessed at the end of primary education in the Netherlands by Edelenbos and Vinjé; a discussion of teacher assessment in relation to psychometric theory by Teasdale and Leung; a description of the Norwegian materials project (referred to in the chapter) by Hasselgren. A handbook and sample papers for the Cambridge tests for young learners can be obtained from the address given on page 73.

1. Attractive as they might seem for young children, true/false and yes/no items, for example, are no more valid or reliable for them than they are for adults.
2. Unfortunately, it was not possible to include colour in this book.
3. I have drawn extensively on the techniques used by Hasselgren in the Norwegian EVA project, and on those to be found in the Cambridge Young Learners tests. Of course children aged five are quite different from children aged twelve, and so not all of the techniques given here will be equally appropriate for young learners throughout this age range.
4. There should always be an example item. To save space, however, these will be omitted for subsequent techniques.
5. I recognise that this example is marginal – between multiple choice and (very) short answer.

16 Test administration

The best test may give unreliable and invalid results if it is not well administered. This chapter is intended simply to provide readers with an ordered set of points to bear in mind when administering a test. While most of these points will be very obvious, it is surprising how often some of them can be forgotten without a list of this kind to refer to. Tedious as many of the suggested procedures are, they are important for successful testing. Once established, they become part of a routine that all concerned take for granted.

Preparation

The key to successful test administration is careful advance preparation. In particular, attention should be given to the following:

Materials and equipment

1. Organise the printing of test booklets and answer sheets in plenty of time. Check that there are no errors or any faulty reproduction.
2. If previously used test booklets are to be employed, check that there are no marks (for example underlining) left by candidates.
3. Number all the test materials consecutively; this permits greater security before, during, and after test administration.
4. Check that there are sufficient keys for scorers, and that these are free of error.
5. Check that all equipment (tape-recorders, loud speaker system, etc.) is in good working order in plenty of time for repair or replacement.

Examiners

6. Detailed instructions should be prepared for all examiners. In these, an attempt should be made to cover all eventualities, though the

unexpected will always occur. These instructions should be gone through with the examiners at least the day before the test is administered. An indication of possible content can be derived from the Administration section, below.

7. Examiners should practise the directions that they will have to read out to candidates.
8. Examiners who will have to use equipment (for example, tape-recorders) should familiarise themselves with its operation.
9. Examiners who have to read aloud for a listening test should practise, preferably with a model tape-recording (see Chapter 12).
10. Oral examiners must be thoroughly familiar with the test procedures and rating system to be used (only properly trained oral examiners should be involved).

Invigilators (or proctors)

11. Detailed instructions should also be prepared for invigilators, and should be the subject of a meeting with them. See the Administration section, for possible content.

Candidates

12. Every candidate should be given full instructions (where to go, at what time, what to bring, what they should do if they arrive late, etc.).
13. There should be an examination number for each candidate.

Rooms

14. Rooms should be quiet and large enough to accommodate comfortably the intended number of candidates. There should be sufficient space between candidates to prevent copying.
15. For listening tests, the rooms must have satisfactory acoustic qualities.
16. The layout of rooms (placing of desks or tables) should be arranged well in advance.
17. Ideally, in each room there should be a clock visible to all candidates.

Administration

18. Candidates should be required to arrive well before the intended starting time for the test.

19. Candidates arriving late should not be admitted to the room. If it is feasible and thought appropriate, they may be redirected to another room where latecomers (up to a certain time) can be tested. They should certainly not be allowed to disturb the concentration of those already taking the test.
20. The identity of candidates should be checked.
21. If possible, candidates should be seated in such a way as to prevent friends being in a position to pass information to each other.
22. The examiner should give clear instructions to candidates about what they are required to do. These should include information on how they should attract the attention of an invigilator if this proves necessary, and what candidates who finish before time are to do. They should also warn students of the consequences of any irregular behaviour, including cheating, and emphasise the necessity of maintaining silence throughout the duration of the test.
23. Test materials should be distributed to candidates individually by the invigilators in such a way that the position of each test paper and answer sheet is known by its number. A record should be made of these. Candidates should not be allowed to distribute test materials.
24. The examiner should instruct candidates to provide the required details (such as examination number, date) on the answer sheet or test booklet.
25. If spoken test instructions are to be given in addition to those written on the test paper, the examiner should read these, including whatever examples have been agreed upon.
26. It is essential that the examiner time the test precisely, making sure that everyone starts on time and does not continue after time.
27. Once the test is in progress, invigilators should unobtrusively monitor the behaviour of candidates. They will deal with any irregularities in the way laid down in their instructions.
28. During the test, candidates should be allowed to leave the room only one at a time, ideally accompanied by an invigilator.
29. Invigilators should ensure that candidates stop work immediately they are told to do so. Candidates should remain in their places until all the materials have been collected and their numbers checked.

Appendix 1 The statistical analysis of test data

The purpose of this appendix is to show readers how the analysis of test data can help to evaluate and improve tests. Note the word 'help'. Statistical analysis will provide the tester with useful information that may then be used in making decisions about tests and test results. But it does not take those decisions. This remains the tester's responsibility and depends not only on the information that statistical analysis provides but also on judgement and experience. The emphasis throughout will be on interpretation of statistics, not on calculation. In fact it will be assumed that readers who want to analyse their own tests statistically will have access to computer software that will do all the necessary calculation. There is no reason these days to do this calculation by hand or to write one's own programs to do it. For that reason, I have not thought it necessary to show any calculations except the most simple, and these only as part of the explanation of concepts. Where the concepts and calculation are more complex, for all but a small minority of readers the inclusion of calculations would only confuse matters. There is no pretence of full coverage of the statistical methods and issues related to testing in this chapter; that would take a book in itself. Rather, the basic notions are presented in a form which it is hoped will be recognised as both accessible and useful. The next step after going through this chapter is to use a test analysis program and analyse your own data. In my experience, it is only then that it all begins to make real sense.

There are essentially two kinds of statistical information on tests. The first relates to the test as a whole (or sometimes to sections of a test); the second relates to the individual items that make up the test. This appendix will deal with each of these in turn, using a single set of data on one test, analysed by ETA (Educational Test Analysis), which readers can obtain cheaply via the book's website. The data is for 186 people taking a 100-item test. The test, which I have here called MYTEST, is intended for use in placement.

Test statistics

Frequency tables

One begins test analysis with a list of the score made by each individual taking the test. In the present case this means we have 186 scores. A list of 186 scores is not very helpful in understanding how the people performed on the test. A first step in getting to grips with the data is to construct a *frequency table*. Here is part of the frequency table for MYTEST.

Score	Frequency
15	6
16	0
17	2
18	1
19	4
20	6
21	2
22	3
23	2
24	4
25	3
26	2
27	3
28	2
29	2
30	2
31	4
32	2
33	2
34	2
35	2
36	5
37	2

The frequency table tells us that 6 people scored 15, nobody scored 16, 2 people scored 17, and so on. Frequency tables are useful when we are considering the effects of different possible cut-off points or pass marks. We can see how many people will pass, fail, or be categorised in some other way (given a particular letter grade, for example).

Histograms

It is still difficult, however, to get a general picture of performance from
a frequency table, especially when there are a large number of different
scores. In order to get this general view of performance, the frequency
distribution can be condensed into what is called a *histogram*. The
histogram for MYTEST appears below.

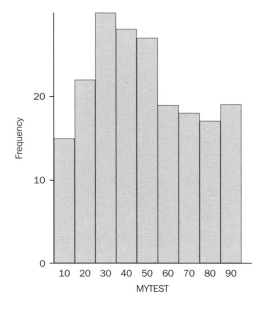

The diagram should be self-explanatory: the vertical dimension indicates the number of candidates scoring within a particular range of
scores; the horizontal dimension shows what these ranges are. It is
always wise to create a histogram in order to be made aware immediately of features of the distribution (for example, many people scoring
high and low, but relatively few scoring in the middle).

Measures of central tendency: the mean, the mode and the median

Once one has a general picture of performance, a next step is to find
what one might think of as a 'typical score'. The most commonly used
of the typical scores (also known as measures of central tendency) is the
mean. The mean is simply the average of all the scores made on the test.
Add up everyone's score on the test and divide by the number of people
taking the test – and you have the mean score on the test.

6 people take a test
Their scores are: 27, 34, 56, 56, 75, 81
The total of their scores is 27 + 34 + 56 + 56 + 75 + 81 = 329
329 divided by 6 = 54.83 which is the mean score on the test.

ETA tells us that the mean score on MYTEST is 41.56

The other measures of central tendency are:
a) The *mode*, which is the most common score. The mode of the scores in the box is 56.
b) The *median*, which can be found by putting all the individual scores in order of magnitude, and choosing the middle one. In the above box the median is 56, the same as the mode. (As there is an even number of test takers, there are two middle scores. In such cases one takes the two middle scores, adds them together and divides by 2. Here that means adding 56 to 56 and dividing it by 2.)

Measures of dispersion: the standard deviation and the range

The mean by itself does not always give an adequate summary of a set of scores. This is because very different sets of scores may have the same mean. For example, one group of five students may score as follows on a test: 48, 49, 50, 51, 52. Another group of five students taking the same test may score: 10, 20, 40, 80, 100. Although for each group the mean score is 50, the distribution of scores is quite different. One set of scores is clustered close to the mean; the other set of scores is more spread out. If we want to compare two such sets of scores, stating the mean alone would be misleading.

What we need is an indication of the ways the scores are distributed around the mean. This is what the *standard deviation* gives us. Just as the mean can be seen as a 'typical' score on a test, the standard deviation can be seen as a typical distance from the mean. I do not think it is worthwhile showing how to calculate the standard deviation here.

The standard deviation on MYTEST is 23.898

> Another useful measure of dispersion is the range. The range is calculated by subtracting the lowest score anyone made on the test from the highest that anyone made. Thus, if the lowest score was 15 and the highest was 86, the range would be 86 − 15 = 71. The range on MYTEST is 86 (88 − 2)

Reliability

We know the meaning and significance of reliability from Chapter 5. It was said there that there are a number of ways of calculating the reliability coefficient. Each way is likely to give a slightly different coefficient. For the data we are looking at, ETA gives four coefficients, which range from 0.94 to 0.98. Without needing to understand the difference between these coefficients, one could quite happily choose the lowest of them, knowing that it is the least likely to be an overestimate. If, of course, one were hoping to sell the test, one might be tempted to choose the highest coefficient!

What all of the estimates given by ETA have in common on this occasion is that they are based on people taking the test only once (see Chapter 5 for the rationale for this). The tester has divided the test into two halves, which are believed to be equivalent. In the present case, one half is made up of the odd-numbered items, and the other half is made up of the even-numbered items.

> **Reliability coefficient 1 = 0.94**
>
> This coefficient is calculated using Analysis of Variance (or ANOVA). It takes into account the fact that, despite the tester's attempt to create two equivalent half-tests, the actual means and standard deviations of those tests are different. The mean of one half is 19.88, while the mean of the other is 21.68. The standard deviation of one is 12.57, while that of the other is 11.59.

> **Reliability coefficient 2 = 0.95**
>
> This coefficient is also calculated using ANOVA. Because it ignores the difference between the two half-tests, it is slightly higher.

Reliability coefficient 3 = 0.98

This coefficient is arrived at by first calculating the correlation between scores on the two half-tests (which is 0.96) and then applying the Spearman-Brown Prophecy Formula. The two half-tests are (obviously!) shorter than the whole test. We know that the longer the test is (if the items are of the same quality), the more reliable it will be. The Spearman-Brown Prophecy Formula estimates the effect on the correlation coefficient of doubling the length of the test.

Reliability coefficient 3 = 0.98

This coefficient is based on the Kuder-Richardson Formula 20. It compares the proportion of correct and incorrect responses on each item. The key thing to remember is that this coefficient is equivalent to the average of all the coefficients that could be calculated using the method that resulted in Reliability coefficient 3.

The reliability of MYTEST is high. If it is thought to be unnecessarily high, one could think of removing items from the test. As this test was intended for low-stakes placement, a second version of the test was created by removing 40 items out of the original 100. The reliability of the shorter version remained high, at around 0.90. How items should be chosen for removal from a test is explained below.

If the reliability of a test is considered to be too low, one possibility is to add items to it. But if the test already has 100 items and isn't reliable enough, this is hardly a sensible course of action. One needs to look closely at all aspects of the test in its present form, including the way it is administered, and think how it might be made more reliable. Advice in doing this was given in Chapter 5.

The Standard Error of Measurement

We know from Chapter 5 that the Standard Error of Measurement (SEM) allows us to make statements about a person's true score in relation to the score they actually obtained on the test. Other things being equal, the greater the reliability, the smaller the SEM[1]. Taking the lowest estimate of reliability (which is 0.94), the SEM of MYTEST is 2.90.

Knowing that the SEM is 2.90, we can make the following statements:

If someone scores 40 on the test we can be 68% certain that their true score is between 37.1 and 42.9

(that is, 40 plus or minus SEM)

And we can be 95% certain that their true score is between 34.2 and 45.8

(that is, 40 plus or minus 2 x SEM)

As was said in Chapter 5, the SEM provides information which is helpful when we have to make decisions about individuals on the basis of their performance on a test. It also helps us to decide whether or not our test is sufficiently reliable.

Before moving on to the second section of this appendix, readers might like to look at the output from ETA, and assure themselves that they understand it.

Overall test mean is 41.56452 with standard deviation 23.89817

Reliability analysis of data in the file **MYTEST.ETA**

There were results from 186 people
Responding to a total of 100 items

First test (part):   Mean = 19.88   St. Dev. = 12.57
Second test (part): Mean = 21.68   St. Dev. = 11.59

The correlation between the two sets of scores is 0.956

Taking into account apparent differences in the form means:
reliability = 0.943   st. error of measurement = 2.90

Within forms analysis:
reliability = 0.953   st. error of measurement = 2.62

Split parts analysis:
Spearman-Brown Coefficient = 0.976 and
Kuder-Richardson 20 = 0.978

Item analysis

The purpose of item analysis is to examine the contribution that each item is making to the test. Items that are identified as faulty or inefficient can be modified or rejected. In this section of the chapter we will look first at so-called classical item analysis, before turning to a fairly recent development – item response theory.

Classical item analysis

This usually involves the calculation of facility values and discrimination indices, as well as an analysis of distractors in the case of multiple choice items.

Facility values

The facility value of an item on which only scores of zero or one can be scored is simply the proportion of test takers that score one on it. Thus, if a hundred people respond to an item and thirty-seven give the correct response, the facility value is 0.37 (37 divided by 100). If 80 people take a test and 56 of them get an item right, the facility value is 0.70 (56 divided by 80).

What use can we make of facility values? This depends on our purpose. If we are developing a proficiency test designed to identify the top 10% of students for a special language course, we won't have much need for easy items, that is, items with high facility values. Those items would not discriminate between the best 10% and most of the other people. Ideally, for this purpose we would want a high proportion of items with a facility value not far from 0.10. If, on the other hand, we are developing a placement test which is meant to cover a wide range of abilities and place people in classes at a number of levels, we will want a wide range of facility values in our items, with no big gaps between them.

The question of facility values for items attracting more than one point is generally not discussed in texts on testing. Nevertheless, it is useful to be able to compare the difficulty of such items. What I would suggest is taking the average score on an item (i.e. total points scored on the item by all test takers divided by the number of test takers) and dividing that by the maximum number of points on the item. Thus, if 100 people take a five-point item and score a

---

total of 375 points on it, the average score is 3.75 (375 divided by 100), and the facility value is .75 (3.75 divided by 5). The advantage of this method is that it gives the same result for zero/one items as the procedure described for them above.

Discrimination indices

A discrimination index is an indicator of how well an item discriminates between weak candidates and strong candidates. The higher its discrimination index, the better the item discriminates in this way. The theoretical maximum discrimination index is 1. An item that does not discriminate at all (weak and strong candidates perform equally well on it) has a discrimination index of zero. An item that discriminates in favour of the weaker candidates (weaker candidates perform better than stronger candidates) – and such items are occasionally written, unfortunately – has a negative discrimination index. Discrimination is important because the more discriminating the items are, the more reliable will be the test.

The discrimination indices are typically correlation coefficients. The usual way of calculating a discrimination index is to compare performance of the candidates on the item with their performance on the test as a whole. If scores on the item (zero or one) correlate well with scores on the test, the resulting correlation coefficient will indicate good discrimination.

Strictly speaking, the correlation should be calculated between the scores made by individuals on an item and their scores on the test *less their score on that item*. Otherwise, scores on the item are included in scores on the test, which will exaggerate the strength of the correlation. This exaggeration is not significant when a test includes a large number of items.

Note that calculation of discrimination indices in this way assumes that, as a group, the people who do better on the whole test (or on some part of it being analysed) should do better on any particular item in it.

Look at the following discrimination indices for items in MYTEST.

ITEM 1	0.386
ITEM 2	0.601
ITEM 3	0.355
ITEM 5	0.734
ITEM 6	0.358
ITEM 7	0.434
ITEM 8	0.207
ITEM 9	0.518
ITEM 10	0.393
ITEM 11	0.590
ITEM 12	0.419
ITEM 13	0.433
ITEM 97	0.265
ITEM 98	0.469
ITEM 99	0.188
ITEM 100	0.124

The items with the greatest indices are the ones that discriminate best. The most discriminating item here, therefore, is Item 5, with an index of 0.734. The least discriminating item is Item 100, with an index of 0.124.

A natural question at this point is: What is regarded as a satisfactory discriminating index? The disappointing answer is that there is no absolute value that one can give. The important thing is the *relative* size of the indices. Remember that we are interested in discrimination for its effect on reliability. The first thing we should do is look at the reliability coefficient. If there is a problem with reliability, we can look at discrimination indices to see if there are items which are not contributing enough to reliability. Any items with a negative index should be first to go. (In fact, they should be candidates for removal from the test even if the reliability coefficient is satisfactory.) After that we look for the items with the lowest positive indices. If the items themselves are clearly faulty, we should either drop them from the test (and try to replace them with better items) or we should try to improve them. A word of warning, though. An item with a low discrimination index is not necessarily faulty. Item 99 in MYTEST is a case in point. The reason for its lack of discrimination is that it is very difficult. Its facility value is only 0.022 (only 2 of the 186 people taking the test responded correctly). When an item is very easy or very difficult, the discrimination index is almost bound to be low. Even if an item does not discriminate well overall, we might wish to keep it in the test. If it is very easy, it might be kept because it is being used to help make the candidates feel confident at the start of the test. If it is very difficult, we may keep it because, while it does not discriminate well over all the people who took the test, it may discriminate between the strongest candidates. When MYTEST was reduced from 100 to 60 items (see above), all the items were grouped into bands according to their facility value. Then the items with the lowest discrimination indices were dropped. This is because the particular purpose of the test called for discrimination at all levels.

Where the scores of only a small number of students (say 30) is available for analysis, formal discrimination indices calculated as described above are not very meaningful. However, it is still worthwhile dividing the students into two groups – top half and bottom half (according to their scores on the complete test) – and then comparing their performance on each item. If there are items where there is no difference between the groups or where the lower group actually do better, then these items are worth scrutinising.

Analysis of distractors

Where multiple choice items are used, in addition to calculating discrimination indices and facility values, it is necessary to analyse the performance of distractors. Distractors that do not work, i.e. are chosen by very few candidates, make no contribution to test reliability. Such distractors should be replaced by better ones, or the item should be otherwise modified or dropped. However, care should be taken in the case of easy items, where there may not be many incorrect responses to be shared among the different distractors (unless a very large number of candidates have been tested).

Item response theory

Everything that has been said so far has related to classical item analysis. In recent years new methods of analysis have been developed which have many attractions for the test writer. These all come under the general heading of item response theory, and the form of it so far most used in language testing is called *Rasch analysis*.

Rasch analysis begins with the assumption that items on a test have a particular difficulty attached to them, that they can be placed in order of difficulty, and that the test taker has a fixed level of ability. Under these conditions, the idealised result of a number of candidates taking a test will be as in Table 1. The candidate with the greatest ability is 'subject 8'; the one with the least ability is 'subject 1'. The most difficult items are items 6 and 7; and the least difficult item is item 1.

Table 1: *Responses of imaginary subjects to imaginary items*

	Items						
Subjects	1	2	3	4	5	6	7
1	1	0	0	0	0	0	0
2	1	1	1	0	0	0	0
3	1	1	1	0	0	0	0
4	1	1	1	0	0	0	0
5	1	1	1	1	0	0	0
6	1	1	1	1	1	0	0
7	1	1	1	1	1	0	0
8	1	1	1	1	1	1	1
Total incorrect	0	1	1	4	5	7	7

(Woods and Baker 1985)

Table 1 represents a model of what happens in test taking, but we know that, even if the model is correct, people's performance will not be a perfect reflection of their ability. In the real world we would expect an individual's performance to be more like the following:

1 1 1 1 0 1 0 1 0

Rasch analysis in fact accepts such departures from the model as normal. But it does draw attention to test performance that is *significantly different* from what the model would predict. It identifies test takers whose behaviour does not fit the model, and it identifies items that do not fit the model.

Here are some examples from the Rasch analysis of MYTEST by ETA. It would be inappropriate (not to say impossible in the space available) to try to explain everything in the analysis. But I will just use the examples to show what it can contribute to our understanding of how items on a test are performing.

ITEM NUMBER	SCORE	FIT
I 9	130	0.3252
I 10	160	31.6097
I 11	135	−3.3231
I 12	154	5.5788
I 13	156	2.2098

Testing for language teachers

The first column identifies the item. The second shows how many correct responses there were on that item (out of 186). The third column shows how well the item fits the Rasch model. The higher the positive value, the *less well* the item fits. It can be seen that the least fitting item is Item 10, which makes us immediately suspicious of it. It's a relatively easy item (130 out of 186 candidates respond correctly); if it's misfitting, therefore, better candidates must be getting it wrong. So we look now at *people* that Rasch analysis identifies as misfitting. Amongst them are two who have an 'unusual' result on Item 10. The first is Person Number 10:

Person	Score	Ability	Misfit value
P10	88	3.1725	48.6729

Items with unusual result:

Item	Residual
I 3	13.90
I 10	29.88
I 34	8.50
I 60	2.54
I 73	3.77
I 76	2.60

We learn from the output that Person 10 had a very high score on the test (88) and performed in an unexpected way on two items in particular (Items 3 and 10 – the ones with high *residuals*[2]). Since these are easy items, we can conclude either that they weren't concentrating (notice that there are 4 other items on which there is an unusual result), or they have very surprising gaps in their knowledge, or that there is something wrong with one or both of the items.

The second is Person Number 166:

Person	Score	Ability	Misfit value
P166	40	−0.6752	4.8836

Items with unusual result:	Item	Residual
	I 7	4.22
	I 10	4.36
	I 61	2.77
	I 67	2.57
	I 70	4.07
	I 72	2.64
	I 81	4.64
	I 92	4.64

This person has unusual results on 8 items. The relatively small residual value for Item 10 reflects the fact that the person is of only middling ability (score 40) and so it is not so surprising that the item was responded to incorrectly.

The situation so far is that we have an item that seems to misfit, and we have two people who behaved unusually on it. If we drop these two people from the analysis, the result for Item 10 is different:

ITEM 10	143	−3.7332	−3.7363

The item now fits well. When we look at the item and can find nothing wrong with it, we come to the conclusion that the problem is with the candidates, not the item. If it is thought worthwhile by the institution using the test, the two people can be followed up in an attempt to find out what is wrong.

If an item is identified as misfitting by Rasch analysis, and we cannot explain the misfit through odd performance on it by a small number of candidates, we can expect to find a problem with the item itself when we come to inspect it.

Rasch analysis assumes that what is being measured by a test is *unidimensional*. This parallels the assumption of classical analysis that people who do better on the test should do better on any item. Of course there may be more than one dimension to what is being learned or acquired, but this does not seem to affect the practical value of Rasch analysis any more than does classical analysis.

Another feature of Rasch analysis is that instead of giving a single standard error of measurement that has to be applied to all candidates, it gives a separate *standard error* for each candidate. Thus:

Person	Ability	Standard error
P28	−5.93	0.82
P31	−3.57	0.41
P3	−0.59	0.27

Person 28 is the weakest of these three candidates (the higher the negative ability value, the weaker the person) and has the highest standard error. Person 3 is of middling ability (near zero) and has the lowest standard error. This fits with what was said in Note 2 below. We can be much more confident that Person 3's true score is close to their actual score, than we can that Person 28's true score is close to their actual score.

There is one more use of Rasch analysis to mention. Rasch analysis can be particularly helpful when we are trialling items on different groups of people. Let's say we want to trial 170 items. We believe that this is too many items to ask one group of people to respond to, so we set up two groups. The problem then is, if the two groups are not equal in ability, how can we compare the facility values of items taken by one group with the facility values of items taken by the other group. The stronger group will be putting the items on a different scale of 'easiness' from that of the weaker group. An item will be given a different facility value than it would have had if it had been taken by the other group.

The answer to this problem is to use what are called *anchor items*. These are items, preferably ones that are known to be 'good', which both groups respond to. So in the situation referred to, 30 items could be anchors. The remaining 140 items would be split into two sets, so that each group took a total of 100 items. Once the items have been administered and scored, Rasch analysis has the ability to use the common anchor items to put all of the other items on the same scale. With the increased use of item banks (Appendix 2), this is a particularly valuable feature.

There is one last thing to say about item analysis. As I hope I have shown, both classical analysis and Rasch analysis have contributions to make to the development of better tests. They should be seen as complementary, not in opposition with one to be chosen over the other.

This chapter on the statistical analysis of tests will not have pleased everyone. For many readers statistics will have little, if any, appeal. Other readers may be frustrated that the treatment of the subject has been so sketchy. My only hope is that there will at least be some people who find it sufficiently interesting and potentially useful to them that they will go on to experiment with statistics and to study the subject in greater depth.

Reader activities

Activities can be found on the book's website.

Further reading

For the use of statistics in language studies, see Woods, Fletcher, and Hughes (1986). For an introduction to item response theory, see Woods and Baker (1985). For a much fuller treatment, see Chapters 5–9 of McNamara (1996). As mentioned above, ETA, the program that has been used for illustration in this chapter (and of which I am joint author), are available at low cost via the book's website, as is a more detailed account of statistics for testing than is possible in this appendix.

1. Statements based on the SEM tend to be less accurate when applied to people at the extremes of the distribution (the strongest and the weakest candidates). Item response theory (see below) is less susceptible to this effect.
2. The residual is an indication of how badly a person's performance on an item fits the Rasch model. Thus, if a candidate does very well on the test as a whole but gets a very easy item wrong, their residual for that item will be high; if they get an item of middling difficulty wrong, then the residual will be smaller. In brief, we are on the lookout for items with high residuals, because these tell us that someone's performance on that item is unexpected, i.e. doesn't fit the model.

Appendix 2 Item banking

When appropriate statistical analysis of test results has been carried out, it is possible to construct what is called an item bank. An item bank is a large collection of previously trialled test items, normally stored nowadays on a computer, which is placed at the disposal of test constructors. Usually stored with each item in the bank are:

1. A number of identifying criteria, relating to such things as its content, class level, stage in the syllabus or course book, the testing technique used, and number of points.
2. Correct response(s) and scoring instructions.
3. Measurement information on the item, such as difficulty level and discrimination index, which has been obtained through previous trialling.
4. Notes on the item (when written, when used, etc.).

Once they have access to an item bank, test constructors simply choose from it the items that they need for a test. They do this by entering into the computer details of the kinds of items they need. They might begin for example, by asking for receptive vocabulary items which have a facility value between 0.4 and 0.6, and which relate to third year study at their institution. The computer will immediately present them with all the items in the bank that meet these criteria, and they are given the opportunity to 'browse' through these, choosing those items that they decide to include in the test. Once they have chosen all the items they need for the test, and have provided details such as the test title and rubrics, the computer provides a printed version of the test.

There are a number of benefits to be had from item banks:

1. Once the bank is constructed, there is a considerable saving of effort. Tests do not have to be constructed over and over again from scratch.
2. Since the trialling of the items (which makes use of anchor items, referred to in Appendix 1) is carried out before they are

entered into the bank, the quality of tests that use them will almost certainly be higher than those made up of untrialled items.

3. The psychometric information on items gathered during trialling means that the measurement qualities (including level of difficulty) of tests made up of these items can be predicted (before the test is taken) with greater accuracy than when predictions are made on the basis of test constructors' judgements. This in turn means that a test constructed in one year can be made to have the same difficulty as tests set in previous years, with implications for the maintenance of standards, fairness, and the evaluation of teaching.

The development of an item bank follows very much the procedures as those for the development of a test. The only differences are that the specifications have to be for a *bank*, not a test; and the trialling process – making use of anchor items – is absolutely essential.

Item banks are now regarded as indispensable to serious testing organisations. With the advent of powerful but inexpensive computers, item banks have become an attractive possibility for all serious testers who are prepared to put in the necessary initial effort.

Further reading

Suggested sources for investigating item banks and banking can be found on the book's website.

Appendix 3 Questions on the New Zealand youth hostels passage

1. New Zealand has a) more than 60 hostels. b) less than 60 hostels. c) exactly 60 hostels.
2. You are unlikely to meet New Zealanders in the hostels. True or false? ....
3. Which hostel is said to be nearly always very full? ....
4. Where can you visit a working sheep-station? ....
5. Give one reason why Mount Cook is so popular with tourists. ....
6. What is the speciality of the hostel near the Franz Josef glacier? ....
7. Does the author recommend one particular hostel above any other which is particularly good for a lazy beach stay with sunbathing and scuba diving? ....
8. How many hostels cater for the Bay of Islands? ....
9. Name two cities which have two hostels. .... and ....
10. At which hostel can you definitely hire a bicycle? ....
11. You can wash your clothes in the hostels. True or false? ....
12. Why do Don and Jean Cameron think they will have to make a world trip next year? ....

Bibliography

Adams, M. L. and J. R. Frith (Eds.). 1979. *Testing Kit*. Washington D.C.: Foreign Service Institute.

AERA, 1999, *Standards for educational and psychological testing*. Washington, D.C.: American Educational Research Association, American Psychological Association, National Council on Measurement in Education.

Alderson, J. C. 1990a. Testing reading comprehension skills (Part one). *Reading in a Foreign Language* 6: 425–438.

Alderson, J. C. 1990b. Testing reading comprehension skills (Part two). *Reading in a Foreign Language* 6: 465–503.

Alderson, J. C. 1995. Response to Lumley. *Language Testing* 12, 121–125.

Alderson, J. C. 2000. *Assessing reading*. Cambridge: CUP.

Alderson, J. C. and G. Buck. 1993. Standards in testing: a study of the practice of UK examination boards in EFL/ESL testing. *Language Testing* 10, 1–26.

Alderson, J. C. and C. Clapham. 1995. Assessing student performance in the ESL classroom. *TESOL Quarterly* 29: 184–187.

Alderson, J. C. and L. Hamp-Lyons. 1996. TOEFL preparation courses: a study of washback. *Language Testing* 13: 280–297.

Alderson, J. C. and A. Hughes (Eds.). 1981. Issues in language testing. *ELT Documents* 111. London: The British Council.

Alderson, J. C., C. Clapham and D. Wall. 1995. *Language test construction and evaluation*. Cambridge: CUP.

Alderson, J. C., K. J. Krahnke and C.W. Stansfield. 1987. *Reviews of English language proficiency tests*. Washington D.C.: TESOL.

Alderson, J. C., R. Percicsich and G. Szabo. 2000. Sequencing as an item type. *Language Testing* 17: 421–447.

Alderson, J. C. and D. Wall. 1993. Does Washback exist? *Applied Linguistics* 14: 115–129.

Allan, A. 1992. Development and validation of a scale to measure test-wiseness in EFL/ESL reading test takers. *Language Testing* 9, 101–122.

Anastasi, A. and S. Urbina. 1997. *Psychological Testing* (7th edition). Upper Saddle River, N.J: Prentice Hall.

Arnold. J. 2000. Seeing through listening comprehension anxiety. *TESOL Quarterly* 34: 777–786.

Bachman, L. F. 1990. *Fundamental considerations in language testing*. Oxford: Oxford University Press.

Bachman, L. F. and A. D. Cohen (Eds.). 1998. *Interfaces between second language acquisition and language testing research*. Cambridge: Cambridge University Press.

Bachman, L. F. and A. S. Palmer. 1981. The construct validation of the FSI oral interview. *Language Learning* 31: 67–86.

Bachman, L. F. and A. S. Palmer. 1996. *Language testing in practice*. Oxford: OUP.

Bachman, L. F. and S. J. Savignon. 1986. The evaluation of communicative language proficiency: a critique of the ACTFL oral interview. *Modern Language Journal* 70: 380–90.

Bailey, K. M. 1996. Working for Washback: a review of the Washback concept in language testing. *Language Testing* 13: 257–279.

Bradshaw, J. 1990. Test-takers' reactions to a placement test. *Language Testing* 7: 13–30.

Brett, P. and G. Motteram. 2000. *A special interest in computers: learning and teaching with information and communications technologies*. Whitstable: IATEFL.

Brown, J. D. 1990. Short-cut estimates of criterion-referenced test consistency. *Language Testing* 7: 77–97.

Brown, J. D. 1993. What are the characteristics of *natural* cloze tests? *Language Testing* 10: 93–115.

Brown, J. D. and T. Hudson. 1998. The alternatives in language assessment. *TESOL Quarterly* 32: 653–675.

Brown, J. D. and T. Hudson. 2002. *Criterion-referenced language testing*. Cambridge: Cambridge University Press.

Buck, G. 1991. The testing of listening comprehension: an introspective study. *Language Testing* 8: 67–91.

Buck, G. 2001. *Assessing listening*. Cambridge: Cambridge University Press.

Buck, G. and K. Tatsuoka. 1998. Application of the rule-space procedure to language testing: examining attributes of a free response listening test. *Language Testing* 15: 119–157.

Bygate, M. 1987. *Speaking*. Oxford: OUP.

Byrne, D. 1967. Progressive picture compositions. London: Longman.

Cameron, L. 2001. *Teaching language to young learners*. Cambridge: CUP.

Canale, M. and M. Swain, 1980. Theoretical bases of communicative approaches to second language teaching and testing. *Applied Linguistics* 1: 1–47.

Carpenter, K., N. Fujii and H. Kataoka. 1995. An oral interview procedure for assessing second language abilities in children. *Language Testing* 12: 157–181.

Carroll, J. B. 1961. Fundamental considerations in testing for English language proficiency of foreign students. In H. B. Allen and R. N. Campbell (Eds.) 1972. *Teaching English as a second language: a book of readings*. New York: McGraw Hill.

Carroll, J. B. 1981. Twenty-five years of research on foreign language aptitude. In K. C. Diller (Ed.) Individual differences and universals in language learning aptitude. Rowley, Mass: Newbury House.

Chalhoub-Deville, M. 1995. Deriving oral assessment scales across different test and rater groups. *Language Testing* 12: 16–33.

Chalhoub-Deville, M. (Ed.) 1999. *Issues in computer adaptive testing of reading proficiency: selected papers*. Cambridge: Cambridge University Press.

Chalhoub-Deville M. and C. Deville. 1999. Computer adaptive testing in second language contexts. *Annual Review of Applied Linguistics* 19: 273–99.

Chapelle, C. A. and R. G. Abraham. 1990. Cloze method: what difference does it make? *Language Testing* 7: 121–146.

Clapham, C. and D. Corson (Eds.). 1997. *Encyclopaedia of Language and Education. Volume 7: Language testing and assessment*. Amsterdam: Kluwer Academic Publishers.

Cohen, A. D. 1984. On taking language tests: What the students report. *Language Testing* 1: 70–81.

Collins Cobuild. 1992. *English Usage*. London: HarperCollins.

Council of Europe. 2001. *Common European framework of references for languages: learning, teaching, assessment*. Cambridge: Cambridge University Press.

Criper, C. and A. Davies. 1988. *ELTS validation project report*. Cambridge: The British Council and Cambridge Local Examinations Syndicate.

Crystal, D. and D. Davy. 1975. *Advanced conversational English*. London: Longman.

Cumming, A. and R. Berwick (Eds.). 1996. *Validation in language testing*. Clevedon: Multilingual Matters.

Davidson, F. 2000. Review of Standards for educational and psychological testing. *Language Testing* 17: 457–462.

Davies, A. (Ed.). 1968. *Language testing symposium: a psycholinguistic perspective*. Oxford: Oxford University Press.

Davies, A. 1988. *Communicative language testing*. In Hughes 1988b.

Davies, A. et al. 1999. *Language testing dictionary*. Cambridge. Cambridge University Press.

DeVicenzi, F. 1995. Examining standardized test content: some advice for teachers. *TESOL Quarterly* 29: 180–183.

Dexter, C. 1986. *The Secret of Annexe 3*. London. Macmillan.

Douglas, D. 1994. Quantity and quality in speaking test performance. *Language Testing* 11: 125–144.

Ebel, R. L. 1978. The case for norm-referenced measurements. *Educational Researcher* 7 (11): 3–5.

Farhady, H. and M. N. Keramati. 1996. A text-driven method for the deletion procedure in cloze passages. *Language Testing* 13: 191–207.

Feldt, L. S. and R. L. Brennan. 1989. *Reliability*. In Linn (Ed.). 1989.

Freedle, R. and I. Kostin. 1993. The prediction of TOEFL reading item difficulty: implications for construct validity. *Language Testing* 10: 133–170.

Freedle, R. and I. Kostin. 1999. Does the text matter in a multiple-choice test of comprehension: The case for the construct validity of TOEFL's minitalks. *Language Testing* 16: 2–32.

Fulcher, G. 1996a. Testing tasks: issues in task design and the group oral. *Language Testing* 13: 23–51.

Fulcher, G. 1996b. Does thick description lead to smart tests? A data-based approach to rating scale construction. *Language Testing* 13: 208–238.

Fulcher, G. 1997. An English language placement test: issues in reliability and validity. *Language Testing* 14: 113–138.

Fulcher, G. 2000. *Computers in language testing.* In Brett and Motteram (Eds.). 2000.

Garman, M. and A. Hughes. 1983. *English cloze exercises.* Oxford: Blackwell.

Gipps, C. 1990. *Assessment: A teachers' guide to the issues.* London: Hodder and Stoughton.

Godshalk, F. L., F. Swineford and W. E. Coffman. 1966. *The measurement of writing ability.* New York: College Entrance Examination Board.

Greenberg, K. 1986. The development and validation of the TOEFL writing test: a discussion of TOEFL Research Reports 15 and 19. *TESOL Quarterly* 20: 531–544.

Hale, G. A. and R. Courtney. 1994. The effects of note-taking on listening comprehension in the Test of English as a Foreign Language. *Language Testing* 11: 29–47.

Hamp-Lyons, L. (Ed.). 1991. *Assessing second language writing in academic contexts.* Norwood, NJ: Ablex.

Hamp-Lyons, L. 1995. Rating non-native writing: the trouble with holistic scoring. *TESOL Quarterly* 29: 759–762.

Hamp-Lyons, L. 1997a. Washback, impact and validity: ethical concerns. *Language Testing* 14: 295–303.

Hamp-Lyons, L. 1997b. Ethical test preparation practice: the case of the TOEFL. *TESOL Quarterly* 32: 329–337.

Hamp-Lyons, L. 1999. The author responds. *TESOL Quarterly* 33: 270–274.

Hasselgren, A. 1999. *Kartlegging av Kommunikativ Kompetanse i Engelsk (Testing of Communicative Ability in English).* Oslo: Nasjonalt læremiddelsenter.

Harris, D. P. 1968. *Testing English as a second language.* New York: McGraw Hill.

Heaton, J. B. 1975. *Writing English language tests.* London: Longman.

Hudson, T. and B. Lynch. 1984. A criterion-referenced approach to ESL achievement testing. *Language Testing* 1: 171–201.

Hughes, A. 1981. Conversational cloze as a measure of oral ability. *English Language Teaching Journal* 35: 161–168.

Hughes, A. 1986. A pragmatic approach to criterion-referenced foreign language testing. In Portal, M. (Ed.). 1986.

Hughes, A. 1988a. Introducing a needs-based test of English for study in an English medium university in Turkey. In Hughes, A. 1988b.

Hughes, A. (Ed.). 1988b. Testing English for university study. *ELT Documents 127.* Oxford: Modern English Press.

Hughes, A. 1993. Backwash and TOEFL 2000. Unpublished paper commissioned by Educational Testing Services.

Hughes, A. and D. Porter. (Eds.). 1983. *Current developments in language testing.* London: Academic Press.

Hughes, A. L. Gülçur, P. Gürel and T. McCombie. 1987. The new Boğaziçi University English Language Proficiency Test. In Bozok, S. and A. Hughes.

Proceedings of the seminar, Testing English beyond the high school. Istanbul: Boğaziçi University Publications.

Hughes, A. and P. Trudgill. 1996. *English accents and dialects: an introduction to social and regional varieties of British English* (3rd edition). London: Edward Arnold.

Hughes, A., D. Porter and C. Weir. (Eds.). 1988. *Validating the ELTS test: a critical review.* Cambridge: The British Council and University of Cambridge Local Examinations Syndicate.

Hughes, A., D. Porter and C. J. Weir. 1996. *ARELS Placement Test* [Written]. London: ARELS.

Hughes, A., D. Porter and C. J. Weir. 1998. *ARELS Placement Test* [Listening]. London: ARELS.

Hughes, A. and A. J. Woods. 2002. *ETA (Educational Test Analysis) Version 2.* Garth: STET.

Jacobs. H. L., S. A. Zingraf, D. R. Wormuth, V. F. Hartfield and J. B. Hughey. 1981. *Testing ESL composition: a practical approach.* Rowley, Mass: Newbury House.

Jafarpur, A. 1995. Is C-testing superior to cloze? *Language Testing* 12: 194–216.

James, C. 1998. *Errors in language learning and use: exploring error analysis.* Harlow: Addison Wesley Longman.

Jennings, M., J. Fox, B. Graves and E. Shohamy. 1999. The test-taker's choice: an investigation of the effect of topic on language test-performance. *Language Testing* 16: 426–456.

Klein-Braley, C. 1985. A cloze-up on the C-Test: a study in the construct validation of authentic tests. *Language Testing* 2: 76–104.

Klein-Braley, C. 1997. C-Tests in the context of reduced redundancy testing: an appraisal. *Language Testing* 14: 47–84.

Klein-Braley, C. and U. Raatz. 1984. A survey of research on the C-Test. *Language Testing* 1: 131–146.

Kormos, J. 1999. Simulating conversation in oral-proficiency assessment: a conversation analysis of role-plays and non-scripted interviews in language exams. *Language Testing* 16: 163–188.

Kunnan, A. J. 2000. *Fairness and validation in language assessment.* Cambridge: Cambridge University Press.

Lado, R. 1961. Language testing. London: Longman.

Lado, R. 1986. Analysis of native speaker performance on a cloze test. *Language Testing* 3: 130–46.

Lazaraton, A. 1996. Interlocutor support in oral proficiency interviews: the case of CASE. *Language Testing* 13: 151–172.

Leech, G., P. Rayson and A. Wilson. 2001. *Word frequencies in written and spoken English.* London: Longman.

Lewkowicz, J. A. (2000). Authenticity in language testing: some outstanding questions. *Language Testing* 17(1) 43–64.

Limb, S. 1983. Living with illness. Migraine. *The Observer*, 9 October.

Linn, R. L. (Ed.). 1989: *Educational measurement* (7th Edition). New York: Macmillan.

Lowe, P. 1986. Proficiency: panacea, framework, process? A reply to Kramsch, Schulz, and particularly to Bachman and Savignon. *Modern Language Journal*. 70: 391–397.

Lumley, T. 1993. The notion of subskills in reading comprehension tests: an EAP example. *Language Testing* 10: 211–234.

Lumley, T. 1995. Reply to Alderson's response. *Language Testing* 12: 125–130.

Lumley, T. and T. F. McNamara. 1995. Rater characteristics and rater bias: implications for training. *Language Testing* 12: 54–71.

Luoma, S. 2001. The test of spoken English. *Language Testing* 18: 225–234.

MacWhinney, B. 1995. Language-specific prediction in foreign language learning. *Language Testing* 12: 292–320.

McLaughlin, B. 1995. Aptitude from an information-processing perspective. *Language Testing* 12: 370–387.

McNamara, T. 1996. *Measuring second language performance*. London: Longman.

Messick, S. 1989. Validity. In Linn, R. (Ed.). 1989.

Messick, S. 1996. Validity and washback in language testing. *Language Testing* 13: 241–256.

Mislevy, R. J. 1995. Test theory and language learning assessment. *Language Testing* 12: 341–369.

Morrow, J. 1979. Communicative language testing: revolution or evolution? In C. J. Brumfit and K. Johnson. *The communicative approach to language teaching*. Oxford: Oxford University Press. Reprinted in Alderson and Hughes.

Morrow, K. 1986. The evaluation of tests of communicative performance. In Portal, M. (Ed.). 1986.

Nitko, A. J. 1989. Designing tests that are integrated with instruction. In Linn, R. (Ed.). 1989.

North, B. and G. Schneider. 1998. Scaling descriptors for language proficiency scales. *Language Testing* 15: 217–263.

Nitko, A. J. 2001. *Educational assessment of students* (3rd edition) Upper Saddle River, NJ: Prentice Hall.

Oller, J. W. 1979. *Language tests at school: a pragmatic approach*. London: Longman.

Oller, J. W. and C. A. Conrad. 1971. The cloze technique and ESL proficiency. *Language Learning* 21: 183–194.

Pilliner, A. 1968. *Subjective and objective testing*. In Davies, A. (Ed.). 1968.

Pimsleur P. 1968. *Language aptitude testing*. In Davies, A. (Ed.). 1968.

Popham, W. J. 1978. The case for criterion-referenced measurements. *Educational Researcher* 7 (11): 6–10.

Portal, M. (Ed.). 1986. *Innovations in language testing*. Windsor: NFER-Nelson.

Powers, D. E., M. A. Schedl, S. W. Leung, F. A. Butler. 1999. Validating the revised Test of Spoken English against a criterion of communicative success. *Language Testing* 1999 16 (4) 399–425.

Raven, J. 1991. *The tragic illusion: Educational testing*. Unionville, NY: Trillium Press: and Oxford: Oxford Psychologists Press.

Read, J. 2000. *Assessing vocabulary*. Cambridge: CUP.

Read, J. and C. Chapelle. 2001. A framework for second language vocabulary assessment. *Language Testing* 18: 1–32.

Rea-Dickens, P. 1997. So, why do we need relationships with stakeholders in language testing? A view from the UK. *Language Testing* 14: 304–314.

Rea-Dickens, P. and S. Gardner. 2000. Snares and silver bullets: disentangling the construct of formative assessment. *Language Testing* 17: 215–243.

Rea-Dickens, P. and S. Rixon. 1997. The assessment of young learners of English as a foreign language. In Clapham and Corson (Eds.). 1997.

Riley, G. L. and J. F. Lee. 1996. A comparison of recall and summary protocols as measures of second language reading comprehension. *Language Testing* 13: 173–189.

Ross, S. 1998. Self-assessment in second language testing: a meta-analysis and analysis of experiential factors. *Language Testing* 15: 1–20.

Salaberry, R. 2000. Revising the revised format of the ACTFL Oral Proficiency Interview. *Language Testing* 17: 289–310.

Scott, M. L., C. W. Stansfield and D. M. Kenyon. 1966. Examining validity in a performance test: the listening summary translation exam (LSTE) – Spanish version. *Language Testing* 13: 83–109.

Sherman, J. 1997. The effect of question preview in listening comprehension tests. *Language Testing* 14: 185–213.

Shohamy, E. 1984. Does the testing method make a difference? The case of reading comprehension. *Language Testing* 1: 147–176.

Shohamy, E. 1994. The validity of direct versus semi-direct oral tests. *Language Testing* 11: 99–123.

Shohamy, E. and O. Inbar. 1991. Validation of listening comprehension tests: the effect of text and question type. *Language Testing* 8: 23–40.

Shohamy, E., T. Reves, and Y. Bejarano. 1986. Introducing a new comprehensive test of oral proficiency. *English Language Teaching Journal* 40: 212–20.

Shohamy, E., S. Donitsa-Schmidt and I. Ferman. 1996. Test impact revisited: Washback effect over time. *Language Testing* 13: 298–317.

Skehan, P. 1984. Issues in the testing of English for specific purposes. *Language Testing* 1: 202–220.

Skehan, P. 1986. The role of foreign language aptitude in a model of school learning. *Language Testing* 3: 188–221.

Spolsky, B. 1981. Some ethical questions about language testing. In C. Klein-Braley and D. K. Stevenson (Eds.). *Practice and problems in language testing 1*. Frankfurt: Verlag Peter D. Lang.

Spolsky, B. 1995. Prognostication and language aptitude testing, 1925–1962. *Language Testing* 12: 321–340.

Sternberg, R. J. 1995. Styles of thinking and learning. *Language Testing* 12: 265–291.

Storey, P. 1997. Examining the test-taking process: a cognitive perspective on the discourse cloze test. *Language Testing* 14: 214–231.

Swan, M. 1975. *Inside meaning*. Cambridge: Cambridge University Press.

Swan, M. and C. Walter. 1988. *The Cambridge English Course. Students' Book 3*. Cambridge: Cambridge University Press.

Timmins, N. 1987. Passive smoking comes under official fire. *The Independent*, 14 March.

Trudgill, P. and J. Hannah. 1982. *International English: a guide to the varieties of standard English*. London: Edward Arnold.

Underhill, N. 1987. *Testing spoken language: a handbook of oral testing techniques*. Cambridge: Cambridge University Press.

University of Cambridge Local Examinations Syndicate. 1997. *First Certificate in English (FCE) handbook*. Cambridge: UCLES.

University of Cambridge Local Examinations Syndicate. 1999. *Certificates in Communicative Skills in English (CCSE) handbook*. Cambridge: UCLES.

University of Cambridge Local Examinations Syndicate. 1998. *Cambridge Young Learners handbook*. Cambridge: UCLES.

University of Cambridge Local Examinations Syndicate. 1999. *Cambridge Young Learners sample papers*. Cambridge: UCLES.

University of Cambridge Local Examinations Syndicate. Undated. *Preliminary English Test (PET) Handbook*.

Urquhart, A. and C. J. Weir. 1998. *Reading in a second language: process, product and practice*. Harlow: Addison Wesley Longman.

van Ek, J. A. and J. L. M. Trim. 2001a. *Waystage 1991*. Cambridge: Cambridge University Press.

van Ek, J. A. and J. L. M. Trim. 2001b. *Threshold 1991*. Cambridge: Cambridge University Press.

van Ek, J. A. and J. L. M. Trim. 2001c. *Vantage*. Cambridge: Cambridge University Press.

Wadden, P. and R. Hilke. 1999. Polemic gone astray: a corrective to recent criticism of TOEFL preparation. *TESOL Quarterly* 33: 263–270.

Wall, D. 1996. Introducing new tests into traditional systems: insights from general education and from innovation theory. *Language Testing* 13: 334–354.

Wall, D. and Alderson, J. C. 1993. Examining Washback: the Sri Lankan impact study. *Language Testing* 10: 41–69.

Wall, D., C. Clapham and J. C. Alderson. 1994. Evaluating a placement test. *Language Testing* 11: 321–344.

Watanabe, Y. 1996. Does grammar translation come from the entrance examination? Preliminary findings from classroom-based research. *Language Testing* 13: 318–333.

Weigle, S. C. 1994. Effects of training on raters of ESL compositions. *Language Testing* 11: 197–223.

Weigle, S. C. 2002. *Assessing Writing*. Cambridge: Cambridge University Press.

Weir, C. J. 1988. The specification, realization and validation of an English language proficiency test. In Hughes, A. (Ed.). 1988b.

Weir, C. J. 1990. *Communicative Language Testing*. Hemel Hempstead: Prentice Hall.

Weir, C. J. 1993. *Understanding and Developing Language Tests*. Hemel Hempstead: Prentice Hall.

Weir, C. J. and D. Porter 1995. The Multi-Divisible or Unitary Nature of Reading: the language tester between Scylla and Charybdis. *Reading in a Foreign Language* 10: 1–19.

Weir, C. J., A. Hughes and D. Porter. 1993 Reading skills: hierarchies, implicational relationships and identifiability. *Reading in a Second Language* 7, 505–510.

Weir, C. J., Yang Huizhong and Jin Yan. 2002. *An empirical investigation of the componentiality of L2 reading in English for academic purposes.* Cambridge: Cambridge University Press.

West, M. (Ed.). 1953. *A general service list of English words: with semantic frequencies and a supplementary word-list for the writing of popular science and technology.* London: Longman.

Wigglesworth, G. 1993. Exploring bias analysis as a tool for improving rater consistency in assessing oral interaction. *Language Testing* 10: 305–335.

Woods, A. and R. Baker. 1985. Item response theory. *Language Testing* 2: 119–140.

Woods, A., P. Fletcher and A. Hughes. 1986. *Statistics in language studies.* Cambridge: Cambridge University Press.

Wu, Y. 1998. What do tests of listening comprehension test? A retrospection study of EFL test-takers performing a multiple-choice task. *Language Testing* 15: 21–44.

Subject Index

Author Index